ALSO BY GLENN GREENWALD

How Would a Patriot Act?

A Tragic Legacy

Great American Hypocrites

WITH LIBERTY AND JUSTICE FOR SOME

WITH
LIBERTY AND JUSTICE
FOR SOME

HOW THE LAW IS USED TO DESTROY EQUALITY
AND PROTECT THE POWERFUL

GLENN GREENWALD

METROPOLITAN BOOKS   HENRY HOLT AND COMPANY   NEW YORK

Metropolitan Books
Henry Holt and Company, LLC
Publishers since 1866
175 Fifth Avenue
New York, New York 10010
www.henryholt.com

Metropolitan Books® and m® are registered trademarks of
Henry Holt and Company, LLC.

Library of Congress Cataloging-in-Publication data is available.
ISBN: 978-0-8050-9205-9

4722 8605 12/11

Henry Holt books are available for special promotions and
premiums. For details contact: Director, Special Markets.

First Edition 2011

Designed by Kelly S. Too

Printed in the United States of America

3   5   7   9   10   8   6   4   2

In the course of this book, I hold certain government officials and corporations
responsible for committing crimes. These assertions constitute my opinions
based on the facts that I set forth in the text.

CONTENTS

WITH LIBERTY AND JUSTICE FOR SOME

INTRODUCTION

As a litigator who practiced for more than a decade in federal and state courts across the country, I've long been aware of the inequities that pervade the American justice system. The rich enjoy superior legal representation and therefore much better prospects for success in court than the poor. The powerful are treated with far more deference by judges than the powerless. The same cultural, socioeconomic, and demographic biases that plague society generally also infect the legal process. Few people who have had any interaction with the justice system would dispute this.

Still, only when I began regularly writing about politics did I realize that the problem extends well beyond such inequities. The issue isn't just that those with political influence and financial power have some advantages in our judicial system. It is much worse than that. Those with political and financial clout are routinely allowed to break the law with no legal repercussions whatsoever. Often they need not even exploit their access to superior lawyers because they don't see the inside of a courtroom in the first place—not even when they get caught in the most egregious criminality. The criminal justice system is now almost exclusively reserved for ordinary Americans, who are routinely subjected to harsh punishments even for the pettiest of offenses.

The wiretapping scandal of 2005 provides a perfect illustration. In December of that year, the *New York Times* revealed that officials in George W. Bush's administration were eavesdropping on Americans' telephone calls and e-mails without warrants or judicial oversight: a felony punishable by up to five years in prison and a ten-thousand-dollar fine for each offense. The lawbreaking could not have been clearer, yet virtually nobody in the political and media class was willing to call those acts "criminal," much less to demand legal investigations or prosecutions.

This was a depressingly familiar pattern for several decades and became particularly pronounced over the last one. America's political and business establishment presided over a series of extraordinary crimes that brought the United States political disgrace and financial ruin: the creation of a global torture regime; the systematic plundering by Wall Street, leading to the 2008 economic crisis; the serial obstruction of justice by high-ranking political officials; the fraudulent home foreclosures by the nation's largest banks. Yet in almost every instance, the perpetrators were shielded from any legal consequences. As these events clearly demonstrate, America's political culture not only provides strategic advantages in the legal system to political and financial elites, but now actually grants them *immunity* when they knowingly break the law. This license—awarded by the same political class that created the world's largest and most merciless prison state for its poorest and most powerless citizens—represents not just a departure from the rule of law but a fundamental repudiation of it.

The central principle of America's founding was that the rule of law would be the prime equalizing force, the ultimate guardian of justice. The founders considered vast inequality in every other realm to be inevitable and even desirable. Some would be rich, and many would be poor. Some would acquire great power, and many would live their entire lives virtually powerless. A small number of individuals would be naturally endowed with unique and extraordinary talents, while most people, by definition, would be ordinary. Due to those unavoidable circumstances, the American conception of liberty was not only consistent with, but premised on, the inevitability of outcome inequality—the success of some people, the failure of others.

The one exception was the rule of law. When it came to the law, no inequality was tolerable. Law was understood to be the sine qua non ensuring fairness, a level playing field, and a universal set of rules. It was the nonnegotiable prerequisite that made all other forms of inequality acceptable. Only if everyone was bound to the same rules would outcome inequality be justifiable.

So central is this founding principle that most Americans absorb it by osmosis via numerous clichés: All are equal before the law. Justice is blind. No man is above the law. We are, in the words of John Adams, "a nation of laws, not men." For Adams, either the law is supreme in all cases, or the arbitrary will of rulers is. Adams and the other founders viewed the preeminence of law over individuals—all individuals—as the only protection against the tyranny that American colonists had launched a revolution to abolish. For that reason, American political liberty was always inextricably bound to the notion that law reigns supreme.

It would be difficult to overstate the essential place of the rule of law in the American political tradition. A principal grievance against King George III was his unilateral power to vest in himself and those he favored the right to act outside of the law. The goal of the American Revolution was to replace this arbitrary will of the monarch with unbending equal application of law to everyone. "Where, say some, is the King of America?" Thomas Paine, the great American revolutionary, asked in his 1776 pamphlet *Common Sense*. His answer:

> Let a crown be placed thereon, by which the world may know, that so far as we approve of monarchy, that in America the Law is King. For as in absolute governments the King is law, so in free countries the law ought to be King; and there ought to be no other.

Alexander Hamilton did not often see eye to eye with Paine, but on this he heartily agreed. "The instruments by which [government] must act are either the AUTHORITY of the laws or FORCE," he wrote in 1794. "If the first be destroyed, the last must be substituted; and where this becomes the ordinary instrument of government there is an end to liberty!" Like Paine and Hamilton, Adams, in his 1776 *Thoughts on Government,* put the rule of law at the top of his list of core principles for a free and legitimate government: "The very definition of a republic is 'an empire of laws, and not of men.' . . . Good government is an empire of laws."

That last line may at first glance appear simple and even trite, but it contains a critical insight. The supremacy of law is not just one among many instruments of good government; it *is* good government itself. The converse is equally true: in the absence of the rule of law, good government cannot be said to exist.

To be sure, there may be exceptional situations where the rule of men might produce better outcomes than the rule of law. A truly magnanimous tyrant, a benevolent dictator, might conceivably lead to more positive results than a regime of unjust laws rigidly applied. Historians can point to emperors who exercised absolute power while advancing the interests of their subjects and the territories they ruled. Nevertheless, such societies should not be confused with "good government," dependent as they are on the fortuitous emergence of an unrestrained leader who is both well-intentioned and relatively immune from the corrupting effects of power (and, even less plausibly, immune from the absolutely corrupting effects of absolute power). A country that prospers by vesting absolute power in a leader who happens to be benevolent could just as easily come under the control of a malevolent leader the next time around. And when that happens, as at some point it surely will, a society without the rule of law will have no means of redress short of violent revolution.

What's more, even the most well-intentioned leader will eventually abuse his power if he is not constrained by law. Indeed, and somewhat paradoxically, a ruler's belief in his own virtue actually renders abuses of power more likely, since he can rationalize all manner of arbitrary and capricious measures: *I am good and doing this for good ends, and it is therefore justifiable.* Power exercised corruptly inevitably degrades and destroys even genuinely benevolent intent.

The founders understood that magnanimity is very rarely an enduring safeguard against the corrupting influences of power, and because they understood this, they insisted on the rule of law as the only effective weapon against such temptations. "Why has government been instituted at all?" Hamilton asked in

Federalist 15. "Because the passions of men will not conform to the dictates of reason and justice without constraint." Thomas Jefferson wrote in 1798: "In questions of power, then, let no more be heard of confidence in man, but bind him down from mischief by the chains of the Constitution." Adams, in 1772, put it this way: "There is danger from all men. The only maxim of a free government ought to be to trust no man living with power to endanger the public liberty." Four years later, his wife, Abigail, memorably echoed the same sentiment in a letter to him: "Remember, all men would be tyrants if they could."

The rule of law does not guarantee good government: an empire of unjust laws can be as tyrannical as an empire of men, perhaps even more so. But though the rule of law is not *sufficient* by itself to ensure a just and free society, it's absolutely *necessary* for it. For that reason, a nation that renounces the rule of law has rendered tyranny not only likely but inevitable.

The fundamental requirement of the rule of law is equality: the uniform application of a set of preexisting rules to everyone, including the rulers. But like the term *rule of law, equality under the law* has become merely a platitude, a phrase recited without much appreciation of its significance. Everyone claims to believe in it, but hardly anyone remembers what it means. And yet the demand that all be treated equally under the law was no secondary concept to the founding of the United States, but its crux, and it is not difficult to understand why.

What the founders feared most was that a centralized federal government would unwittingly replicate the abuses they had suffered under the king. Unless aggressively constrained, a federal government could erode every precept of liberty that they were attempting to enshrine. It could forcibly override local rule, obliterate self-governance, and, through its sheer weight, transgress every limit. Preventing the government from succumbing to the temptations inherent in its power was the founders' central concern when they were creating the Constitution.

Of course, the law itself also wields tremendous power. The legal system's reach is unparalleled: it can deprive a person of property, liberty, even life. It may compel people to transfer their material goods to others, block them from engaging in planned actions, destroy their reputations, consign them to cages, or even inject lethal chemicals into their veins. Unequal application of the law is thus not merely unjust in theory but devastating in practice. When the law is wielded only against the powerless, it ceases to be a safeguard against injustice and becomes the primary tool of oppression. Unjust acts perpetrated in defiance of the law are relatively easy to fight against, but unjust acts perpetrated under cover of law are much harder to challenge. Thus, not only does unequal application of law result in the loss of something good and necessary; it becomes a potent means for entrenching and protecting exactly that which law is designed to prevent.

In his 1795 essay *Dissertations on First Principles of Government,* Paine thus insisted that "the true and only true basis of representative government" is equal application of law to all citizens: rich and poor, strong and weak, powerful and powerless, landowner and tenant. Without equal application of the laws, Benjamin Franklin warned in his 1774 *Emblematical Representations,* society would fracture into two tiers: the "favored" and the "oppressed." The result, he said, would be "great and violent jealousies and animosities" between these classes, and a "total separation of affections, interests, political obligations, and all manner of connections, by which the whole state is weakened."

Revealingly, the central function of the Constitution as

law—the supreme law—was to impose limitations not on the behavior of ordinary citizens but on the federal government itself. The government, and those who ran it, were not placed outside the law, but expressly targeted by it. Indeed, the Bill of Rights is little more than a description of the lines that the most powerful political officials are barred from crossing, even if they have the power to do so and even when the majority of citizens might wish them to do so.

The vital aim of law, then, was to ensure that the powerful were subjected to its dictates on equal terms with the powerless. As Jefferson put it in an April 16, 1784, letter to George Washington, the foundation on which any constitution must rest is "the denial of every preeminence." In his 1786 *Answers to Monsieur de Meusnier's Questions*, Jefferson argued that the essence of America was that "the poorest laborer stood on equal ground with the wealthiest millionaire, and generally on a more favored one whenever their rights seem to jar." Even Hamilton, who made no attempt to conceal his belief in a strong executive, argued in *Federalist 71* that the president had to be "subordinate to the laws." The notion of *law* simply makes no sense, and has no good purpose, unless all are bound by its dictates.

The dangers of abandoning this principle were well recognized. In *Federalist 57*, James Madison emphasized that equal application of the law to political elites was a prerequisite for a free and cohesive society ("one of the strongest bonds by which human policy can connect the rulers and the people together"), and warned that in its absence "every government degenerates into tyranny." Perhaps most tellingly of all, the founder who was the least philosophically inclined but the most practiced in the exigencies of governance—George Washington—vowed, in a letter written in December 1795, that there would never be immunity for wrongdoing by high government officials on his watch: "The executive branch of this government never has, nor will suffer, while I preside, any improper conduct of its officers to escape with impunity."

What the founders recognized was that unless the law were applied equally, subjecting all citizens to its mandates, the Constitution would simply consist of a set of guidelines or suggestions, compliance being optional. In view of that danger, equal enforcement was embedded in formal American jurisprudence from early on as the linchpin of the rule of law. The seminal 1803 Supreme Court case *Marbury v. Madison* is widely remembered for having established the foundation for how the U.S. government functions: Congress enacts laws, the president executes them, and the courts "say what the law is." But the Supreme Court's ruling was just as meaningful for what it signaled about how the principle of equality under the law would work in practice. The central dispute in *Marbury* was whether the courts had the authority to subject officials in the executive branch to their rulings—that is, whether officials who violated the law could be compelled to submit to judicial decrees. The court's unanimous decision announced that the judicial branch had not only the right but the duty to enforce the law on all citizens, including high-level officials in the executive branch. "The very essence of civil liberty certainly consists in the right of every individual to claim the protection of the laws," the chief justice wrote.

What makes the founders' insistence on equality under the law all the more striking is that none believed in equality as a general proposition. Indeed, the opposite is true: they considered inequality on every level, other than in law, to be the natural, inevitable, and just state of affairs. Even Jefferson, one of the most egalitarian of the founders, held that there was "a natural aristocracy" among men, based on "virtue and talents." And he saw its existence as not only inevitable but desirable: "The natural aristocracy I consider as the most precious gift of nature for the instruction, the trusts, and government of society." Similarly, for Adams, inequality was both inevitable and natural, even divinely ordained: "It already appears, that there must be in every society of men superiors and inferiors, because God has laid in the constitution and course of nature the foundations of the distinction." Yet the founders concurred that nothing constituted a greater threat to the Republic than to allow this inequality of wealth or political power to determine the treatment of citizens before the law. In particular, they disdained superior and inferior positions imposed by the state rather than determined by merit. Paine, for instance, loathed inherited titles on the ground that they doled out rewards based on assigned status rather unrelated to entitlement. He declared:

> Nature is often giving to the world some extraordinary men who arrive at fame by merit and universal consent, such as Aristotle, Socrates, Plato, etc. They were truly great or noble. But when government sets up a manufactory of nobles, it is as absurd as if she undertook to manufacture wise men. Her nobles are all counterfeits.

To Paine, a system of legally enforced inequality would enable the elite to exploit the law to entrench unearned prerogatives or shield ill-gotten gains. And those counterfeit nobles would turn the law into a tool to promote and protect injustice rather than to correct it. Though Paine's liveliest polemics were devoted to scorning the accumulation of wealth, he had no quarrel with income inequality *provided* that there was no such inequality under law. The rich could buy what they desired, dress and eat as they wished, and wallow in the most effete comforts and luxuries. But the law was the one realm where their money and property would count for nothing.

One point is vital to acknowledge: like all of the other principles espoused by the founders, equality under the law was not always observed in practice. Indeed, it was often violently breached from the very beginning of the Republic. Slavery, the dispossession of Native Americans, the denial of voting rights to women, and the granting of superior legal rights to property owners are a few of the most glaring deviations.

But even when the principle of equal treatment was betrayed, American leaders in every era have emphatically affirmed it, not so much out of hypocrisy as out of aspiration. Indeed, for those who were devoted to justice, the persistence of inequality was precisely what made equality before the law so imperative. Over time, this principle would provide the road map for eradicating injustice. It was the impetus for the abolition of slavery; the enactment of the Fourteenth Amendment, with its overarching guarantee of "equal protection of the laws"; the enfranchisement and empowerment of women; the civil rights movement; enhanced protections for the poor in the criminal justice process; and numerous other legal and social reforms of the last two centuries.

Today, equal application of the law remains a sacrosanct principle among virtually all legal theorists. Contemporary scholars routinely emphasize that the rule of law cannot exist without legal equality. As the constitutional legal scholar Michel Rosenfeld argues, the rule of law is not merely weakened if "the ruler and his or her associates consistently remain above the law"; it ceases to exist by definition. When the powerful can effectively exempt themselves from law's punishments, we live under "the rule of men," even if we maintain a facade of laws and other trappings of a legal system, such as courts, legislatures, and judges. Indeed, it's nearly impossible to find a definition of the *rule of law* that does not contain some requirement that the law be applied equally. As Judge Diane Wood, of the Seventh Circuit Court of Appeals, observes, the consensus view is that "there is no one in a society governed by law who is above the law or immune from some form of legal constraint."

This conception is practically universal, certainly in the West. In the early 1990s, the World Bank and International Monetary Fund announced that any states wishing to receive financial assistance were required to respect the rule of law, prompting debate over what exactly that entailed. In a 1998 essay in *Foreign Affairs*, Thomas Carothers of the Carnegie Endowment for International Peace articulated the standard used by the Western world to dictate to developing nations what the rule of law minimally demands. The rule of law, he wrote, is "a system in which the laws . . . apply equally to everyone." Unless the political and financial elites are subject to the same laws as everyone else, he argued, there could be no rule of law—only its trappings. He cited Latin America, Asia, the former Soviet Union, and parts of the former Eastern bloc as examples of "the ruling elite's tendency to act extralegally" wherever "legal systems remain captive of the powers that be." The most crucial challenge in developing countries, as Carothers put it, is that elites "must give up the habit of placing themselves above the law."

We face a similar challenge in the United States today. For

all the homage we pay to equality under law, we have virtually abolished it in practice. Indeed, beyond isolated, politically motivated rhetoric, we hardly even pretend to believe in its validity any longer. Instead, the United States now has the exact opposite of a single set of laws before which everyone is equal. It has an entrenched two-tiered system of justice: the country's most powerful political and financial elites are virtually immunized from the rule of law, empowered to commit felonies with full-scale impunity and to act without any constraints, while the politically powerless are imprisoned with greater ease and in far greater numbers than in any other country on the planet.

Over the past several decades, we have witnessed numerous examples of serious lawbreaking on the part of our most powerful political and financial leaders with no consequences of any kind. It is no exaggeration to state that the current consensus among journalists and politicians is that except in the most blatant and sensationalistic cases (typically ones in which other powerful factions are aggrieved—a Bernie Madoff here, a Rod Blagojevich there), criminal prosecutions are simply not appropriate for the country's elites. Courtrooms, indictments, and prisons are there for ordinary Americans, not for the ruling classes, and virtually never for our highest political leaders.

The central promise of the American founding—that all would stand equal before the rule of law no matter what other political and economic inequality was allowed—has been abandoned. Two features of contemporary American political life are particularly significant in this regard. First, the elites' exemption from the rule of law has been strengthened at exactly the same time that the law has become an increasingly draconian instrument of punishment for the rest of Americans—particularly the poor and racial minorities. Not only does the law fail to equalize the playing field; it perpetuates and even generates tremendous social inequality.

Second, though unequal application of the law has always been pervasive in American society, until recently such inequality was regarded as a problem: something to be deplored and, if possible, corrected. Today, however, substantial factions in our political culture explicitly renounce the principle of legal equality itself. It is now quite common for American political discourse to include arguments expressly justifying the elites' legal impunity and openly calling for radically different treatment under the law for various classes of people based on their power, status, and wealth.

Historically, our collective insistence on the principle of equality under law has been principally responsible for our forward progress, our ability to identify and eliminate major and minor transgressions. Conversely, our abandonment of that principle precludes such progress and, worse, shields legal inequality from reform. A society that demands equality under the law will move inexorably toward it. A society that renounces this virtue will move in the opposite direction. We have, manifestly, become a society that no longer even rhetorically affirms the necessity for this equality, and the outcome is exactly as dangerous, oppressive, and antidemocratic as the American founders warned it would be.

1

THE ORIGIN OF ELITE IMMUNITY

Wealth and power have always conferred substantial advantages, and it is thus unsurprising that throughout history the rich and well-connected have enjoyed superior treatment under the law. In the past, those advantages were broadly seen as failures of justice and ruefully acknowledged as shortcomings of the legal system. Today, however, in a radical and momentous shift, the American political class and its media increasingly repudiate the principle that the law must be equally applied to all. To hear our politicians and our press tell it, the conclusion is inescapable: we're far better off when political and financial elites—and they alone—are shielded from criminal accountability.

It has become a virtual consensus among the elites that their members are so indispensable to the running of American society that vesting them with immunity from prosecution—even for the most egregious crimes—is not only in their interest but in our interest, too. Prosecutions, courtrooms, and prisons, it's hinted—and sometimes even explicitly stated—are for the rabble, like the street-side drug peddlers we occasionally glimpse from our car windows, not for the political and financial leaders who manage our nation and fuel our prosperity. It is simply too disruptive, distracting, and unjust, we are told, to subject them to the burden of legal consequences.

This is no hyperbole. As multiple episodes demonstrate, a belief that elite immunity is both necessary and justified has indeed become the prevailing ethos in the nation's most influential circles. In countless instances over recent years, prominent political and media figures have insisted that serious crimes by the most powerful should be overlooked—either in the name of the common good, or in the name of a warped conception of fairness according to which those with the greatest power are the most entitled to deference and understanding.

This is what makes the contemporary form of American lawlessness new and unprecedented. It is now perfectly common, and perfectly acceptable, to openly advocate elite immunity. And this advocacy has had its intended effect: the United States has become a nation that does not apply the rule of law to its elite class, which is another way of saying that the United States does not apply the rule of law.

The last decade in particular is full of examples. Consider the way our political class responded to the crimes committed by the Bush administration during the "war on terror." Even as recently as 2007, allegations that the administration was breaking laws and committing felonies were dismissed as shrill, groundless rhetoric. But now it is understood even in the most mainstream opinion-making circles that numerous actions undertaken by top Bush officials—torture, warrantless eavesdropping, the Central Intelligence Agency's black sites, politicized prosecutions, obstruction of justice—violated the law. This recognition, however, did not lead to calls by our politicians or by the establishment press for what should naturally follow from the discovery of serious crimes: criminal investigations and prosecutions. Instead, nothing happened, even though the United States is a party to two separate treaties—the Geneva Conventions and the Convention Against Torture—that obligate all signatory countries to prosecute any officials who ordered, authorized, or otherwise perpetrated torture. And since the U.S. Constitution states that international treaties made "under Authority of the United States" shall be "the Supreme Law of the Land," not only are the radical acts of the Bush administration illegal, but so, too, is the ongoing refusal to investigate and prosecute those crimes.

The consensus that even the most serious Bush crimes need not—and should not—be prosecuted reflects our political class's central belief: that the law simply does not apply to them. And the result of that mind-set is exactly what one would expect: a group that knows it can break the law with impunity increasingly does so. If the threat of real punishment for criminality is removed, for many rational people there will be little incentive to abide by the law and much incentive to break it. Alexander Hamilton, in *Federalist 15*, explained why.

> It is essential to the idea of a law, that it be attended with a sanction; or, in other words, a penalty or punishment for disobedience. If there be no penalty annexed to disobedience, the resolutions or commands which pretend to be laws will, in fact, amount to nothing more than advice or recommendation.

For the nation's most powerful elites, the law has indeed been whittled down to "nothing more than advice or recommendation." Although there have been episodes of unpunished elite malfeasance throughout American history, the explicit, systematic embrace of the notion that such malfeasance should be shielded from legal consequences begins with the Watergate scandal—one of the clearest cases of widespread, deliberate criminality at the highest level of the U.S. government.

THE EVOLUTION OF ELITE IMMUNITY

When first presented to the public, Watergate was broadly dismissed as an insignificant affair, a "third-rate burglary" that few imagined could topple a popular president. Once it was subjected to intense media focus, reaction to the scandal largely broke down along partisan lines. Most (though not all) leading Republicans belittled its importance or insisted that President Richard Nixon had no direct culpability in the crimes. Democratic leaders, for their part, tried to exploit the scandal for political gain, but without much vigor or conviction that it could actually sink the president. As segments of both Congress and the media tenaciously pursued the truth, however, it became undeniable that serious criminality had pervaded the upper reaches of government.

By the scandal's conclusion, few contested that not only Nixon's top aides but Nixon himself had committed serious felonies—either in authorizing the break-in and related illegalities, or in obstructing the ensuing investigation. Nonetheless, Nixon was ultimately shielded from all legal consequences thanks to the pardon granted by his handpicked vice president, Gerald Ford—who, it was widely believed, secured his appointment by agreeing to protect Nixon from prosecution.

In his 1983 book *The Price of Power*, Seymour Hersh compiled extensive evidence suggesting an implicit if not overt deal. As he makes clear, Ford was selected because Nixon and his secretary of state, Alexander Haig, were confident that they could count on Ford's protection. "Nixon and Haig thought of Ford as a proven commodity," writes Hersh, "a man who placed loyalty to Nixon and the Republican presidency above his personal ambitions and his political well-being. They assumed, according to the aides, that Ford would take care of his former boss as soon as he became President."

Americans would condemn this sort of arrangement as cronyism and corruption of the sleaziest sort if they witnessed it in another country. In the United States, however, political and media elites (though not the general public) widely agreed that immunizing the felony-committing president from the criminal justice system was the right thing to do.

Ford first explained his decision to pardon Nixon in a speech to the nation on September 8, 1974. The new president began by paying lip service to the rule of law: "I deeply believe in equal justice for all Americans, whatever their station or former station. The law, whether human or divine, is no respecter of persons; but"—and here he tacked on a newly concocted amendment designed to gut that phrase's meaning—"the law is a respecter of reality." Ford then proceeded to recite what have by now become the standard clichés our political class uses to justify immunity. Watergate, he intoned,

is an American tragedy in which we all have played a part. It could go on and on and on, or someone must write the end to it. I have concluded that only I can do that, and if I can, I must. . . .

The facts, as I see them, are that a former President of the United States, instead of enjoying equal treatment with any other citizen accused of violating the law, would be cruelly and excessively penalized either in preserving the presumption of his innocence or in obtaining a speedy determination of his guilt in order to repay a legal debt to society.

During this long period of delay and potential litigation, ugly passions would again be aroused. And our people would again be polarized in their opinions. And the credibility of our free institutions of government would again be challenged at home and abroad. . . .

My conscience tells me clearly and certainly that I cannot prolong the bad dreams that continue to reopen a chapter that is closed. My conscience tells me that only I, as President, have the constitutional power to firmly shut and seal this book. My conscience tells me it is my duty, not merely to proclaim domestic tranquility but to use every means that I have to insure it.

Remarkably, Ford explicitly pointed to Nixon's lofty status as a reason to exempt him from the accountability applied to ordinary Americans—a complete reversal and rejection of the central covenant of the American founding. Ford's signature line—"Our long national nightmare is over"—put a heroic spin on the betrayal of the rule of law: we end the "nightmare" of high-level criminality by sweeping it under the rug, protecting the wrongdoers, and pretending their crimes never happened.

Upon Ford's death in December 2006, prominent figures rushed forth to consecrate his pardon of Nixon as an act of great nobility, magnanimity, and self-sacrifice, and thus to glorify its underlying premises. Leading the charge, not surprisingly, was Dick Cheney, Ford's former chief of staff and the then–vice president. By 2006, Cheney himself had been accused of involvement in a wide variety of illegal acts, from establishing a worldwide torture regime and spying on Americans without warrants to outing a covert CIA agent and obstructing the resulting investigation. Cheney's own interests were thus clearly served by exploiting Ford's death to bolster the propagandistic notion that elite immunity is dispensed not for the benefit of the powerful but rather in patriotic service of the common good. At Ford's funeral, Cheney eulogized his former boss by heralding the pardon as an act of national salvation.

> This President's hardest decision was also among his first. And in September of 1974, Gerald Ford was almost alone in understanding that there can be no healing without pardon. . . . It was this man, Gerald R. Ford, who led our republic safely through a crisis that could have turned to catastrophe. We will never know what further unravelings, what greater malevolence might have come in that time of furies turned loose and hearts turned cold. But we do know this: America was spared the worst. And this was the doing of an American President. For all the grief that never came, for all the wounds that were never inflicted, the people of the United States will forever stand in debt to the good man and faithful servant we mourn tonight.

In fairness to Dick Cheney, we heard the same message from others, almost note for note. The *Washington Post*'s David Broder—the so-called dean of the Washington press corps—spoke for many journalists, past and present, when asked what would have happened had Nixon not been immunized.

> My guess is that there would have been strong public pressure for prosecution of Richard Nixon, since several of his White House associates were already facing criminal charges. A

lengthy trial would have been a difficult ordeal for the country, something President Ford wanted to spare Americans.

The actual beneficiary of the pardon, of course, was not "Americans" but Richard Nixon. Thanks to Ford's act, Nixon himself was shielded from the kind of punishment that, as a "law-and-order Republican," he had devoted his career to imposing on ordinary Americans when they broke the law, no matter how petty the offense. Yet this grant of immunity to the nation's most powerful figure was endlessly cast as a generous gift to the American public, which—we were repeatedly told—had been spared the agony, acrimony, and shame of seeing their leader held accountable for his crimes as any other citizen would be.

The Nixon pardon, and the way it was sold to the country, became the template for justifying elite immunity. Nowadays, with only rare exceptions, each time top members of the nation's political class are caught committing a crime, the same reasons are hauled out to get them off the hook. Prosecuting public officials mires us in a "divisive" past when we should be looking forward. It is wrong to "criminalize policy disputes"—meaning crimes committed with the use of political power. Political elites who commit crimes in carrying out their duties are "well-intentioned" and so do not deserve to be treated as if they were common criminals; moreover, politicians who are forced out of office and have their reputations damaged already "suffer enough." To prosecute them would only engender a cycle of retribution. Political harmony thus trumps the need to enforce the rule of law.

Of course, all criminal prosecutions are, by definition, exercises in looking to the past rather than the future. All prosecutions impose substantial burdens on the accused, cost enormous amounts of time and money to resolve, and are plagued by

numerous imperfections. The nation always faces pressing chal-
lenges and urgent problems from which headline-grabbing
prosecutions will distract attention. All individuals accused of
serious crimes suffer in multiple ways long before—and completely independent of—any actual punishment. And while it is
true that criminal proceedings involving politicians who commit crimes in office inevitably engender partisan divisions and
undermine political harmony, citing these circumstances as just
cause for legal immunity is, by definition, creating a license to
break the law.

In his memoirs, Ford explicitly acknowledged that he had
dispensed with the rule of law when pardoning Nixon, but he
went on to defend his decision anyway. Indeed, Ford claimed
that political leaders have not only the right to act as he did, but
the obligation. As he put it in *A Time to Heal*: "I learned that
public policy often took precedence over a rule of law. Although
I respected the tenet that no man should be above the law, public
policy demanded that I put Nixon—and Watergate—behind
us as quickly as possible." One would be hard-pressed to find an
instance of the American founders—or anyone who genuinely
believed in the rule of law—claiming that "public policy often
took precedence" over justice. To believe that public policy considerations, as assessed by a particular individual, override the
rule of law is simply a euphemism for declaring that the rule of
law is dead and the rule of men reigns supreme. Yet starting with
Ford, such explicit repudiations of the rule of law have become
an increasingly common and perfectly respectable view.

Notably, there were a handful of influential people at the
time of the Watergate scandal, including some in government,
who vehemently objected to Ford's pardon. They pointed out
that the pardon subverted the central American premise that all

are equal before the law, and warned that immunizing Nixon would create a dangerous precedent. Ford's own press secretary, Jerald terHorst, resigned in protest a mere thirty days after being appointed. In his September 8, 1974, resignation letter, terHorst condemned the two-tiered system of justice he believed the pardons would entrench.

> As your spokesman, I do not know how I could credibly defend that action in the absence of a like decision to grant absolute pardon to the young men who evaded Vietnam military service as a matter of conscience and the absence of pardons for former aides and associates of Mr. Nixon who have been charged with crimes—and imprisoned—stemming from the same Watergate situation. . . .
>
> These are also men whose reputations and families have been grievously injured. Try as I can, it is impossible to conclude that the former president is more deserving of mercy than persons of lesser station in life whose offenses have had far less effect on our national wellbeing.

TerHorst's view was shared by large numbers of ordinary Americans. Hersh reports that "seventeen thousand telegrams were sent to the White House within two days, running at 'about six to one,' by a White House spokesman's count, against the pardon." And a handful of liberal Democrats, including Elizabeth Holtzman, Bella Abzug, and John Conyers, demanded an investigation into Ford's conduct. But theirs was clearly the minority view in America's most influential circles.

Instead, appeals to empathy were deployed to defend the pardon. As *Time* reported in October 1974:

Some of the members of Congress were worried about what Ford's pardoning of Nixon did to the nation's standards of equality under the law. California's Don Edwards, a liberal Democrat, wondered how Ford would explain American justice to his students if he were a high school teacher in Watts or Harlem. Ford's reply was that Nixon was the only President to resign in shame and disgrace; that, he implied, was punishment enough. South Carolina's James R. Mann, a conservative Democrat, asked if Ford agreed with "the maxim that the law is no respecter of persons." Ford's reply: "Certainly it should be." The gentle, courtly Mann seemed about to follow up the question but hesitated and then said softly, "Thank you, Mr. President."

Needless to say, the empathy Ford expressed for Nixon is rarely invoked as a means of arguing for leniency, let alone immunity, for ordinary Americans. That's because Ford's call for "empathy" is merely disguised aristocratic privilege.

THE PRECEDENT EXPLOITED

The precedent established by the Nixon pardon would be exploited little more than a decade later, when another group of high-level offenders—the Iran-Contra criminals of the Ronald Reagan and George H. W. Bush administrations—were seeking immunity from prosecution. Sure enough, they got it: White House officials who clearly and knowingly broke the law, and then deliberately lied to Congress about what they had done (also a felony), were systematically protected from any consequences for their crimes.

The Iran-Contra scandal erupted in 1986, when it was revealed that the Reagan administration had sold arms—antitank and antiaircraft missiles—to the Ayatollah Khomeini's regime in Iran. The purpose of the deal was twofold. Initially, it was meant to help secure the release of six American hostages who were being held by Iranian-backed Shia militants in Lebanon. At the same time, the money received from the sale of these weapons to Iran was used to fund the Contras, a CIA-backed rebel group fighting to overthrow the Sandinista government in Nicaragua.

Reagan's approval of a weapons-for-hostages deal was an astonishing act of hypocrisy for a self-styled tough guy who had boasted that he would never "negotiate with terrorists." Indeed, Reagan had imposed a harsh embargo against Iran because of the hostage crisis, so the news that he was covertly shoveling high-tech arms to the Iranian government was politically shocking.

But the funding of the Contras—a guerrilla group responsible for brutal atrocities against civilians, widely denounced in many parts of the world as a terrorist organization—was not just shocking. It was a clear-cut crime. In 1982, Congress had enacted and Reagan had signed into law the Boland Amendment, which explicitly banned any government assistance to the Contras for the purpose of overthrowing the Nicaraguan government. (The law had been prompted by the revelation that the CIA had been funding and providing assistance to those guerrillas without the knowledge of Congress.) The 1986 Iran-Contra disclosures revealed that Reagan officials had done exactly that which the law prohibited: they had funneled millions of dollars to the Contras in order to facilitate the overthrow of the Sandinistas.

When the covert program was revealed, numerous legal

proceedings were initiated. Among them was an action brought by Nicaragua against the United States in the International Court of Justice, charging that the United States had illegally attempted to overthrow the Nicaraguan government. The court ruled in favor of Nicaragua and ordered the United States to pay substantial compensation, but the Reagan administration refused to comply with the court's order and then used the United States' seat on the Security Council to veto any efforts by the United Nations to enforce the judgment.

Domestically, the Justice Department appointed an independent prosecutor, Lawrence Walsh, to investigate Iran-Contra. Over the next several years, numerous Reagan appointees—including high-level officials at the National Security Agency, the Defense Department, the CIA, and the State Department—were indicted, both for the crimes themselves and for lying to federal investigators and to Congress in order to cover up the scandal. In the end, though, not a single one of them would serve even a day in prison.

Two key Reagan aides—Lieutenant Colonel Oliver North and John Poindexter—had their convictions overturned on appeal, on the ground that information they provided under a grant of immunity had been improperly used against them. National Security Adviser Robert McFarlane and Assistant Secretary of State Elliott Abrams pleaded guilty to several misdemeanor counts of illegally withholding information, but they were pardoned by George H. W. Bush during his last month in office. Yet it was the treatment of the highest-ranking official to be indicted— Defense Secretary Caspar Weinberger—that best illustrates the prevailing ethos of elite immunity.

Weinberger had been charged with multiple felony counts of perjury and obstruction of justice after the 1991 discovery of diaries that contradicted much of what he had told investigators. Though he had been required to turn over those diaries to prosecutors, Weinberger had failed to do so. Once the contents of the diaries were publicly revealed, the reasons for his concealment became obvious. Not only did they contradict his own denials of knowledge of the transactions, but the diaries directly implicated other key officials, including President Reagan himself. As Walsh put it, "Weinberger's early and deliberate decision to conceal and withhold extensive contemporaneous notes of the Iran-contra matter radically altered the official investigations and possibly forestalled timely impeachment proceedings against President Reagan and other officials." The special prosecutor added that the "notes contain evidence of a conspiracy among the highest-ranking Reagan Administration officials to lie to Congress and the American public."

Weinberger's trial was set to begin in January 1993. However, on December 24, 1992, the former Pentagon chief, along with five others (four of whom had already been convicted and one of whom was set to stand trial), was pardoned by Bush 41, who was less than a month away from leaving office, having been defeated by Bill Clinton in the 1992 election. A December 25, 1992, editorial in the *New York Times*—one of the very few mainstream institutions to condemn the pardons—noted that the rationale invoked by Bush 41 to justify his actions was a replica of the excuses Ford had relied on to protect Richard Nixon.

> If Mr. Bush had rested his pardon of Mr. Weinberger on the former Defense Secretary's health alone, he might deserve credit for compassion. But he went on to lecture Lawrence

Walsh, the independent prosecutor, against what he called "the criminalization of policy differences."

That's a bogus complaint. Mr. Weinberger was not charged with lying to Congress because of policy differences; lying to Congress for any reason is criminal conduct. . . .

When President Ford pardoned Richard Nixon for Watergate crimes—a precedent Mr. Bush ignored in his pardon message—he said he acted to restore harmony and move on. Mr. Bush invoked the same sentiments. But the Nixon pardon was wrong, too.

And like Ford's pardon, Bush's won praise from the overwhelming majority of politicians and journalists. Weinberger, after all, was a member in good standing of the political class generally and the Washington establishment in particular. He had been a close associate of Reagan's since the 1960s, when Reagan was governor of California, and he had held a number of key posts under Nixon—including director of the Office of Management and Budget, where his merciless cost-cutting measures had earned him the nickname "Cap the Knife." In a pattern no one considers unusual anymore, "Cap the Knife" had then converted the praise earned as Nixon's OMB cost cutter into a plum position as vice president and general counsel of the Bechtel Corporation, which must have found his contacts in DC to be very useful indeed.

In other words, in the eyes of the political and media establishment, Weinberger was not someone who belonged in a prison cell—not even when there was clear evidence that he had committed serious felonies. As Robert Parry detailed in *Consortium News*, journalists and political operatives from across the political spectrum closed ranks to celebrate the immunity bestowed on Weinberger and his coconspirators.

> The Washington elites rallied to Weinberger's defense. In the salons of Georgetown, there was palpable relief in December 1992 when President Bush pardoned Weinberger and five other Iran-contra defendants, effectively ending the Iran-contra investigation.
>
> *Washington Post* columnist Richard Cohen spoke for many insiders. In a column [on December 30, 1992], Cohen described how impressed he was that Weinberger would push his own shopping cart at the Georgetown Safeway, often called the "social Safeway" because so many members of Washington's establishment shopped there.
>
> "Based on my Safeway encounters, I came to think of Weinberger as a basic sort of guy, candid and no nonsense—which is the way much of official Washington saw him," Cohen wrote in praise of the pardon. "Cap, my Safeway buddy, walks, and that's all right with me."

Let us pause for a moment to reflect on how perverse that is. Richard Cohen describes himself as a journalist and is presented as such to his readers by the *Washington Post*. Our journalist class never tires of touting their vital role as intrepid, adversarial watchdogs keeping a keen eye on the politically powerful. Yet here was an influential pundit explicitly defending the immunity granted to Caspar Weinberger on the grounds that the Pentagon chief was in his social circle and was a fine, admirable man and thus—unlike the many common Washingtonians convicted and imprisoned every day for petty crimes without the slightest objection from Cohen—deserved to be shielded from the criminal justice system. A more naked rejection of Jefferson's "natural equality of man, the denial of every preeminence" can scarcely be imagined.

What made the pardon even more pernicious was that the person issuing it—George H. W. Bush—had been centrally involved in many of the incriminating acts as Reagan's vice president and was widely believed to be at risk himself if the trials of Weinberger and the others proceeded. A major effect of pardoning the remaining Iran-Contra criminals was to put an end to the investigations and thus to exempt Bush from accountability for his own crimes. The post-Nixon pattern was reaffirmed: those who are most politically powerful in our society could break the law with impunity. Lawrence Walsh, the Iran-Contra special prosecutor (and lifelong Republican), said as much.

> President Bush's pardon of Caspar Weinberger and other Iran-contra defendants undermines the principle that no man is above the law. It demonstrates that powerful people with powerful allies can commit serious crimes in high office— deliberately abusing the public trust without consequence.
>
> Weinberger, who faced four felony charges, deserved to be tried by a jury of citizens. Although it is the President's prerogative to grant pardons, it is every American's right that the criminal justice system be administered fairly, regardless of a person's rank and connections.

The path from the Watergate and Iran-Contra pardons to the immunity now routinely enjoyed by political elites is easy to see. In 1987, when a House committee issued a report finding that Reagan officials had broken the law, a dissenting claim (authored by future Bush 43 White House aide David Addington) was filed by then–GOP congressman Dick Cheney. Despite obvious evidence of lawbreaking, Cheney defiantly argued that the Reagan administration had done nothing wrong, but rather had acted patriotically. Cheney claimed that Article II of the Constitution, by anointing the president "commander in chief," vests him with virtually absolute power in foreign policy-making; the other branches cannot restrict him even by duly enacted statutes of the Congress. Two decades later, when the *New York Times* reported that the Bush administration had ordered the National Security Agency to spy on Americans without the warrants required by law, Cheney likewise insisted that it had done nothing wrong and relied on that same theory of presidential omnipotence. When asked how he could advance such a claim in light of the clear dictates of the law, he responded, "If you want to understand why this program is legal . . . go back and read my Iran-Contra report."

Moreover, during the Bush 43 years, serial lying under oath by high-level political officials became the norm. To gain an appreciation of this culture of crime, one might consider the case of Bush attorney general Alberto Gonzales, whose lies about multiple scandals became so blatant that he was eventually forced to leave office. In 2008, the Bush Justice Department's own inspector general issued a report on Gonzales's testimony concerning the NSA's warrantless eavesdropping program, finding, as *Congressional Quarterly* reported, that there was "strong evidence. . . that the former attorney general lied to federal investigators probing his careless handling of highly classified documents." A separate inquiry in 2009 by the DOJ's inspector general—this one involving the scandal arising out of Gonzales's firing of eight U.S. attorneys—found that he "may have lied to Congress." And a 2009 report jointly issued by the inspectors general of five different cabinet agencies concerning the NSA wiretapping concluded that Gonzales had provided "confusing, inaccurate" statements when testifying to Congress about government eavesdropping. Yet even though lying to Congress and federal investigators is a felony under U.S. law, none of those incidents led to any criminal investigations of Gonzales, let alone indictments or prosecutions.

This nonchalant attitude toward Gonzales's lawbreaking followed the template established during the Watergate and Iran-Contra scandals, where high-level officials had similarly been let off the hook. Tellingly, Oliver North, a key figure in Iran-Contra, became a beloved folk hero on the right *because* of how proudly he boasted of lying to Congress. Consider the following exchange between North and John Nields, counsel to the congressional joint committee investigating Iran-Contra—an exchange that boosted North into superstardom among the Republican faithful and many in the media class.

NORTH: I will tell you right now, counsel, and to all the members here gathered, that I misled the Congress.

NIELDS: At that meeting?

NORTH: At that meeting.

NIELDS: Face to face?

NORTH: Face to face.

NIELDS: You made false statements to them about your activities in support of the Contras?

NORTH: I did.

North then proceeded to proclaim that lying to Congress had been the patriotic thing to do. Days later, North's loyal secretary, Fawn Hall, captured the prevailing ethos at the Reagan

National Security Council when she declared, "Sometimes you have to go above the written law."

Indeed, many of the key culprits from Iran-Contra—including Elliott Abrams, John Poindexter, John Negroponte, and Otto Reich—went on to occupy important positions in George W. Bush's administration, while several others ascended to positions of influence in the political and media establishment. Less than a decade after his indictment, Oliver North became the GOP Senate nominee in Virginia. After almost unseating the incumbent, Senator Chuck Robb, he was rewarded with a Fox News contract. Reagan's defense secretary, Caspar Weinberger, left the government under a heavy cloud of scandal but soon ascended to the position of publisher at *Forbes* magazine. In 2002, he was the featured witness at a Senate Foreign Relations Committee hearing, where he advocated an attack on Iraq while all the senators in attendance—led by committee chairman Joe Biden—treated him with the utmost deference.

That Iran-Contra participants were rewarded with high-profile media posts and sensitive jobs in the Bush 43 administration highlights that lying to Congress is no longer considered a shameful act and is indeed seen by some as perfectly normal, an exercise of a legitimate right by the president and those who work under him. This lenient attitude completely disregards the fact that the law, as enacted by the American people through their representatives in Congress, unambiguously classifies such behavior as a felony.

The embrace of elite immunity is by no means confined to one party. The conviction that political elites should be shielded from accountability is fully bipartisan and has been embraced by every administration over the past several decades. When Bill Clinton campaigned for president against the incumbent, George

H. W. Bush, in 1991, he repeatedly argued that there was serious wrongdoing requiring urgent investigation and possibly prosecution. Clinton was referring not only to the Iran-Contra affair but also to the so-called Iraqgate scandal. Iraqgate entailed well-documented allegations that officials in both the Reagan and Bush administrations, in their efforts to fuel Iraq's war with Iran, had secretly and illegally supplied Saddam Hussein with large amounts of money, weapons technology, training, military intelligence, and even nuclear components. The iconic photograph of Donald Rumsfeld, who was then Reagan's special envoy to the Middle East, smiling and shaking hands with Saddam in 1985 captured the essence of Iraqgate: the highest-level Reagan and Bush officials unlawfully supporting a regime that had, only a few years before, headlined the U.S. list of "State Sponsors of Terrorism." (Indeed, when officials in the Bush 43 administration spent all of 2002 and early 2003 beating the drums for war against Iraq, they frequently cited atrocities such as Saddam's "gassing of his own people"—atrocities perpetrated during the very period when Reagan and Bush 41 were illegally building up Saddam's military and financial strength and concealing his crimes. Another result of the U.S. support for the Iraqi dictator during the 1980s, of course, was that a stronger and emboldened Saddam soon decided to invade Kuwait.)

But as soon as Clinton was safely elected president, he quickly took steps to suppress any real inquiries into Iraqgate, invoking the same reasoning that had been used to justify the pardons of Nixon and the Iran-Contra criminals. In November 1993, when some establishment journalists still took seriously their role as adversarial checks on those in power, the *Washington Post* columnist Mary McGrory excoriated the new president for his role in blocking accountability.

During the campaign, Bill Clinton indignantly promised to get to the bottom of [Iraqgate]. But a deep incuriosity has set in, and so far his Justice Department has accepted the finding of an in-house whitewash headed by retired judge Frederick Lacey. Attorney General Janet Reno has indicated she will make an investigation of her own. But who would take seriously any probe that Justice might make of its own outrageous behavior?

The president, it is said, wants to forget yesterday and concentrate on tomorrow, because he needs the help of Republicans in Congress. But truth has its uses in a republic, and is especially beneficial to presidents who may be contemplating loony and illicit foreign policies, as Bush did, even with Iran-contra fresh in his mind.

McGrory's protests fell on deaf ears. By then, the proclamation that we must "forget yesterday and concentrate on tomorrow" was ingrained Beltway orthodoxy.

ABERRATIONS QUICKLY FIXED

On one occasion during the Bush 43 years, elite immunity did seem to suffer an exceedingly rare setback. On March 6, 2007, a unanimous federal jury found Vice President Dick Cheney's chief of staff, Lewis "Scooter" Libby, guilty of four of the five felonies for which he had been indicted. Libby was convicted of two counts of perjury, one count of obstruction of justice, and one count of making a false statement, all of which arose from the lies he told to the Federal Bureau of Investigation and the grand jury as they were investigating the "outing" by Bush officials of CIA operative Valerie Plame. (He was acquitted on another count of making a false statement.)

Libby's importance in the Bush administration went far beyond his title. He had long been one of the most well-connected politicians in the country. Along with Cheney, Donald Rumsfeld, Paul Wolfowitz, Jeb Bush, and Norman Podhoretz, he was one of the twenty-five signatories to the 1997 founding statement of Bill Kristol's pro-imperial Project for a New American Century, which had called for an invasion of Iraq more than four years before the 9/11 attacks. Scooter Libby was at the very apex of the neoconservative movement that dominated Washington during the Bush 43 years, a top Bush aide and close intimate of America's most powerful political and media figures.

But with the announcement of the verdict, Dick Cheney's leading adviser became a convicted felon. This rare triumph for equality before the law could not have happened but for an improbable set of circumstances. First, Libby had made the mistake of crossing the CIA, which loathes any outing of covert agents. Because it was the CIA that had asked the Department of Justice to investigate the leak, the request had to be taken seriously. Thus, it was not only the perpetrators of the crime in this case who wielded elite status but also one of their prime victims. The CIA insisted that the leak of Plame's identity violated the Intelligence Identities Protection Act, which criminalizes the disclosure by anyone of the identity of a covert CIA operative.

Second, because the primary culprits were all top Bush aides and perhaps even Bush himself, the president's political appointees at the DOJ had to recuse themselves from the investigation; the possible conflict of interest they faced—having to investigate their own bosses—was too severe even for our highly permissive political culture. Thus the DOJ was forced to assign full autonomy to a prosecutor who would remain independent of the DOJ hierarchy and could therefore conduct the investigation free from the control of the president's loyal staff. And third, the independent prosecutor chosen by DOJ officials to lead the investigation, Patrick Fitzgerald, happened to possess an unusual degree of tenacity and aggressiveness when it came to pursuing prominent targets. These circumstances combined to produce the rarest of all Washington events: the prosecution of a truly powerful individual for serious crimes committed while in office.

In his October 28, 2005, announcement of the grand jury's indictment, Fitzgerald underscored the significance of the event: "I think what we see here today, when a vice president's chief of staff is charged with perjury and obstruction of justice, it does show the world that this is a country that takes its law seriously; that all citizens are bound by the law."

The progress of Libby's trial bore out the lofty ideals expressed by Fitzgerald. On June 5, 2007, the Bush 43–appointed federal judge presiding over the trial sentenced Libby to thirty months in prison. As the Associated Press reported, "In the end, U.S. District Judge Reggie Walton said Libby's lies in the Valerie Plame affair outweighed his public service." For a moment, it looked as though a hole had been blasted in the shield of immunity enjoyed by America's elites. On the day Libby was sentenced, I wrote—rather optimistically, probably naively—in my *Salon* column:

> This event sends a potent and unmistakable message, one that is absolutely reverberating in the West Wing: If Libby can be convicted of multiple felonies, then any Bush official who has committed crimes can be as well. . . . Having the nation watch this powerful Bush official be declared a criminal—despite having been defended by the best legal team money can buy—resoundingly reaffirms the principle that our highest political officials can and must be held accountable when they break the law.

The affirmation of that principle did not last very long. Less than a month later, on July 2, 2007, President Bush announced his decision to commute the sentence completely down to zero— despite Libby's conviction on multiple felony counts, Libby would serve no jail time whatsoever. And just as his father's pardon of Iran-Contra criminals ended an investigation that threatened to expose his own wrongdoing, so, too, did Bush's commutation of Libby's sentence provide presidential protection to an individual who could well have incriminated the president. Once again, with a wave of the presidential hand, the rule of law was abolished and the rule of men restored.

Remarkably, the same right-wingers who had created the framework of merciless punishment for ordinary Americans rushed to celebrate Libby's being spared from prison. This attitude was particularly striking given the lack of any partisan angle to the prosecution. The Plame investigation, after all, had been urged by the Bush CIA; the prosecution had been pursued by a Bush-appointed federal prosecutor, and Libby's prison sentence was imposed by a Bush-appointed federal judge, all in line with the sentencing laws long advocated by the "tough-on-crime" wing of America's political class. Simply put, the system that directed Scooter Libby to prison had been zealously constructed over the course of decades by the very conservative movement that was now aghast at his plight.

Still, the stench of hypocrisy did not prevent the American right from elevating Libby's protection to the ranks of its most impassioned causes. Indeed, many conservatives were more furious than grateful toward Bush when he announced his decision. In their eyes, commuting Libby's sentence did not go far enough; they wanted a full presidential pardon. The crusade to free Scooter Libby became the cause célèbre of the year among the nation's conservative elites. The list of Bush supporters agitating for an immediate pardon included Bill Kristol and *National Review*'s Ramesh Ponnuru, while former Bush aide David Frum declared the prosecution a "travesty" and demanded: "Pardon Libby Now." Fred Barnes, cofounder of the *Weekly Standard*, went on Fox News and assured viewers that it was only "a minor case," that Libby has "been a loyal and effective member of this administration," and therefore "there's every reason to pardon him." *National Review*'s Byron York, meanwhile, cast aspersions on the integrity of the jurors.

Marty Peretz, then the owner of the *New Republic*, proudly announced he was on the board of the Libby Defense Fund, a group of influential political and media figures who raised millions to pay for Libby's high-priced team of lawyers. Pronouncing Libby "brilliant, very honest, and brave," Peretz concluded that "the charges against Libby should go into the trash." The *Wall Street Journal* editorial page insisted that "Mr. Bush owes the former aide a pardon, and an apology" and "the time for a pardon is now." In an interview he gave after leaving office, Dick Cheney admitted that Bush's refusal to grant Libby a full pardon was among his most contentious disputes with the president in the eight years they worked together.

In demanding full-scale exoneration of Libby, his elite defenders were completely unconcerned with precepts of law and with questions of his guilt or innocence. What preoccupied them was not what Libby had done, but who he was. As they saw it, Libby was the kind of person who did not deserve to be branded a felon—and thus could not be a felon—even if he had committed felonies. For a man like Libby, punishment was simply inappropriate.

One of the very few Republicans to speak out against special protection for Libby was the long-shot presidential candidate and former Virginia governor Jim Gilmore. When candidates were asked during a 2007 GOP presidential debate whether Libby should be pardoned, Gilmore opposed the notion, attributing his position to the fact that he was "steeped in the law." He then eloquently elaborated in an interview with the *Los Angeles Times*: "If the public believes there's one law for a certain group of people in high places and another law for regular people, then you will destroy the law and destroy the system." Of course, Gilmore could afford to take such positions because he had virtually no chance of winning the nomination. Almost every other GOP candidate came out on Libby's side.

MEDIA "WATCHDOGS" DEMAND ELITE IMPUNITY

Support for Scooter Libby did not come from conservatives alone. It soon became apparent that establishment journalists would be as vigorous in demanding protection for Bush's disgraced aide as they had been in advocating immunity for Richard Nixon and Caspar Weinberger.

Shortly after Libby's sentencing, *Time*'s Joe Klein was just one of numerous prominent media figures fuming over the prospect that One of Their Own might end up in prison. In a piece titled "Thoughts on Sentencing," Klein actually prefaced his defense of Libby by insisting that it was of the utmost importance for Paris Hilton to receive jail time for driving with a suspended license because "it is exemplary: It sends the message . . . that even rich twits can't avoid the law." That same reasoning, however, apparently did not apply to Dick Cheney's top adviser.

> I have a different feeling about Libby. His "perjury"—not tell-
> ing the truth about which reporters he talked to—would never

be considered significant enough to reach trial, much less sentencing, much less time in the stir if he weren't Dick Cheney's hatchet man. . . . Jail time? Do we really want to spend our tax dollars keeping Scooter Libby behind bars? I don't think so. This "perjury" case only exists because of his celebrity.

There are so many false and misleading assertions crammed into these few sentences that it is difficult to know where to begin. It is worth the effort to unpack them, though, because Klein's defense of Libby reveals just how our media class reasons when it comes to the political figures whom they claim to hold accountable.

Note, for instance, the snide use of quotation marks for "perjury"—as though Libby's conviction constitutes that crime only in the most technical and meaningless sense, if at all. In fact, Libby's lies to the FBI and the grand jury obscured the actual leakers' identities and thereby significantly obstructed the government's efforts to determine what happened. As Fitzgerald had put it when he announced Libby's indictment: "What we have when someone charges obstruction of justice, the umpire gets sand thrown in his eyes. He's trying to figure what happened and somebody blocked their view." The University of Arizona professor Jonah Gelbach elaborated (emphasis in original).

> Libby's lies struck at the heart of Fitzgerald's—indeed, the prior DOJ investigation's—ability to tell whether Libby had violated [the Intelligence Identities Protection Act]. . . . It's not just the usual principle that obstruction and perjury can't be tolerated—it's that *these* instances prevented Fitzgerald from being able to decide whether any underlying crime (violation of the IIPA) had been committed.

Contrary to Klein's breezy efforts to trivialize them, Libby's crimes were serious not only in the abstract but for the substantial impediments they deliberately put in the way of the government's efforts to determine whether underlying crimes had occurred.

It is also worth noting that Klein deliberately made no mention of the several felony counts of obstruction of justice and false statements for which Libby was convicted; his only crime, Klein implied, was "mere" perjury. More dishonest still was Klein's manner of insinuating that Libby's conviction and sentencing were politically motivated (that none of this would have happened "if he weren't Dick Cheney's hatchet man") while inexcusably concealing from his readers that Libby's prosecutor and the judge who sentenced him were both Republicans and appointees of George W. Bush's administration.

But the most glaring falsehood in Klein's Libby defense is also the most significant for our purposes: namely, his claim that "perjury" is something for which people are not convicted and imprisoned unless they are "celebrities," and that Libby was being persecuted because of his elevated position. In fact, the opposite is true: many far less famous or powerful Americans have been sent to prison or otherwise punished for the crimes of obstruction of justice and perjury. Here are just a few illustrative examples.

- "The United States Attorney in Manhattan, Rudolph W. Giuliani, declared yesterday that the one-year prison sentence that a Queens judge received for perjury was 'somewhat shocking.' 'A sentence of one year seemed to me to be very lenient,' Mr. Giuliani said, when asked to comment on the sentence imposed Wednesday on Justice Francis X. Smith, the former Queens administrative judge" (*New York Times*, September 11, 1987).

- "A Boston police officer was sentenced late yesterday to 2 years and 10 months in prison after being convicted in federal court for perjury and obstruction of justice during a grand jury investigation of the unlawful beating of a fellow plain clothes police officer" (*Business Wire*, September 30, 1998).
- "Still insisting that he never took a payoff or tried to hide evidence, former East St. Louis Police Chief Ronald Matthews began serving 33 months in prison Monday after a judge sentenced him for obstruction of justice and perjury" (*St. Louis Dispatch*, March 21, 2006).
- "Prison sentence for perjury in a bankruptcy case: A federal judge today sentenced Douglas W. Cox, 44, to ten months in prison. In April, Cox admitted that, during a bankruptcy deposition, he testified falsely about the ownership of five vending machines" (U.S. Department of Justice Press Release, November 2006).

Clearly, Klein and other media defenders of Libby have it exactly backward: it is not uncommon for people to be punished for obstruction of justice and perjury. What is uncommon is for anyone to pay attention when it happens, let alone object on their behalf, because they typically are not people with powerful connections.

Klein's indignation over Libby's unfair treatment was echoed by many in the establishment media. The former *Time* editor in chief Norman Pearlstine wrote a book denouncing Fitzgerald's investigation, while the *New York Times* columnist David Brooks condemned the prosecution in multiple venues as a "farce."

But perhaps the most revealing pro-Libby defense came from the *Washington Post*'s Richard Cohen, who—as we just saw—had gleefully celebrated the pardon bequeathed to his "Safeway buddy" Caspar Weinberger. Cohen's June 2007 defense of Libby was a true tour de force of apologia, highlighting the function of our Beltway media stars when it comes to elite immunity. Grieving over what he considered the grave and tragic injustice brought down upon the newly convicted felon, Cohen unleashed a paragraph that perfectly captures how many establishment journalists view their role vis-à-vis top political leaders.

> With the sentencing of I. Lewis "Scooter" Libby, Fitzgerald has apparently finished his work, which was, not to put too fine a point on it, to make a mountain out of a molehill. At the urging of the liberal press (especially *The New York Times*), he was appointed to look into a run-of-the-mill leak and wound up prosecuting not the leaker—Richard Armitage of the State Department—but Libby, convicted in the end of lying. This is not an entirely trivial matter since government officials should not lie to grand juries, but neither should they be called to account for practicing the dark art of politics. As with sex or real estate, it is often best to keep the lights off.

Just as Klein did, Cohen managed to pack multiple falsehoods into his Libby defense. He told his readers, for instance, that a special prosecutor was appointed to investigate the Plame leak "at the urging of the liberal press," and later on in the column he pinned the blame for Libby's terrible plight on "antiwar sanctimony," "an unpopular war," "opponents of the Iraq war," and "a vestigial Stalinist-era yearning for abasement." Somehow, Cohen attributed Libby's prosecution to left-wing culprits even though the investigation began when a complaint was filed by

the CIA, proceeded when the Bush DOJ appointed a GOP prosecutor, and then ended when a Bush 43–appointed federal judge
sentenced Libby to prison.

Cohen went on to chastise Fitzgerald for having been
unfairly harsh in his investigation, especially for terrifying the
famous journalists whom he subpoenaed to testify. Cohen protested: "As any prosecutor knows—and Martha Stewart can
attest—white-collar types tend to have a morbid fear of jail."
Of course, blue-collar types, and poorer ones still, do not mind
prison at all. Why would they? It's their natural habitat, where
they belong. Prison is for people like them.

Under this view, law is needed to control and constrain the
ignoble masses (that is, the powerless), who will otherwise spread
chaos and disorder. But the noble among us need no constraints.
Indeed, the opposite is true: society is better off if the most privileged are free to act without limits, for that will maximize the
good they can produce for everyone.

In all the media outrage over the plight of poor Scooter
Libby, *that* was the point all along. And the spirit of Cohen's
objection infuses the crusade for elite immunity in general. The
real injustice is to consign the powerful to prison, even if they
are guilty of crimes. There is a grave indignity to watching our
vaunted political elite being dragged through criminal proceedings and threatened with jail time as though they were common
criminals. How disruptive and disrespectful and demeaning it
all is.

The overriding allegiance of our permanent Beltway class—
including its media—is to the royal court that accords them
their status and prestige. That overarching allegiance overrides
any supposed partisan, ideological, or other divisions. That is
what explains why the neoconservative Lewis Libby and the

"liberal pundits" Joe Klein and Richard Cohen are colleagues and comrades in every way that matters. High members of the royal court are, first and foremost, defenders of their swamp. And the most revered and highest-ranking among them shouldn't ever be punished, let alone imprisoned, for practicing what Cohen admiringly called their "dark art"—whether that comes in the form of illegal eavesdropping, illegal torture, illegal arming and funding of outlaw regimes, or illegal obstruction of justice.

To be sure, this dynamic has prevailed in imperial capitals for centuries. And it is what explains much of official Washington. The crux of political power (the White House) is the royal court, the most powerful leader (the American president) is the monarch, and his highest and most trusted aides are the gatekeepers. Those who are graced with admission and access to the royal court—including "journalists"—are grateful to those who grant them that privilege. They are equally grateful to the political culture on which their special status, privileges, and wealth depend. Naturally, the journalists' impulse is to protect those who bestowed such favors on them and to promote the culture that sustains them, even as they sentimentally invoke their supposed role as watchdogs over the powerful—a role that they long ago ceased to perform.

SELF-PERPETUATING ELITE IMMUNITY

In a culture of immunity, powerful elites quickly learn that they can act without constraints, that lawbreaking entails no consequences. Even more striking, they come to believe that they actually *merit* their privileged standing. The notion that the most powerful are too important to be subjected to prosecution becomes not merely a pretext to justify lawlessness to the public, but a genuine conviction on the part of those vested with those prerogatives.

A 2009 study conducted by Joris Lammers at Tilburg University in the Netherlands and by Adam Galinsky at Northwestern University in Illinois sought to determine how power and powerlessness affect a person's moral pliability. The researchers found that those in positions of power not only violate rules much more readily but feel far less contrition about their violations because their power leads them to a consuming, blinding sense of entitlement. As the *Economist* summarized the study's findings: "Powerful people who have been caught out often show little sign of contrition. It is not just that they abuse the system; they also seem to feel entitled to abuse it." Further, "people with power that they think is justified break rules not only because they can get away with it, but also because they feel at some intuitive level that they are entitled to take what they want. This sense of entitlement is crucial to understanding why people misbehave in high office. In its absence, abuses will be less likely. The word 'privilege' translates as 'private law.'"

During the Bush 43 years, the culture of elite lawlessness slouched toward its most extreme, though logical, conclusions. The Bush administration expressly adopted the theory that the president is greater than the law, that his obligation to protect the nation means that nothing can limit what he does—not even the laws enacted by the American people through their Congress.

Indeed, during the Bush presidency, the Harvard professor of government and well-known neoconservative Harvey Mansfield published an article in the *Weekly Standard* perfectly summarizing the dominant view of America's political and media class. Mansfield wrote that our "enemies, being extra-legal, need to be faced with extra-legal force"; that the office of the president is "larger" than the law; that "the rule of law is not enough to run a government"; that "ordinary power needs to be supplemented or corrected by the extraordinary power of a prince, using wise discretion"; and, most shockingly, that the American legal system is so constraining that it suggests the need for "one-man rule." Mansfield's advocacy may have been starker than most, but it was far from unusual. Its fundamental premise— that elites are the owners of law and thus cannot really violate it—echoes Nixon himself, who infamously told David Frost in a 1977 interview, "When the president does it, that means it is not illegal."

In response to Bush-era declarations of elite lawlessness and presidential omnipotence, our sober guardians of political wisdom shrugged. Those who objected too strenuously, who used terms such as *criminal* and *illegality* or who raised the specter of impeachment—one of the tools created by the founders to redress executive lawbreaking—were branded as radicals, as unserious, partisan hysterics. The only crime recognized by official Washington was using impetuous or excessively irreverent language to object to the lawbreaking and radicalism of the Leader, or acting too aggressively to investigate them.

Bush 43 and his followers knew that they could freely break the law because our Washington establishment, our "political press," would never object too strenuously, if at all. During the Bush presidency, the American media directed its hostility almost exclusively toward those who investigated or attempted to hold accountable the most powerful members of our political system; hence their attacks on the GOP prosecutor investigating the Bush administration's crimes, their anger at the very few investigative reporters trying to uncover Washington's secrets, and their righteous condemnation of each of the handful of attempts by Congress to exercise investigative oversight of the administration.

In *Federalist 70*, Alexander Hamilton explained why the defining power of the king rendered the British monarchy intolerably corrupt: "In England, the king is a perpetual magistrate; and it is a maxim which has obtained for the sake of the public peace, that he is unaccountable for his administration, and his person sacred." We have now come to approximate that state of affairs. In the aftermath of the George W. Bush years, replete with one act of high-level lawbreaking after the next, it cannot be reasonably denied that we have become exactly the country that Iran-Contra prosecutor Lawrence Walsh warned us we might turn into: one where "powerful people with powerful allies can commit serious crimes in high office—deliberately abusing the public trust without consequence."

Evidence of domestic felonies and war crimes committed by high-level Bush administration officials is now so blatant and abundant that few bother to deny any longer that pervasive lawbreaking occurred. Indeed, acts that our highest government officials *acknowledge* they authorized—torture, imprisonment without trials, the kidnapping and disappearing of detainees, warrantless domestic spying, the destruction of incriminating evidence—are among those for which the United States has routinely condemned other nations.

And any hope that this culture of immunity would be challenged by Barack Obama was soon dashed. Although as a candidate he had offered emphatic defenses of the rule of law when asked whether he would consider investigations and prosecutions of Bush-era crimes, Obama quickly abandoned that pretense once he was safely elected—just as Bill Clinton had immediately lost interest in enforcing accountability for his predecessor's crimes upon assuming office. On January 12, 2009, before Obama was even inaugurated, an article appeared on the front page of the *New York Times* under the headline "Obama Reluctant to Look Into Bush Programs." The first sentence reported: "President-elect Barack Obama signaled in an interview broadcast Sunday that he was unlikely to authorize a broad inquiry into Bush administration programs like domestic eavesdropping or the treatment of terrorism suspects." Echoing almost verbatim the excuse Bill Clinton had offered for abandoning his pledge to bring accountability to the crimes of Bush 41 officials, Obama was quoted in the article as explaining that he had "a belief that we need to look forward as opposed to looking backwards."

To date, Obama has succeeded in blocking and suppressing virtually every investigation into Bush crimes, whether by congressional committees, courts, international tribunals, or even internal executive branch inquiries. The specific methods Obama has adopted to strengthen and expand elite immunity are the subject of a later chapter, so for now, it suffices to note how seamlessly this continuity of Washington's culture of consequence-free lawbreaking has extended into the era of the self-proclaimed Agent of Change.

Why has Obama been so intent on shielding his politically powerful predecessors from accountability? A *New York Times* article from November 2008, examining the possibility that Obama would authorize investigations into Bush-era crimes, provides a key insight: "Because every president eventually leaves office, incoming chief executives have an incentive to quash investigations into their predecessor's tenure." In other words, by letting criminal bygones be bygones within the executive branch, presidents uphold a gentlemen's agreement to shield each other from accountability for any crimes they might want to commit in office.

That dynamic expresses the underlying motive of the political and media classes' general defense of elite immunity: by protecting the lawbreaking license for other powerful individuals, they strengthen a custom of which they might avail themselves if they too break the law and get caught. It is class-based, self-interested advocacy. That is why belief in this prerogative and the devotion to protecting it transcend political ideology, partisan affiliation, the supposed wall between political and media figures, and every other pretense of division within elite classes. It is in the interest of every member of the privileged political and financial class, regardless of role or position, to maintain the vitality of this immunity. And what we have seen over the last decade is the inevitable by-product of elite immunity: pervasive, limitless elite corruption and criminality.

2

IMMUNITY IN THE PRIVATE SECTOR

What began with the Nixon pardon as legal immunity for the most powerful political officials has now been extended to those who wield the most power in the private sector. The defining event in this expansion was the Bush-era warrantless wiretapping scandal, which revealed that executive branch officials had worked for years with the nation's largest telecommunications companies to spy on American citizens without a shred of oversight from courts or Congress. In the ensuing uproar, the political class demanded legal immunity not only for the government officials who ordered this lawbreaking but also for their indispensable "corporate partners," who had enabled the spying by indiscriminately turning over to the government the telephone calls and e-mail records of millions of their customers.

In addition, the wiretapping controversy demonstrated the severe erosion of the wall traditionally separating government functions and the private sector. It showed that America's surveillance state is not maintained by public officials alone but relies crucially on their partnership with the private telecom industry. Such melding of public and private forces now characterizes most areas of government, and has resulted in the creation of a single large, self-protecting entity. In the process, corporate elites have gained equal footing with political officials when it comes to being shielded from consequences for their illegal acts.

The telecom immunity battle marked the point when politicians and corporations perfected the process of immunizing elites in the private sector. There is no more compelling example of the death of the rule of law in America than the bipartisan scheme to vest the nation's largest telecoms with retroactive immunity, both criminal and civil, for the transgressions they committed on a grand scale.

TELECOMS AND THE LAW

Torture and aggressive war may have been the most serious crimes that the Bush administration committed, but the warrantless wiretapping of American citizens was its clearest and most undeniable act of lawbreaking. In a *New York Times* article published on December 16, 2005, the reporters James Risen and Eric Lichtblau made the situation plain: in early 2002, "President Bush secretly authorized the National Security Agency to eavesdrop on Americans and others inside the United States . . . without the court-approved warrants" required by law. For three years, Risen and Lichtblau revealed, the intelligence agency had illegally monitored and intercepted the "telephone calls and international e-mail messages of hundreds, perhaps thousands, of people inside the United States."

When the spying program was exposed, Bush showed no hint of contrition. Instead, he went on national television and proudly admitted that he had done exactly what the *Times* had described, and defiantly vowed that he would continue doing it. That there was a criminal law in place explicitly prohibiting warrantless eavesdropping did not seem to concern him in the slightest.

The dictates of that law—the Foreign Intelligence Surveillance Act—could not have been clearer. FISA specifically barred government officials from intercepting the "electronic communications" of American citizens, and of foreigners on U.S. soil, without first obtaining a warrant from a specially created court. And while some Bush officials attempted to justify their illegal spying on the ground that they were doing it to stop terrorism, FISA's warrant requirements explicitly applied to surveillance of anyone believed to be "engaged in international terrorism or activities in preparation therefor."

Some background is in order. FISA had been enacted in response to the shocking discoveries made in the mid-1970s by the U.S. Senate's Church Committee investigation. That investigation, which had been prompted by reports of serious eavesdropping improprieties by the Nixon administration, uncovered decades of surveillance abuses by the executive branch under every president since World War II. For all those years, the government's eavesdropping power had been publicly justified as necessary to fight communism, but the Church Committee found that those powers were in fact continuously misused to spy on the communications of thousands of American citizens for purely political purposes. The most notable abuse documented by the committee was the FBI's malicious, years-long eavesdropping on the telephone calls of Martin Luther King Jr., carried out in an attempt to obtain embarrassing personal information with which King could be blackmailed.

The FISA bill was meant to remedy these abuses. It stipulated that before government officials could listen in on private communications, they had to obtain judicial approval in the form of a warrant. That requirement was designed to ensure that government agencies would eavesdrop on Americans only if they first were able to present convincing evidence to a federal judge that the target of the eavesdropping was acting as an agent of a foreign power or a terrorist group. In the face of intense public anger over the abuses revealed by the Church Committee, FISA passed both houses of Congress with large majorities and substantial bipartisan support, and was signed into law in 1978.

In language as clear as English permits, section 1809 of FISA provided that anyone who violates its mandates by eavesdropping without the requisite judicial approval has committed a felony punishable by up to five years in prison and a $10,000 fine for each offense. And there was no question that George W. Bush, Dick Cheney, former NSA and CIA director Michael Hayden, and many other Bush officials had violated FISA's requirements by spying on Americans without warrants. Not only had the *New York Times* article exposed that illegality, but Bush himself had confirmed the findings on national television. If we were a country that actually lived under the rule of law, the illegal actions would have carried grave consequences for the lawbreakers—just as if they had been caught robbing a bank, embezzling money, or dealing drugs. But since we're not such a country, it has done nothing of the kind. From the start of the wiretapping scandal, the nation's media stars and the leaders of both political parties unanimously adhered to the same piety: whatever else one might want to say about the NSA spying program, it was simply wrong—inappropriate, unserious, and reckless—to talk about it as though it were a crime.

Time's Joe Klein, for example, echoed the rapidly emerging consensus of the Beltway class. In an article titled "How to Stay out of Power," he sternly warned Democrats not to criticize

Bush for his illegal surveillance, let alone demand accountability for it. Conceding the long history of government abuse of surveillance powers when exercised without oversight, and further acknowledging the mountains of public evidence that the Bush administration had transgressed the limits of the law when acting in other areas, Klein nonetheless insisted that "these concerns pale before the importance of the program." He then ventured this guess: "I suspect that a strong majority would favor the NSA program . . . if its details were declassified and made known." He concluded by denouncing what he called "civil-liberties fetishism" as "a hangover from the Vietnam era" and warned, "Until the Democrats make clear that they will err on the side of aggressiveness in the war against al-Qaeda, they will probably not regain the majority in Congress or the country."

That the eavesdropping was illegal, criminal, a felony under long-standing statutes was not mentioned by Klein at all. It simply did not enter the calculus. Nor did that issue get noted by the overwhelming majority of media figures or, for that matter, by politicians from both parties who commented publicly on this scandal. After all, it was the president who had ordered this program. And as Richard Nixon announced long ago, "When the president does it, that means it is not illegal." The NSA scandal left no doubt that what was once a strange Nixonian formulation had become unchallenged orthodoxy. It is difficult indeed to find any media figure with a national platform in 2005 who was willing to even refer to Bush's program as a "crime," let alone call for legal accountability. The vast majority, with very few exceptions, affirmatively defended it.

Critically, it was not only Bush and his aides who were implicated in this criminality, but also the nation's telecom giants. In the 1970s, the Church Committee investigation revealed to

Americans that domestic eavesdropping abuses by the government had been carried out with the cooperation of the telecommunications companies. AT&T, for example, had allowed the government unfettered access to its customers' telephone calls for years, while Western Union had turned over to government agents all private telegrams that it transmitted throughout the 1950s and 1960s.

To prevent such abuses, Congress, in addition to passing FISA, had enacted stringent new laws that specifically criminalized such conduct on the part of telecommunications firms. These laws imposed on telecom companies an absolute duty—under pain of severe criminal sanctions as well as civil liability—never to allow government access to their customers' communications without a court warrant authorizing such spying.

But a series of revelations in 2006 and 2007 left no doubt that most of the major telecoms had indeed allowed the Bush administration full access to their customers' private telephone and e-mail communications without warrants of any kind. In other words, these telecoms, in collusion with the government's illegal domestic spying program, had for years knowingly engaged in precisely the behavior that federal statutes prohibited and criminalized.

In May 2006, *USA Today* reported that "the National Security Agency has been secretly collecting the phone call records of tens of millions of Americans, using data provided by AT&T, Verizon and BellSouth." One AT&T whistleblower, Mark Klein, disclosed that AT&T had gone out of its way to give the government access to all its customers' communications. Specifically, Klein revealed in an interview, the company had "installed a fiber optic splitter at its facility at 611 Folsom Street in San Francisco that makes copies of all emails, web browsing, and other Internet traffic to and from AT&T customers, and provides those copies to the NSA."

At least four federal laws were clearly violated by the telecoms when they decided to cooperate with the Bush administration. FISA made it illegal for any party—not only government officials—to intentionally engage in electronic surveillance unless authorized by a court. The Wiretap Act prohibits any person from illegally intercepting, disclosing, or using, phone calls or electronic communications. The Communications Act prohibits carriers from unauthorized divulgence or publication of customer communications. And the Stored Communications Act makes it unlawful for carriers to disclose the contents of customers' stored communications and to pass along records of such communications to a governmental entity without valid legal process.

Notably, these laws had all been written with the active participation of the telecoms themselves. After the Church Committee investigation, when it became clear that Congress intended to set up a strict new legal regime regulating the telecoms' interactions with the government, the telecoms had one principal demand: that their legal obligations be set forth as clearly as possible so that there would be no ambiguity regarding their duties. The congressional committees that drafted these statutes worked directly with the lawyers for the telecom giants to ensure clarity.

In deference to the telecoms' primary concern that their duties be clearly spelled out, and that they not end up suffering liability for accidental violations, Congress included broad immunity provisions in these statutes. Specifically, with regard to any criminal or civil accusations against the telecoms, FISA and the other laws provided full-scale amnesty in the event that telecoms could show that they acted in good faith—that even if they violated the law, they did not do so knowingly. Section

2520 of Title 18 of the U.S. Code created as broad and absolute an immunity provision as could be imagined: it provided that a demonstration of good faith by the telecoms "is a complete defense against any civil or criminal action brought under this chapter or any other law." In other words, under the laws in place at the time the illegal spying began, the only situation in which telecoms could be sued or prosecuted for working with the government was when they *clearly and knowingly* violated their legal duties to their customers and the country by enabling plainly illegal government spying.

When the Bush administration originally approached the telecoms about cooperating with its new warrantless eavesdropping program—and there are credible reports that some of these discussions took place prior to 9/11—a small handful of the companies emphatically refused. They did so based on their conviction that the proposed program was so obviously illegal that taking part in it would leave them outside the scope of the statutory immunity rights conferred by Congress.

One company that refused was Qwest. To see just how reckless most telecoms were in deliberately violating the law, consider what motivated Qwest's refusal, as reported by *USA Today*.

> Qwest's CEO at the time, Joe Nacchio, was deeply troubled by the NSA's assertion that Qwest didn't need a court order—or approval under FISA—to proceed. Adding to the tension, Qwest was unclear about who, exactly, would have access to its customers' information and how that information might be used. . . .
>
> Unable to get comfortable with what NSA was proposing, Qwest's lawyers asked NSA to take its proposal to the FISA court. According to the sources, the agency refused.

The NSA's explanation did little to satisfy Qwest's lawyers. "They told (Qwest) they didn't want to do that because FISA might not agree with them," one person recalled. For similar reasons, this person said, NSA rejected Qwest's suggestion of getting a letter of authorization from the U.S. attorney general's office. A second person confirmed this version of events.

But the rest of the telecom industry had no such qualms about FISA. In fact, the government even attempted to pressure Qwest by telling the firm that "it was the lone holdout among the big telecommunications companies." Most telecoms had readily agreed to cooperate fully with the government's illegal program, lured by the mammoth profits to be earned from the growing surveillance state. To induce Qwest to capitulate, Bush officials threatened it with the possibility of losing government contracts. As *USA Today* explained: "In addition, the agency suggested that Qwest's foot-dragging might affect its ability to get future classified work with the government. Like other big telecommunications companies, Qwest already had classified contracts and hoped to get more."

As the Qwest case demonstrates, telecoms had the option to refuse to participate in the NSA program and thus abide by the law. Yet most of them chose not to. The evidence seems clear that virtually the entire American telecom industry—AT&T, Sprint, Verizon, BellSouth, and numerous others—broke the law by allowing the U.S. government to invade their customers' private communications without the warrants required by the federal statutes that the telecoms themselves had actively participated in writing. And it is not insignificant that their actions generated hundreds of millions of dollars in government surveillance contracts.

When the NSA program was revealed, the telecoms' customers, represented by nonprofit groups such as the Electronic Frontier Foundation and the American Civil Liberties Union, sued these firms for enabling the government to spy on their phone calls and e-mails without warrants. Suing the telecoms was particularly important because the Bush administration had succeeded in blocking the eavesdropping-related suits that had been brought directly against the government—even though all three federal judges who had considered the legal issues had concluded that the NSA program broke the law. (To get the lawsuits against the government dismissed, the Bush Justice Department argued that the eavesdropping program was a state secret and therefore could not be evaluated by the courts; it also maintained that since no specific individual could prove that he or she had been spied upon by the secret program, no one had legal standing to sue the administration.) Suing the telecoms was thus the only way for American citizens to learn the central facts about what the spying program entailed: Which citizens were targeted? How many? How were they selected? With lawsuits against the government blocked, the telecom suits were also the only means for obtaining an official court ruling on whether Bush's warrantless spying program was illegal.

From the start, the telecom cases were a classic David-versus-Goliath battle. The plaintiffs were ordinary, powerless Americans: customers of the telecoms whose e-mail records and telephone conversations had been turned over to the Bush administration without warrants. Their lawyers came from the EFF, a small nonprofit organization with a tiny budget. By stark contrast, the defendants were all telecom giants, represented by armies of the nation's most expensive law firms. Nonetheless, as the lawsuits proceeded, courts began ruling against the telecoms.

In one of the most important developments, in July 2006 the federal judge Vaughn Walker refused to dismiss the lawsuits brought against AT&T by its customers. AT&T had cited FISA's immunity provisions as a ground for dismissal, but Judge Walker rejected that argument, ruling that the conduct in which the telecoms were accused of engaging was so clearly illegal that they could not hide behind the immunity provisions provided by law. Judge Walker wrote that "AT&T cannot seriously contend that a reasonable entity in its position could have believed that the alleged domestic dragnet was legal."

But in the United States, the most powerful corporations need not fear when they break the law or even when courts begin to rule against them. They can simply have the law changed—even retroactively—by the Congress which they own. Once they began losing in court, that is exactly what the telecom industry proceeded to do: it flooded the coffers of key members of Congress with money, deployed a veritable army of the highest-paid and most politically well-connected lobbyists from both parties, and began demanding that Congress block courts from ruling on their conduct and retroactively immunize them from any consequences for their lawbreaking.

ELITES CONSPIRE TO PROTECT THEIR OWN

It is difficult to overstate the extent to which congressionally bestowed retroactive immunity represents a profound departure from basic norms of justice. Ordinary Americans are sued every day and forced to endure the severe hardships and sometimes ruinous costs of litigation. When that happens, it is the role of the courts alone to determine who is at fault and whether liability should be imposed. The Constitution vests "the judicial

Power of the United States" in courts, not Congress. And when it comes to lawsuits brought against ordinary Americans, that is how such suits are always resolved: by courts issuing rulings on the merits. The very idea that Congress would intervene in such proceedings and act to protect ordinary Americans from lawsuits is too outlandish even to entertain.

But when the wealthiest, most powerful, and most well-connected financial elites are caught red-handed violating the privacy rights of their customers and committing clear felonies, their lobbyists call for a new law that has no purpose other than to declare that the old laws do not apply to them. That is the living, breathing embodiment of our two-tiered justice system—a lawless Wild West for elites in which anything goes. Examining how the telecoms pursued the amazing feat of getting full immunity for their systematic lawbreaking highlights how and why the rule of law is so easily discarded in the United States.

The very idea of *retroactive immunity* for lawbreaking corporations is so antithetical to the most basic principles of the rule of law that I have been able to find only one other such attempt in recent history. That case involved the efforts by some in Congress in 1965 to enact a law retroactively legalizing the mergers of six large banks—mergers which, as a federal court found, were clearly illegal under antitrust laws.

The banks knew when they merged that they were almost certainly violating antitrust regulations. But they did it anyway, assuming that once the mergers were effectuated it would be impossible to undo them. And when, postmerger, courts began ruling that their behavior was indeed illegal, the banks ran to Congress to demand that a law be passed granting them amnesty, claiming that the consequences would be ruinous if they were held accountable under the law.

In 1965, this brazen demand met with stiff resistance. Senator Robert Kennedy pointed out that if retroactive immunity were granted to the banks, it might equally well be applied to "murder or any other crime." And Attorney General Nicholas Katzenbach was equally appalled. An August 22, 1965, article in the *New York Times* described his response as "one of the most sternly-worded statements ever delivered by a Cabinet-rank official." The attorney general denounced as "outrageous" the very idea that Congress might retroactively immunize clearly illegal corporate behavior, and condemned the proposal as "nothing more or less than a private relief bill for the banks" that "can in no way be justified." Such fervent objections had their effect. While disentangling the illegally merged banks ultimately proved to be impossible from a practical standpoint, the opposition did succeed in imposing substantial limits on the banks' ability to act anticompetitively.

Kennedy and Katzenbach stood up eloquently and aggressively for the rule of law—even when the nation's wealthiest bankers claimed that undoing their mergers would cripple the economy—but our political class today is bound by no such principles. Instead, leading Democratic members of Congress spent months in secret discussions with Dick Cheney, looking for ways to protect lawbreaking telecoms from the court battles that they were losing, and trying to save the telecoms from the consequences of their criminal conduct. That steeply downward fall—from Robert Kennedy and his emphatic insistence on equality under the law to the Cheney/Democratic telecom amnesty scheme—illustrates much about what has happened to our country and its rule of law.

The public campaign for retroactive telecom immunity relied on two main arguments. On one hand, there was the familiar fearmongering about terrorism: the idea that if we do not immunize them, telecoms might no longer cooperate with the government's eavesdropping programs and we will thus be unable to detect terrorist plots. At the same time, immunity advocates proclaimed that the telecoms had been motivated only by feelings of patriotic duty to the nation and should therefore not be punished for their actions.

Both of those claims were patently false. Telecoms are already required by law to assist the government with any legal requests for eavesdropping (that is, requests accompanied by a judicial warrant) and thus do not have the option to refuse to cooperate. And whatever the claims to patriotism by the telecoms, their cooperation resulted in massive profits. (Of course, breaking the law is not permitted even if patriotic motives are involved.) But none of that mattered much. So absolute was the telecoms' control over Congress and the lawmaking process that their success was virtually a fait accompli as soon as they decided that they wanted retroactive immunity.

The first public move made by immunity advocates came in the form of an op-ed published in the *Washington Post* on May 21, 2007, by Bush's director of national intelligence (DNI), Admiral Michael McConnell. It was a stealthy opening to the campaign. McConnell said nothing about immunity, focusing instead on an apparently unrelated matter: he repeatedly called for wholly unspecified "updates" and "changes" to FISA that would expand the government's powers of eavesdropping on Americans.

But McConnell's central argument—that such updates were needed because FISA had "not been changed to reflect technological advancements" since its original enactment—was a red herring. FISA had been changed numerous times for exactly that purpose, including shortly after the 9/11 attacks, when Congress agreed to every expansion and modernization of FISA powers requested by the Bush administration. Indeed, on signing the post-9/11 updates to FISA into law, Bush told the nation:

> The bill before me takes account of the new realities and dangers posed by modern terrorists. . . . This new law I sign today will allow surveillance of all communications used by terrorists, including e-mails, the Internet, and cell phones. As of today, we'll be able to better meet the technological challenges posed by this proliferation of communications technology.

The fact that McConnell's op-ed called for revisions to FISA based on a patently false claim indicated that the true reasons why the Bush administration wanted a new eavesdropping law were not yet on view. But these reasons would not remain hidden for very long.

In July 2007, Bush officials followed up on McConnell's op-ed by proclaiming that there was an emergency need to revise FISA because its scope was too limited and because the eavesdropping authorizations on which they were relying were set to expire. The claims were dubious at best, but they had their effect. As the *Washington Post* reported, McConnell and other Bush officials secretly met with leading Democrats and warned them that failure to enact the revisions proposed by the White House—and to do so by the very fast deadline the White House had imposed—could prevent the administration from protecting the Capitol from serious terrorist plots, plots which intelligence agencies had been recently picking up in vague "chatter." The new bill the Bush administration wanted would drastically expand eavesdropping powers and allow spy agencies to act without a warrant, thus essentially legalizing the program that had been exposed by the *New York Times*.

The demand that the Democratic-led Congress enact a statute vesting the administration with increased eavesdropping powers was audacious indeed; after all, Democrats had spent months complaining that their efforts to learn about the Bush NSA program had been completely stonewalled. In other words, Democrats were being told to legalize and expand an eavesdropping program that had been carried out illegally for years and that they knew virtually nothing about. What's more, they were being pressed to do so in such a rapid timeframe, and under the specter of such grave warnings, that they barely had time even to learn what exactly they were supposed to approve.

But as they always did whenever the Bush administration invoked terrorism, the Democratic Congress quickly and meekly obeyed. At 10:00 p.m. on Saturday, August 4, 2007 (the day after Congress was scheduled to begin its summer recess), with virtually no debate, and with most of the caucus having little idea what they were voting on, they passed an "emergency" eavesdropping bill. Oh-so-subtly christened the Protect America Act, the bill essentially legitimized the president's warrantless spying program. The only concession to the fact that the Democrats had enacted the new law with such haste—Senator Chris Dodd told me in an interview the day after the vote that senators had no idea why the new provisions were warranted but were "not secure enough in their own beliefs" to object—was a "sunset" provision they inserted into the bill, which called for the new regulations to expire in six months. The plan was that the six-month period would give Congress time to craft a new, permanent eavesdropping bill that would be considered in a more deliberative manner.

The hurried FISA revision accomplished one of the Bush administration's goals: eliminating the need for warrants for future eavesdropping. But what about the liability of the telecoms who had illegally helped them over the previous years? It was later reported by numerous Senate sources that during the frenzied campaign of pressure, the Bush administration had several times raised the issue of immunity for telecoms, but there was simply too little time for it to be drafted and included in the new bill. The White House made clear to congressional Democrats, however, that inclusion of telecom immunity in the permanent eavesdropping bill would be a nonnegotiable condition.

Indeed, as soon as the temporary six-month bill was passed in early August, the White House issued a statement unveiling, for the first time in public, a demand for full retroactive legal immunity—both criminal and civil—for all telecommunications companies that had participated in the warrantless eavesdropping program. The demand for telecom immunity was spelled out in the very first paragraph of the press release posted on the official White House Web site:

> Our Work Is Not Done—This Act Is A Temporary, Narrowly Focused Statute To Deal With The Most Immediate Needs Of The Intelligence Community To Protect The Country. When Congress returns in September, the Intelligence Committees and leaders in both parties will need to complete work on the comprehensive reforms requested by Director of National Intelligence Mike McConnell, including the important issues of providing meaningful liability protection to those who are alleged to have assisted our Nation following the attacks of September 11, 2001.

That same month, McConnell gave an interview in which he finally unveiled the real impetus behind his op-ed call for a "modernized" FISA bill. Like the White House press release, McConnell expressly stated for the first time in public that the new FISA bill must include retroactive immunity for telecoms that had participated in the administration's illegal eavesdropping activities.

McConnell began by unintentionally providing an unusually clear and straightforward summary of federal law regarding eavesdropping on Americans by the U.S. government—unusually clear in that it highlighted how patently illegal Bush's domestic spying activities had been. McConnell explained:

> The reason that the FISA law was passed in 1978 was an arrangement was worked out between the Congress and the administration, we did not want to allow this community to conduct surveillance, electronic surveillance, of Americans for foreign intelligence unless you had a warrant, so that was required.

What McConnell euphemistically referred to as an "arrangement . . . worked out between the Congress and the administration" is what most people call a "federal law." But McConnell's basic point—that FISA required a warrant to conduct surveillance of Americans—was exactly correct. Despite that, McConnell now insisted that the bill he expected Congress to pass would vest full immunity in the administration's "private partners" who had broken that law. The real goal of the new bill, he explained, was to force the termination of the lawsuits that were proceeding in court against the telecoms.

The government's "terrorist surveillance program"—which McConnell also referred to as the "president's program"—had needed a partner, and the private sector had come to its assistance. Now those partners were being sued, and if the lawsuits were allowed to go forward, McConnell said, they would "bankrupt" those companies. McConnell's suggested remedy was simple: "We have to provide liability protection to these private sector entities." Bush's DNI acknowledged that the idea had been on the administration's mind for a while and had encountered some resistance: "When I went through and briefed the various senators and congressmen, the issue was alright, look, we don't want to work that right now, it's too hard because we want to find out about some issues of the past." But now the time had come, McConnell said: "The retroactive liability protection has got to be addressed."

It is hard to imagine open contempt for the rule of law being expressed more explicitly than this. What possible reason is there to protect anyone—let alone the nation's largest, richest, and most powerful telecom companies—with a special law enacted to declare that they are relieved of all accountability for illegal behavior? Ordinary individuals and small companies are routinely confronted with lawsuits that could bankrupt them, yet Congress does nothing to intervene or protect them. The theory of our justice system is that any person or corporation that breaks the law is obliged to pay for the resulting damages, even if—*especially if*—those damages are substantial.

The underlying premise of McConnell's demand for immunity was even more dangerous than his conclusion. The argument was grounded in the claim that these companies were only acting at the behest of George W. Bush—carrying out "the President's program"—and therefore were entitled, even obligated, to do what they did. In other words, to hear McConnell tell it, the president has the power not only to violate the law at will but also to authorize or even order private actors to break the law—who then have no choice but to submit. And when those illegal orders are obeyed, the private actors are to be immune from the consequences of their lawbreaking because they acted at the president's behest.

Retroactive immunity makes complete mockery of the rule of law. The United States is not supposed to be a country where private actors are permitted to commit crimes and violate laws whenever the president tells them that they should. The president has no greater power to authorize others to break the law than he does to break the law himself. On the contrary, Article II of the Constitution, which defines the powers of the executive, imposes the exact opposite obligation: "He shall take Care that the Laws be faithfully executed." Lawbreaking is still illegal even if the president says it should be done.

It is also no minor matter that immunizing telecom corporations would effectively prevent any official ruling on the question of whether the president himself committed crimes in his insistence on warrantless wiretapping. The White House was so eager to secure immunity not only because of the benefits it would confer on their industry "partners," but because of this crucial self-protective benefit as well. Terminating lawsuits against the telecoms by retroactively granting them immunity would forever shield the actions of the president and the telecom industry alike from judicial review—that is, from the rule of law.

ADMIRAL MICHAEL MCCONNELL:
THE FACE OF PRIVATE SECTOR IMMUNITY

It was both important and revealing, though not at all surprising, that the man who led the crusade for retroactive amnesty for the telecoms was Michael McConnell. In many ways, he is the living, breathing embodiment of the decadent political culture that reigns among America's most powerful.

Even in a political culture drowning in conflicts of interest, McConnell stands out. Few people have blurred the line between public office and private profit more egregiously and shamelessly than he. McConnell's career is the classic illustration of the "revolving door" syndrome: public officials serve private interests while in office and are then lavishly rewarded by those same interests once they leave. He went from being head of the National Security Agency under Bush 41 and Clinton directly to Booz Allen, one of the nation's largest private intelligence contractors, then became Bush 43's director of national intelligence, then went back to Booz Allen, where he is now executive vice president.

But that's the least of what makes McConnell such a perfect symbol for the legalized corruption that dominates Washington. More important, his overarching project while at Booz Allen and in public office was exactly the same: the outsourcing of the American government's intelligence and surveillance functions (including domestic surveillance) to private corporations, where those activities are even less subject to oversight than they are as part of government operations, and where they generate massive profit for the corporations at the public expense.

Accelerating the merger between the private and public spheres is the cause to which McConnell devoted himself for decades, both in and out of government. While at Booz Allen, McConnell was chairman of the Intelligence and National Security Alliance, the primary business association of NSA and CIA contractors devoted to expanding the privatization of government intelligence functions. Then, as Bush's DNI, McConnell

dramatically expanded the extent to which intelligence functions were outsourced to the same private industry that he long
represented. Worse, he became the government's leading advocate for giving full immunity to the telecoms. In other words, as
DNI he worked to win the dismissal of lawsuits against the very
industry he had represented as INSA chairman. Once the Bush
administration ended, McConnell returned to Booz Allen's lov-
ing arms, where he resumed his work on behalf of the private
intelligence industry.

It's vital to understand how this process truly works. People
like Mike McConnell don't really move from public office to the
private sector and back again; that implies more separation than
actually exists. Rather, the U.S. government and industry interests essentially form one gigantic, amalgamated, inseparable
entity—with a public division and a private one. When someone
like McConnell goes from a top private sector position to a top
government post in the same field, it's more like an intracor-
porate reassignment than it is like changing employers. When
McConnell serves as DNI he's simply in one division of this
entity, and when he's at Booz Allen he is in another. It's precisely
the same way that Goldman Sachs officials endlessly move in
and out of the Treasury Department and other government positions with financial authority, or the way that health care and oil
executives move in and out of government agencies charged with
regulating those fields.

In every way that matters, the separation between government and corporations is nonexistent, and this is especially true
when it comes to national security and the surveillance state.
Indeed, so extreme is this overlap that McConnell, when he was
nominated to be Bush's DNI, told the *New York Times* that his
ten years of working for Booz Allen would not impede his ability

to run the nation's intelligence functions. That's because his Booz Allen work was indistinguishable from working for the government. As McConnell himself put it, "In many respects, I never left the business."

The NSA scandal made it clear that private telecom giants had come to occupy a central role in carrying out the government's domestic surveillance and intelligence activities—almost always in the shadows, beyond the reach of oversight or the law. Just how central a part they played was revealed in October 2007 by documents made public as part of the criminal prosecution of Joseph Nacchio, the former CEO of the telecom giant Qwest, for insider trading. Under Nacchio's leadership, Qwest had steadfastly refused to participate in the surveillance programs of the Bush administration; now, Nacchio was accused by Bush's DOJ of selling his Qwest shares based on nonpublic knowledge that the company was about to lose substantial value. To defend himself, Nacchio was attempting to prove that, at the time he sold his shares, he actually anticipated the opposite: a rise in Qwest's value, based on highly lucrative government contracts that the company expected to receive. Notably, these contracts were being negotiated almost immediately upon Bush's inauguration in 2001—months before the 9/11 attacks.

To prove his case, Nacchio submitted voluminous documentation detailing the vast number of projects that the Bush administration was pursuing jointly with the telecom industry. (The Clinton administration had engaged in similar projects, though to a lesser extent.) The documents revealed an extraordinary degree of cooperation between the various military and intelligence branches of the federal government—particularly the Pentagon and the NSA—and the private telecommunications corporations. The federal government had its hands deep in the ostensibly "private" telecommunications infrastructure, while the nation's telecoms—in exchange for huge revenues—had dedicated themselves to carrying out most of the state's surveillance functions.

Nacchio's documents show that telecom corporations and the military and intelligence agencies of the federal government were so close as to be virtually indistinguishable. They met and planned and agreed so frequently, and at such high levels, that they essentially formed a consortium. Just in Nacchio's limited and redacted disclosures there were descriptions of numerous pre-9/11 meetings between the largest telecoms and multiple Bush national security officials, including Paul Wolfowitz, Condoleezza Rice, NSA director general Michael Hayden, and the counterterrorism adviser Richard Clarke. State secrets posed no obstacle to this cooperation: the top telecom officials were devoting substantial amounts of their energy to working with the Bush administration on highly classified telecom projects, including plans to develop whole new joint surveillance networks with unlimited governmental access.

At the center of this private/public convergence stood Mike McConnell. As Tim Shorrock documented in his definitive 2007 *Salon* investigative article on the relationship between McConnell, Booz Allen, and the intelligence community, Booz Allen employed more than ten thousand individuals with "top secret" clearance and was thus "one of the largest employers of cleared personnel in the United States." Among those on Booz Allen's payroll were James Woolsey, a former CIA director and a neoconservative extremist; Joan Dempsey, former chief of staff to CIA director; George Tenet and Keith Hall, a former director of the National Reconnaissance Office, the supersecret organization that oversees the nation's spy satellites. As Shorrock noted, "Under McConnell's watch, Booz Allen has been deeply involved in some of the most controversial counterterrorism programs the Bush administration has run, including the infamous Total Information Awareness data-mining scheme" and "is almost certainly participating in the agency's warrantless surveillance of the telephone calls and e-mails of American citizens."

Aside from the general dangers of vesting government power in private corporations, all of this is big business on an astonishing scale. The attacks of 9/11 greatly increased the already-huge (and secret) intelligence budget. Shorrock estimated that "about 50 percent of this spending goes directly to private companies" and that "spending on intelligence since 2002 is much higher than the total of $33 billion the Bush administration paid to Bechtel, Halliburton and other large corporations for reconstruction projects in Iraq."

To sum up: McConnell left a career in government to go profit from the private telecom industry. Then he returned to government, where he devoted himself to protecting and shielding that industry from any accountability. Once the Bush administration ended, McConnell went back directly to his lucrative position at Booz Allen, where he advocates for massive expansions of surveillance policies—such as increased, joint government/corporate control over the Internet in the name of fighting "cyber wars"—from which his firm and its clients would profit greatly.

This is the toxic pattern that leads government officials to try to shield not only themselves but their most favored private corporations from any consequences for what they do, no matter how legally dubious.

LAWBREAKING STUDIOUSLY IGNORED

When McConnell first publicly demanded full immunity for the telecom industry he served, it seemed implausible in the extreme that it would actually happen. Even highly cynical observers (such as myself) who had been working extensively on these issues for several years did not expect his brazen efforts to succeed. For a Democratic-controlled Congress, which claimed to be offended by Bush's illegal spying, to grant retroactive immunity to the entire telecom industry after it had spent years breaking the law and invading the privacy of Americans—it just seemed a bridge too far, even for the culture of impunity that reigns in Washington.

After all, leading Democrats in Congress were expressing righteous outrage not only about the illegal spying but also about how little they were being told regarding what the program entailed and about how contemptuously Bush officials were stonewalling their investigations. In September 2006—two months before Democrats won control of Congress—the then–ranking member of the Senate Intelligence Committee, Jay Rockefeller, made clear in a letter to the White House how little even he knew about the most basic elements of the NSA spying program.

> For the past six months, I have been requesting without success specific details about the program, including: how many terrorists have been identified; how many arrested; how many convicted; and how many terrorists have been deported or killed as a direct result of information obtained through the warrantless wiretapping program.
>
> I can assure you, not one person in Congress has the answers to these and many other fundamental questions.

The problem for McConnell wasn't merely that Congress was in the dark about what the eavesdropping program entailed. A potentially even greater obstacle was that it had become indisputably clear that, even using the right-wing DOJ's view of the law, the Bush administration's spying on Americans had been blatantly illegal. Indeed, Congress and the nation would soon learn that at one point, the wiretapping had been so shockingly lawless that even Bush's own top DOJ officials had revolted when they learned of it.

In May 2007, James Comey—Bush's deputy attorney general in 2003 and 2004—testified about the NSA program before the Senate Judiciary Committee. (Bush's attorney general, Alberto Gonzales, had spent two years working to block Comey from testifying, but once Democrats gained control of the Senate they were finally able to compel his appearance.) Comey reported that shortly after he became deputy attorney general, he reviewed the warrantless NSA spying program Bush had ordered back in 2001 and concluded that it was patently illegal. As a result, Comey refused to sign a DOJ certification attesting to the program's legality, a certification which was required every forty-five days under Bush's original executive order that implemented the program.

When the new DOJ certification was due, Attorney General John Ashcroft was in the hospital recovering from serious gallbladder surgery. Before entering the hospital, he had transferred the powers of attorney general to his deputy. Comey's refusal to certify the legality of the NSA program thus left the Bush administration without legal cover. After all, the second-highest ranking DOJ official was insisting that their actions broke the law, and had told White House officials that Ashcroft—who had previously signed off on the program—now agreed with his assessment.

The aspect of Comey's testimony that received the most media attention was his dramatic tale—later confirmed by all parties—of how President Bush sent Gonzales and Chief of Staff Andrew Card to Ashcroft's hospital room, where Ashcroft was barely lucid, in order to induce him to sign off on the program. Upon hearing that the president had dispatched his two aides on this mission, Comey rushed to the hospital, explaining that he did not trust Gonzales and Card to be alone in the room with Ashcroft. Indeed, so distrustful were Comey and FBI director Robert Mueller of the lengths to which Gonzales and Card might go in order to extract Ashcroft's signature that, Comey explained, "Director Mueller instructed the FBI agents present not to allow me to be removed from the room under any circumstances."

Comey arrived at the hospital immediately before Gonzales and Card. When the two White House officials entered the room and demanded that Ashcroft certify the legality of the NSA program, the attorney general lifted his head from his pillow and announced that he refused to override Comey's judgment. Though he was clearly mentally and physically impaired—Comey said he had "witnessed an effort to take advantage of a very sick man"—Ashcroft informed Gonzales and Card that he agreed with Comey that the spying program was illegal, and that, in any event, it was Comey's call to make.

The media's fixation on this hospital melodrama obscured the substance of Comey's monumentally important revelations. Hearing from his own Justice Department that his spying program was in violation of criminal law did not faze Bush. Instead, vividly demonstrating his complete indifference to the rule of law and his confidence that he was free to violate it at will, Bush ordered the NSA spying program to go on even in the face of the emphatic conclusion of his own top DOJ appointees that it was illegal.

In response, Comey and the entire top level of Bush's Justice Department team—including Ashcroft, FBI director Mueller, and Jack Goldsmith, the newly appointed chief of the Office of Legal Counsel—threatened to resign en masse unless Bush immediately put an end to the unlawful spying. This was in March of 2004, the year Bush was running for reelection, and he concluded that he could not afford to suffer a public scandal of that magnitude. As a result, though he refused to terminate the program completely, Bush agreed to "refashion" it so as to pacify Comey, Ashcroft, and the others.

A month later, these rebelling DOJ officials signed off on Bush's newly "refashioned" program. And it was this "modified" approach that the *New York Times* exposed in December 2005 to such great controversy.

To date, we still don't know what the original program entailed. In 2007, Marty Lederman, then a Georgetown law professor, asked in a piece titled "Can You Even Imagine How Bad It Must Have Been?": "Just how radical were the Administration's legal judgments? How extreme were the programs they implemented? How egregious was the lawbreaking?" Given that the DOJ protesters were eventually willing to endorse the spying program that the *New York Times* reported on, the activities that almost prompted their resignation must have been illegal in the extreme.

Such shocking revelations made even the most cynical civil libertarians doubtful that McConnell's mid-2007 demands for a new FISA law that would legalize Bush's program and grant retroactive immunity to the telecoms would ever be fulfilled.

How could Congress, controlled by the ostensibly "opposition" Democratic Party, possibly whitewash the years of criminal spying on American citizens by legalizing it all and then retroactively immunizing the criminals?

But in our culture of lawlessness, there is no such thing as too much cynicism. Sure enough, on September 19, 2007, there appeared in the *New York Times* an article by James Risen on a variety of surveillance issues. Buried toward the end was the following passage, strongly suggesting that congressional Democrats were indeed ready, as always, to do as they were told.

> Mr. McConnell . . . pushed for a provision that would grant legal immunity to the telecommunications companies that secretly cooperated with the N.S.A. on the warrantless program. Those companies, now facing lawsuits, have never been officially identified.
>
> Democratic Congressional aides say they believe that a deal is likely to provide protection for the companies.

This anonymously leaked announcement came with little warning and was initially confounding. Even leaving aside righteous considerations of the rule of law and the like, why would Democrats want to help bury a potentially costly Republican crime scandal as they headed into an election year?

IMMUNITY FOR SALE, TELECOMS BUYING

The answer—which should have been obvious from the start—quickly became clear: Democrats were being deluged with massive amounts of money and other forms of corporate largesse from the telecom industry in exchange for supporting full-scale retroactive immunity, which the telecoms viewed as particularly necessary given that the customer lawsuits against them were rapidly advancing through the courts. In September, *Newsweek*'s Michael Isikoff and Mark Hosenball reported: "Congressional staffers said this week that some version of the [telecom immunity] proposal is likely to pass—in part because of a high-pressure lobbying campaign warning of dire consequences if the lawsuits proceed."

The *Newsweek* reporters detailed a "secretive lobbying campaign to get Congress to quickly approve a measure wiping out all private lawsuits" against the telecoms. The campaign was being waged by "the nation's biggest telecommunications companies, working closely with the White House." Isikoff and Hosenball made clear that the drive for immunity was fueled by the likelihood of more losses for the telecoms in America's courts of law: immunity, they wrote, had "taken on new urgency in recent weeks because of fears that a U.S. appellate court in San Francisco is poised to rule that the lawsuits should be allowed to proceed."

The *Newsweek* reporters further revealed that the lobbyist army deployed by the telecom industry was fully bipartisan. It included leading former GOP officials, such as Bush 41 attorney general William Barr, then serving as Verizon's general counsel; Brad Berenson, a former assistant White House counsel under Bush 43, on behalf of AT&T; and former (and now again current) GOP senator Dan Coats on behalf of Sprint. Also toiling for the telecoms were former high-level Democratic officials, such as the Clinton deputy attorney general Jamie Gorelick and the Clinton State Department official (and current national security adviser to Obama) Tom Donilon, both on behalf of Verizon. Many of the most powerful lobbyists in Washington—former officials from both political parties—were thus using their relationships with current political officials to help extract retroactive immunity for the telecom giants and getting paid quite well for the influence peddling.

Lobbyist disclosure statements revealed that just in the first three months of 2008, AT&T spent $5.2 million on lobbyist fees (putting it well ahead of its 2007 pace, when it spent about $17 million for the entire year). In the same first quarter of 2008, Verizon spent $4.8 million on lobbyist fees, and Comcast spent $2.6 million. In only ninety days, as the telecom immunity debate raged, those three corporations—which were to be among the biggest beneficiaries of telecom amnesty—spent a combined total of almost $13 million just on lobbyists, leaving aside campaign donations and other means of influencing the lawmaking process. Had the telecom battle lasted through the end of 2008, those three telecoms alone were on pace to spend more than $50 million on lobbying for the year.

Also revealing are the specific lobbying arrangements these telecoms had constructed for influencing how FISA was rewritten. AT&T, for instance, paid $120,000 in the first three months of 2008 to the lobbying firm BSKH & Associates—a firm which counts Charlie Black, the top campaign adviser to John McCain in 2008, as a founding partner. According to BSKH's lobbyist disclosure form, Black himself, at the same time that he was advising McCain, was one of the individuals paid by AT&T to lobby Congress on FISA. McCain, needless to say, became a vocal proponent for telecom immunity.

On the other side of the aisle, the "Blue Dogs," a powerful faction within the Democratic Party at the time, became instrumental in demanding that their party enact telecom immunity. In early 2008, twenty-one members of that caucus wrote a public letter to Speaker Nancy Pelosi demanding amnesty for the telecoms.

A major factor in getting them to take this position was the influence of the C2 Group—a lobbying firm that includes Jeff Murray, former chief of staff to Blue Dog congressional representative Bud Cramer of Alabama, and Robert Van Heuvelen, former chief of staff to Democratic senator Kent Conrad of North Dakota. Comcast paid the C2 Group $90,000 for its efforts in the first three months of 2008 and more than $300,000 in 2007. It was money well spent. C2 has extraordinary access to and influence over the Blue Dog coalition, which it proudly touts in an article prominently posted on its Web site.

> When lobbyist Jeff Murray and his firm, the C2 Group, held a reception . . . to honor Members of the conservative Democratic Blue Dog Coalition on the occasion of their swearing-in for the new Congress, the event drew a crowd of 300.
>
> That's six times the number it was two years ago, Murray said.
>
> The increase is a clear sign of the business community's redoubled affection for the Blue Dogs, a group that lobbyists for corporate America view as a natural ally in the Democratic-controlled Congress. . . .
>
> "On every issue that comes up, I am having clients ask, 'Where are the Blue Dogs on this?'" said Quinn Gillespie & Associates lobbyist Bruce Andrews, a former aide to Blue Dog Rep. Tim Holden (D-Pa.).

Unsurprisingly, Murray's former boss, Representative Cramer, was one of twenty-one Blue Dogs who wrote to Pelosi demanding immunity for Murray's client, Comcast, along with the rest of the nation's telecoms.

The Quinn Gillespie firm, mentioned in the article as the home of a former aide to Blue Dog representative Tim Holden, was also active in the telecom fray: it received $60,000 from AT&T in the first quarter of 2008 and more than $300,000 in 2007. And it is no coincidence that Holden was also one of the twenty-one Blue Dogs writing to Pelosi to promote amnesty for the client of his former top aide.

The list goes on and on. In the first three months of 2008 alone, for example, AT&T paid $200,000 to Roberti Associates, a small lobbying firm led by Vincent Roberti, a former Democratic congressman and current member of the Democratic Senatorial Campaign Committee's finance group. The firm's managing partner is Harmony Knutson, who had been a finance director for the Democratic Congressional Campaign Committee and for Democratic senator Kent Conrad, among many others. One could spend all day documenting the large sums paid by immunity-seeking telecoms to lobbying firms stuffed with former executive officials and key congressional staffers from both political parties.

This kind of spending, of course, is what leads to having major corporations literally write our nation's laws, and what made it possible for the telecoms to demand from Congress such an extraordinary and transparently corrupt gift as retroactive immunity for blatant lawbreaking. A *Politico* article published during the immunity debate shed light on the sleazy and corrupt process.

> Telecom companies have presented congressional Democrats with a set of proposals on how to provide immunity to the businesses that participated in a controversial government electronic surveillance program, a House Democratic aide said Wednesday. . . .

Although it remains to be seen if congressional Democrats will accept the telecom companies' proposal, the communication between the two sides signifies that progress is being made.

The "two sides" mentioned here are the House Democratic leadership and the telecoms. In other words, congressional leaders were "negotiating" with the telecoms—the defendants in pending lawsuits—on the best way of immunizing them from liability, no doubt with the help of the former Democratic members and staffers being paid by the telecoms to speak to their ex-bosses and colleagues about what they should do. This banana-republic-like corruption is generally how our laws are written today.

And on top of that multimillion-dollar lobbying assault came many thousands more in campaign contributions—money that the telecoms poured directly into the coffers of members of Congress in order to purchase amnesty for their lawbreaking. One prime target of the telecoms' legalized bribery was Democratic senator Jay Rockefeller, who had become chairman of the Senate Intelligence Committee when Democrats won control of Congress in 2006 and was thus the linchpin for securing the immunity they sought.

Back in 2003, Rockefeller had been one of the tiny handful of senators who were informed by the Bush administration about the warrantless spying on Americans. At the time, he did nothing other than send a short, meaningless handwritten letter to Dick Cheney expressing "concerns." But his concerns—along with the anger he had publicly expressed regarding his inability to learn anything about the spying program—quickly evaporated. Indeed, by the fall of 2007 Rockefeller emerged as the most vocal congressional advocate for full telecom immunity;

as the *New York Times* reported, he jointly created a proposal for such immunity directly with Dick Cheney. With the Bush White House and Director of National Intelligence McConnell already fully on board, the telecoms' ability to secure the support of the key Democratic senator on intelligence issues was a major coup.

The reason for their success is not difficult to understand. In October 2007, *Wired* wrote an article about Rockefeller titled "Democratic Lawmaker Pushing Immunity Is Newly Flush With Telco Cash." It documented that as Rockefeller was "steering the secretive Senate Intelligence Committee to give retroactive immunity to telecoms that helped the government secretly spy on Americans," he was the recipient of a substantial increase in telecom money. If he wanted to stay in the Senate, Rockefeller was required to run for reelection in 2008, and the *Wired* article, using public finance records, detailed how much assistance the telecom industry was suddenly providing.

> Top Verizon executives, including CEO Ivan Seidenberg and President Dennis Strigl, wrote personal checks to Rockefeller totaling $23,500 in March, 2007. Prior to that apparently coordinated flurry of 29 donations, only one of those executives had ever donated to Rockefeller (at least while working for Verizon).
>
> In fact, prior to 2007, contributions to Rockefeller from company executives at AT&T and Verizon were mostly nonexistent.
>
> But that changed around the same time that the companies began lobbying Congress to grant them retroactive immunity from lawsuits seeking billions for their alleged participation in secret, warrantless surveillance programs that targeted Americans.

The Spring '07 checks represent 86 percent of money donated to Rockefeller by Verizon employees since at least 2001.

AT&T executives discovered a fondness for Rockefeller just a month after Verizon execs did and over a three-month span, collectively made donations totaling $19,350.

AT&T Vice President Fred McCallum began the giving spree in May with a $500 donation. 22 other AT&T high fliers soon followed with their own checks.

Wired included two charts (see next page) to illustrate the telecom industry's sudden fondness for Rockefeller.

The significance of these donations extends far beyond mere money. To be sure, the money matters. Although Jay Rockefeller lives off a vast family fortune, after he was first elected to the Senate—which he accomplished by flooding his small West Virginia state with $12 million of his own money—Rockefeller vowed that he would never again spend personal funds on a political race. Like most other politicians, then, Rockefeller relies upon donors to maintain his political power.

But beyond that, these endless interactions between senators and the executives, lawyers, and lobbyists for large corporations also create a culture, a community, that is closed to those who cannot afford the admission fee—namely, the vast majority of Americans. With donations comes access; after AT&T and Verizon delivered large checks to Senator Rockefeller, for example, they were able to hold a cocktail party attended by numerous key Democrats. Similarly, lobbyists are almost always former officials in Congress or the executive branch and thus friends of those who are still in political office. Soon enough, lawmakers find themselves spending most of their time with representatives of the corporations that fund their careers and that have

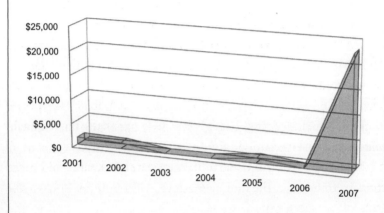

VERIZON EMPLOYEE CONTRIBUTIONS TO SENATOR JAY ROCKEFELLER

$25,000
$20,000
$15,000
$10,000
$5,000
$0

2001 2002 2003 2004 2005 2006 2007

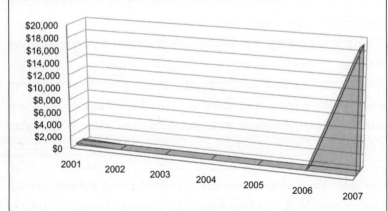

AT&T EMPLOYEE CONTRIBUTIONS TO SENATOR JAY ROCKEFELLER

$20,000
$18,000
$16,000
$14,000
$12,000
$10,000
$8,000
$6,000
$4,000
$2,000
$0

2001 2002 2003 2004 2005 2006 2007

the power to end them. Such communion only further acceler-
ates the intermingling of government and private industry. The
public/private merger exists not only on the tangible levels of
policy and money but on intangible—though equally potent—
social, cultural, and socioeconomic levels as well.

Providing crucial support to this army of corporations and
lobbyists was, as usual, the establishment media. In 2008, the vast
majority of establishment journalists emphatically advocated for
telecom immunity. The self-proclaimed watchdogs over power
thereby yet again devoted themselves to suppressing facts, quash-
ing investigations, and demanding protection for elites from all
accountability. They did so by invoking the same batch of clichés
now hauled out every time elite immunity is to be sold to the
public.

The *Washington Post*'s David Ignatius casually proclaimed,
as though it were the most natural thing in the world: "A key
administration demand is retroactive immunity for telecommunications companies that agreed to help the government in
what they thought was a legal program. That seems fair enough."
Time's Joe Klein cast the telecoms as the victims in need of protection: "I have no problem with telecommunications companies being protected from lawsuits brought by those who may or
may not have been illegally targeted simply because the Bush
Administration refused to update the law." The *Washington
Post* editorial page repeatedly urged the granting of immunity,
claiming—in perfect lockstep with McConnell and other Bush
officials—that telecoms could not afford the liability to which
they would be subjected, that their cooperation was urgently
needed to keep us safe from terrorists, and that it was terribly
unfair to punish them for having unquestioningly complied with
the president's requests ("the telecommunications providers

seem to us to have been acting as patriotic corporate citizens in a difficult and uncharted environment").

Perhaps most tellingly, the *Washington Post* editorial page actually argued that it was unfair to subject telecoms to the "high costs" of defending against these lawsuits—meaning their attorneys' fees. In October 2007, they demanded amnesty, arguing, "We do not believe that these companies should be held hostage to costly litigation in what is essentially a complaint about administration activities."

In 2007, the total revenue of Verizon was $93 billion. AT&T's total 2007 revenue was $119 billion, which gave it after-tax income of $12 billion. The costs of paying their attorneys to defend a few lawsuits was a minuscule—really undetectable— amount to these companies. Whatever the telecoms' motives were in desperately seeking amnesty for their lawbreaking, being relieved from "costly litigation" had nothing to do with it.

(Notably, this sort of populist rhetoric about the "high costs" of litigation is actually valid when it comes to lawsuits against small businesses or individuals. There, attorneys' fees and other expenses really do make lawsuits expensive to defend—often prohibitively so. But no matter; individuals of modest means and small businesses, when sued, still have to go to court to prove they did nothing wrong; they don't have Congress intervene to shield them.)

The customers' lawsuits would have proved "costly" to the telecoms only if they were found to have knowingly and deliberately broken the law—in which case the penalties would have been fully deserved. But so complete is the identification of journalists such as those who write *Post* editorials with the nation's most powerful that they indignantly demanded that the telecoms— among the wealthiest corporations in the world—be shielded by a special act of Congress in order to spare them the burdens of "costly litigation." That such deep concern was expressed for the extraordinarily profitable telecoms as they battled the under-funded, tiny nonprofit groups representing ordinary Americans highlighted the exclusive fixation on the interests of elites by much of our media class.

The *Post* also misled its readers when it characterized the lawsuits as nothing more than "a complaint about administration activities." In fact, the lawsuits alleged that the telecoms had violated multiple federal laws—laws enacted as a result of the discoveries by the Church Commission of massive invasions of the privacy rights of American citizens and decades-long abuses of surveillance powers by the government. Corporations do not have license to break the law because the president tells them to. It is truly unbelievable that this even needs to be pointed out at all.

The lawsuits against the telecoms were the sole hope for obtaining a judicial ruling on whether the spying was illegal and for bringing about a minimum amount of disclosure and accountability. But as always happens when the interests of financial and political elites are in play, journalists helped lead the chorus in demanding that all such proceedings be quashed.

THE UNSTOPPABLE MACHINE OF ELITE LAWLESSNESS

Once it became clear in the fall of 2007 that the White House was seriously demanding retroactive amnesty for the telecoms and that congressional Democrats were preparing to grant it, a coordinated and sustained public campaign was launched—largely via the Internet—to oppose telecom immunity.

In October, as the Democratic presidential primary was

heating up, various blogs organized a mass call-in campaign to insist that each candidate clearly state his or her position on telecom immunity and vow to do everything possible to oppose it. In response, all of the major Democratic candidates issued statements vehemently opposing amnesty for the telecoms, and Barack Obama went even farther, vowing to filibuster any bill containing such immunity. Obama's campaign spokesman, Bill Burton, put the promise in a way that could not have been more absolute: "To be clear, Barack will support a filibuster of any bill that includes retroactive immunity for telecommunications companies."

Opponents of telecom immunity also asked Senator Chris Dodd—who had made a defense of civil liberties and restoration of the rule of law a centerpiece of his campaign for the Democratic nomination—to take the lead in blocking Senate enactment of the immunity. He agreed to do so and publicly announced that he would not only filibuster any bill containing amnesty for telecoms but also use his power as a senator for the first time in his career to place a so-called hold on any such bill.

> The Military Commissions Act. Warrantless wiretapping. Shredding of Habeas Corpus. Torture. Extraordinary Rendition. Secret Prisons.
>
> No more.
>
> I have decided to place a "hold" on the latest FISA bill that would have included amnesty for telecommunications companies that enabled the President's assault on the Constitution by illegally providing personal information on their customers without judicial authorization.

So eager were many citizens for leadership against corporate lawlessness that, as a result of this bold commitment, Dodd's anemic presidential campaign received literally hundreds of thousands of dollars in donations overnight from small donors.

Hundreds of thousands of dollars were also raised from small donors to pay for political ads opposing telecom immunity. With that money, "robocalls" were run in the districts of Democratic leaders, such as then–House minority whip Steny Hoyer, who were signaling their support for immunity. And full-page advertisements were placed in the *Washington Post* in the days before the vote, warning of the threat to the rule of law posed by retroactive immunity for telecoms.

Working with Dodd, bloggers and online activist groups were able to catapult the issue of telecom immunity from the darkened back rooms in Washington where bills are typically drafted into the light of mainstream political debate. What would have otherwise been a measure quietly passed without much public notice became a genuine source of contention and conflict. Other allies in Congress were recruited to the cause, and with Dodd fulfilling his promise to use every obstructionist measure available, telecom immunity—which looked to be on the easy road of lobbyist-driven, quick, and painless bipartisan enactment—lingered in Congress for months and months. In March 2008, it even appeared that the measure had suffered a potentially fatal defeat, when the Democratic-led House rejected a new FISA bill (which came complete with full-scale immunity) by a narrow margin.

But democratic activism is no match for the army of corporate money, lobbyists, national security officials, and media servants. Ordinary Americans, even when united in a coordinated campaign, may be able to delay or disrupt this limitlessly funded onslaught, but they eventually will be steamrolled by it. And that's precisely what happened.

In late June, the Democratic-controlled House passed a new FISA bill that vastly expanded the warrantless eavesdropping powers of the government, in the process legalizing most of what had previously been illegal. On July 9, 2008, the U.S. Senate did the same. Titled the FISA Amendments Act of 2008, the bill also granted full retroactive immunity, both civil and criminal, to the entire telecom industry, thus guaranteeing an end to the multiple lawsuits that had been filed against them. All possibility for further investigation into the massive spying program, and for a judicial review of its legality, permanently ended on that day.

The bill passed with the support of virtually the entire Democratic congressional leadership. Barack Obama, by then the Democratic nominee for president, blatantly violated his vow to filibuster any bill containing telecom immunity. Instead, he voted *against* the Dodd-sponsored filibuster; with the filibuster defeated, Obama then voted *in favor* of the underlying bill itself. (Hillary Clinton, no longer a presidential candidate, fulfilled her campaign promise by voting against it.) The vote in the Democratic-controlled Senate was not even close: 69–28 in favor of the bill. The vote in the House was similarly lopsided (293–129), with Democrats evenly split but with the entire Democratic leadership—including Speaker Nancy Pelosi, Majority Leader Steny Hoyer, and Rahm Emanuel—supporting the bill.

The day after the Senate vote, President Bush celebrated the harmless end to a scandal that began almost three years earlier when the *New York Times* told the nation that he had been illegally spying on American citizens for years. He invited numerous leaders of both political parties to the White House for the ceremony at which the new FISA bill was signed into law. Those members of Congress mingled with Admiral McConnell and the other national security officials who had worked so tirelessly to ensure that telecoms (and therefore the president) would be shielded from all liability. In his remarks, the president heaped particular praise on Senator Rockefeller for leading the way in ensuring the bill's passage.

Very soon after Bush's signing ceremony, the telecoms filed papers in the federal court where the lawsuits against them were proceeding and—citing the immunity they had just received—demanded the summary dismissal of those suits. The judges, their hands bound by the new law, threw those cases out of court, and the telecoms were forever shielded from paying any compensation to the customers whose privacy they had sacrificed. They were also shielded from any criminal investigations or prosecutions for those crimes.

The Washington establishment and the telecom industry exulted over their great victory, and understandably so. It signaled that there is literally no limit on the ability of corporate elites, using their control of government, to be immunized from the rule of law, potently foreshadowing Wall Street's full-scale protection after the 2008 financial crisis.

The telecom industry issued fulsome expressions of gratitude. As it happened, the new FISA bill was passed shortly before the Democratic National Convention was to meet in Denver and formally announce Barack Obama as the party's presidential nominee. Within two weeks after the bill's passage, the steering committee of the DNC unveiled AT&T's generous sponsorship of various aspects of the convention, including products such as an AT&T-branded tote bag to be distributed to all convention delegates.

At the convention itself, AT&T's signature globe was prominently placed at virtually every DNC event. While this sponsorship was relatively trivial from a financial perspective, few
things were more appropriate than having a telecom logo hover
over the Democratic Party's principal gathering. After all, the
party had just delivered an extraordinary gift to that industry.
The omnipresence of AT&T was a refreshingly, if not intentionally, honest expression of the Democrats' true allegiance.

The second day of the Democratic convention fell on August
25, 2008. That night, at the Mile High Station—next to Invesco
Stadium, where Barack Obama was to accept the party's nomination in front of a crowd of eighty thousand people two nights
later—AT&T threw a lavish private party for Blue Dog House
Democrats. This was one of the listings for the event:

> **8 P.M.**
> Just because the Blue Dogs are fiscally
> conservative doesn't mean they can't
> have a good time, especially when AT&T
> is picking up the bill. Mile High Station,
> 2027 W. Lower Colfax Ave. By invitation.

Armed with full-scale convention press credentials issued
by the DNC (though lacking an invitation to the party), I went
with several other people to report on the festivities. Deployed
around the building was a wall of private security guards, who
informed us that the press was barred from the gathering—even
though what was taking place inside was a meeting between one

of the nation's largest corporations and the numerous members of one of the most influential elected factions in Congress.

Denied access to the building, we stood in front of the entrance and began videotaping and trying to interview the parade of Blue Dog representatives, AT&T executives, assorted lobbyists, and convention delegates pulling up in their rented limousines, chauffeured cars, and SUVs. We wanted to find out who was attending and why AT&T would be throwing such a lavish party for the Blue Dog members of Congress.

Amazingly, not a single one of the twenty-five to thirty people we tried to interview would speak to us about who they were, how they got invited, what the party's purpose was, or why they were there. One attendee said that he was with an "energy company," and another confessed that she was affiliated with a "trade association," but this was the full extent of anyone's willingness to describe themselves or this event. After just a few minutes, the private security teams demanded that we leave. When we refused and continued trying to interview the reticent attendees, the Denver police forced us to move farther and farther away from the entrance until finally we were unable to approach any more of the arriving guests.

It was really the perfect symbol for how the Beltway political system functions: those who dictate the nation's laws (the largest corporations and their lobbyists) cavorting with those who are elected to write those laws (members of Congress) while completely prohibiting the public from having any access to and knowledge of—let alone involvement in—what they are doing. All of this was arranged by AT&T, the corporation that paid for part of the Democrats' national convention after having just received an extraordinary gift of retroactive amnesty from the Congress controlled by that party. And all of it took place right next to the stadium where the Democratic presidential nominee—who had spent months righteously claiming that, if elected, he would cleanse the Beltway of corporate and lobbying influences—was to accept the presidential nomination.

The telecom immunity law was one of the most striking pieces of evidence demonstrating that the royal Beltway court and its corporate partners placed themselves above and beyond the reach of the law even for the most blatant transgressions. But more important, it also proved that they no longer cared who knew it. And the vital enabling role that the Democratic Party and Barack Obama played in those events was a powerful fore-shadowing of how—once they consolidated their hold on political power—the Democrats would not just maintain, but entrench and expand, this culture of elite impunity.

3

TOO BIG TO JAIL

In July 2010, Martin Joel Erzinger, a hedge fund manager for extremely wealthy investors at Morgan Stanley Smith Barney, was driving his car near Vail, Colorado, when he hit a bicyclist from behind and then sped away. The *Vail Daily* reported that the victim, Steven Milo, suffered "spinal cord injuries, bleeding from his brain and damage to his knee and scapula," which left him facing multiple surgeries. The newspaper's account of the incident makes clear that Erzinger should have been prosecuted for this incident.

> Milo was bicycling eastbound on Highway 6 just east of Miller Ranch Road, when Erzinger allegedly hit him with the black 2010 Mercedes Benz sedan he was driving. Erzinger fled the scene and was arrested later, police say.
>
> Erzinger allegedly veered onto the side of the road and hit Milo from behind. Milo was thrown to the pavement, while Erzinger struck a culvert and kept driving, according to court documents.
>
> Erzinger drove all the way through Avon, the town's round-abouts, under I-70 and stopped in the Pizza Hut parking lot

where he called the Mercedes auto assistance service to report damage to his vehicle, and asked that his car be towed, records show. He did not ask for law enforcement assistance, according to court records.

Committing a hit-and-run is a felony in Colorado, and leaving the scene of a crime constitutes a felony as well. Nevertheless, the district attorney, Mark Hurlbert, announced that Erzinger would be charged only with a misdemeanor, which carries no jail time. Hurlbert's explanation for not charging Erzinger with any felonies was blunt: "Felony convictions have some pretty serious job implications for someone in Mr. Erzinger's profession."

In other words, Erzinger engages in such vital activity that charging him with a felony would be wrong because it might seriously disrupt his work: managing the money of multimillionaires and billionaires. According to *Worth* magazine, Erzinger "oversees over $1 billion in assets for ultra high net worth individuals, their families and foundations." If he were charged with a felony, he would be required to report that fact to licensing agencies; a felony conviction could result in his fund manager license being rescinded. Apparently, as far as the district attorney was concerned, it would be terribly unfair to subject someone like Erzinger to the risk of damaging his career, though presumably someone with less to lose could—and would—be charged as a felon without any such worries.

Hurlbert added that Erzinger's willingness to pay restitution to his victim also militated against prosecuting him: "The money has never been a priority for [the victim]. It is for us. Justice in this case includes restitution and the ability to pay it." As Felix Salmon of Reuters put it, the Erzinger case was thus a classic demonstration of how to "buy your way out of a felony charge." But it was also more than that. Hurlbert's decision was grounded in what has become a well-entrenched principle: certain individuals are simply too important to be subjected to criminal prosecution.

Once the Erzinger case was publicized by the talk radio host David Sirota and by Colorado newspapers, there was a public uproar. More than ten thousand local residents signed petitions demanding the filing of felony charges, to no avail. And although the incident eventually attracted significant attention, Hurlbert's logic is notable precisely because it is so common. Indeed, the same type of immunity from legal consequences is continuously granted to the financially powerful on a much larger and more consequential scale.

The shielding of the Colorado hedge fund manager illustrates how reflexively exemption from the rule of law is now bestowed on the nation's wealthiest, and it highlights the means used to accomplish that. Even the massive recklessness and fraud that in 2008 spawned one of the worst financial crises in modern history has produced very little legal accountability—and almost no criminal liability—for the perpetrators so far, and is quite unlikely to do so in the future. Nor have the 2010 revelations of systematic industry-wide fraud by mortgage-holding banks prompted anything besides efforts by the political class to protect that plundering industry. And to justify this lack of accountability for the nation's wealthiest lawbreakers, the all-too-familiar excuses long used to shield the politically powerful are trotted out on cue. Once again, we are told that prosecutions are too disruptive; that it's more important to fix the system than to seek retribution for the past; that because the wrongdoers' reputation is in tatters, they have already suffered enough; that we need the goodwill of financial titans to ensure our common prosperity; and so on.

The granting of immunity to the telecoms after the Bush wiretapping program was a travesty because corporate giants were able so flagrantly to purchase retroactive exemption from the rule of law. But the steadfast refusal to hold financial elites accountable for the 2008 financial crisis and 2010 mortgage fraud scandal represents a whole new level of lawlessness. As disgraceful as the telecom amnesty was, at least it was given by an act of Congress and thus had some legal pretense to it. By contrast, in protecting Wall Street, the executive branch simply violated its core constitutional duty: to "take care that the laws be faithfully executed." Moreover, while the immunized telecoms had broken the law in conjunction with government programs, the crimes for which Wall Street barons are being protected are purely private ones. Worse still, the scope of these financial crimes is so vast, and the suffering they have caused so deep and enduring, that the refusal to impose any consequences on the culprits proves the near-absolute nature of this elite lawbreaking license. It is now clear that there are virtually no limits on the magnitude of the crimes that the nation's most powerful private actors can commit with impunity.

MASS ECONOMIC DESTRUCTION

In the fall of 2008, the American and world economies were brought to the brink of complete collapse. On September 19 of that year, the *New York Times* reported on a secret congressional briefing given by top financial officials at which they described the extraordinary threat as they perceived it. According to that account, when the Federal Reserve chairman, Ben Bernanke, "laid out the potentially devastating ramifications of the financial crisis before congressional leaders ... there was a stunned silence." The New York senator Chuck Schumer, who was present at the meeting, told the *Times*: "When you listened to [Bernanke] describe it, you gulped."

The warnings issued to the congressional leaders were apocalyptic. According to the Connecticut senator Chris Dodd, chairman of the Banking, Housing, and Urban Affairs Committee, the senators were informed that the country was "literally maybe days away from a complete meltdown of our financial system, with all the implications here at home and globally." In his thirty years in Congress, Dodd told *Good Morning America*, he had "never heard language like this."

Full-scale destruction of the economy was averted by quickly transferring $700 billion in taxpayer money to the very banks that spawned the crisis. That infusion of cash not only saved the banks but enabled them to return almost immediately to great profitability, which in some cases surpassed even the massive earnings they had been generating throughout the prior decade.

Outside the banks, meanwhile, the worldwide economic disruption was so severe that nothing since the Great Depression could compare to it. A full two years after the crisis began, the human misery it wrought had barely been mitigated. Further, the harmful effects have almost certainly not completely materialized yet, and more suffering is still to come.

In the United States alone, more people have been unemployed for a longer period of time than at any point since the 1930s. In August 2009, the *New York Times* reported that "almost 45 percent of today's unemployed workers have been without a job for at least 27 weeks. In no other downturn since World War II did the share exceed 26 percent." Andrew Stettner of the National Employment Law Project told the *Huffington Post* in January 2010 that "long term unemployment is more than ever the norm . . . and it's across the country and across the economy that this is happening."

Long-term unemployment has serious consequences. People who are out of the workforce for even a few months suffer severe erosion of self-esteem, great stress, and dramatic changes to their lives. People who are out for a year or more are at risk of becoming permanently unemployable. Brian Bethune, chief financial economist at IHS Global Insight, warned in *Daily Finance* in March 2010: "People who are unemployed tend to get de-skilled. Anytime you go through a recession and there is an extended time of unemployment, there is a dead-weight loss of skills."

The unemployment crisis not only led to suffering and lost opportunity in its own right, but further entrenched and exacerbated America's already-shocking inequality. The hardest-hit, by far, were those in the lower income brackets. In late 2009, when the Center for Labor Market Studies at Northeastern University analyzed labor conditions for ten groups of American households based on annual household income, it found that the poorest group had a jobless rate of 30.8 percent—which, as the *New York Times* columnist Bob Herbert pointed out, is "more than five points higher than the overall jobless rate at the height of the Depression."

The next-lowest group suffered a still-staggering jobless rate of 19.1 percent. As one ascended into the higher levels of income earners, though, the unemployment rate steadily decreased. Pervasive joblessness afflicted the middle classes less severely than the poor, while at the two richest levels only 3.2 percent and 4 percent of job seekers, respectively, were without work. As the

Center for Labor Market Studies explained in its report, "A true labor market depression faced those in the bottom two deciles of the income distribution; a deep labor market recession prevailed among those in the middle of the distribution, and close to a full employment environment prevailed at the top."

Beyond the miseries of long-term unemployment, the impact of the financial crisis was visible in many other ways. In 2009, 2.8 million American homes had foreclosure proceedings filed against them. As Reuters put it at the beginning of 2010: "U.S. foreclosure actions shattered all records in 2009 and will do so again this year." Deep into 2010, that trend showed no signs of abating. In September, as Reuters reported, "The number of homes taken over by banks topped 100,000 for the first time."

In sum, the financial crisis caused by Wall Street was easily one of the most devastating and misery-producing events in American history. To the limited extent its causes have been investigated, it has become increasingly clear that the crisis was the result of plundering, fraud, lawlessness, and criminality on a massive scale. Major sectors of the financial industry turned out to be little more than glorified Ponzi schemes. Credit agencies on which investors relied routinely gave their stamp of approval to debt and loan instruments that were backed by "assets" of little or no value. Wall Street flooded the nation with toxic "derivative products," which Warren Buffett had denounced back in 2003 as "financial weapons of mass destruction" posing a "mega-catastrophic risk." And yet there has been virtually no punishment for the perpetrators, and it is highly unlikely that there will ever be any.

On the contrary, those who have brought the world economy to its knees are the ones who have prospered—the only ones who have prospered. "A lot of people who are responsible (for the crisis) seem to have gotten awfully rich," Barbara Roper, the director of investor protection for the Consumer Federation of America, told a McClatchy reporter on the one-year anniversary of the crisis. It's not hard to see why that happened. The political responses to this crisis have been shaped by the very financial elites whose recklessness caused the crisis in the first place, and thus it is those very elites who have been the prime beneficiaries.

In August 2009, Simon Johnson, the former chief economist at the International Monetary Fund and current economics professor at MIT, wrote a widely hailed article in the *Atlantic* titled "The Quiet Coup." He documented the similarities between the U.S. response to the financial crisis and the response of "emerging markets" countries to similar upheavals of the past. Arguing that a "financial oligarchy" exerts nearly full control over America's political institutions, Johnson pointed to parallels with the elites that caused previous financial meltdowns in places such as Ukraine, Russia, Thailand, Indonesia, and South Korea. In all those cases, the same financial elites whose recklessness and illegality brought on the economic crisis used their power over political institutions to ensure that they were the prime beneficiaries of the governments' response. Johnson writes:

> At the outset of the crisis, the oligarchs are usually among the first to get extra help from the government, such as preferential access to foreign currency, or maybe a nice tax break, or— here's a classic Kremlin bailout technique—the assumption of private debt obligations by the government. Under duress, generosity toward old friends takes many innovative forms. Meanwhile, needing to squeeze someone, most emerging-market governments look first to ordinary working folk—at least until the riots grow too large. . . .

In its depth and suddenness, the U.S. economic and financial crisis is shockingly reminiscent of moments we have recently seen in emerging markets (and only in emerging markets): South Korea (1997), Malaysia (1998), Russia and Argentina (time and again). . . .

But there's a deeper and more disturbing similarity: elite business interests—financiers, in the case of the U.S.—played a central role in creating the crisis, making ever-larger gambles, with the implicit backing of the government, until the inevitable collapse. More alarming, they are now using their influence to prevent precisely the sorts of reforms that are needed, and fast, to pull the economy out of its nosedive. The government seems helpless, or unwilling, to act against them.

This unwillingness is easily explained. Our government institutions are so dominated by financial elites that the very idea that the former would hold the latter accountable under the law is ludicrous. Indeed, it is impossible—as impossible as, say, an employee firing his boss, a tenant evicting a building owner, or inmates punishing the warden. America's financial elites have not only stockpiled vast amounts of material wealth but also acquired control over all the government and legal institutions that might stand in the way of their corruption and stealing.

To say such things about America, particularly in such stark terms, was once deemed radical and unserious; it was self-marginalizing. But no longer. The ability of financial elites to avoid any legal consequences even for the most egregious acts of wrongdoing is now so self-evident that it has been acknowledged even in the most establishment-sympathetic venues.

In April 2009, the second-highest-ranking Democrat in the United States Senate, Dick Durbin of Illinois, blurted out on a local Chicago radio station: "The banks—hard to believe in a time when we're facing a banking crisis that many of the banks created—are still the most powerful lobby on Capitol Hill. And they frankly own the place." Paul Blumenthal of the transparency group Sunlight Foundation emphasized the eye-popping dollar amounts behind Durbin's comment.

> You would think that this might be an exaggeration, or just a rhetorical bit of anti-bank populism, but if you look at the numbers, Durbin isn't wrong. . . . Since 1997, the financial sector has spent a combined total of $3.6 billion on lobbying the federal government. The total lobbying expenses have increased by 260% since 1997. Over that same time financial sector corporate profits have gone through the roof, with the financial sector reporting up to 40% of corporate profits in recent years.

Blumenthal offered just a "sampling" of what that money has bought:

> the deregulation of financial derivatives and credit default swaps, the elimination of the line between investment banks and commercial banks, the increased hardship for those filing for bankruptcy, and the total free hand for Fannie Mae and Freddie Mac to muddle their books and evade responsibility. And all of this has been fueled by the 3,000 or so finance sector lobbyists meeting with, calling up, and emailing congressional offices and executive branch agencies.

It should have come as no surprise, then, that in April 2009—a mere six months after Wall Street was in such desperate straits that it needed almost $1 trillion in bailout money—

Goldman Sachs reported a $1.8 billion profit for its first quarter. That summer, with serious understatement, the *New York Times* noted, "Goldman has turned the crisis to its advantage." And in early 2010, as the unemployment rate hovered close to 10 percent, Goldman Sachs revealed that its earnings for 2009 had topped $13 billion.

OWNERS OF GOVERNMENT

Of course, ownership of the government is not confined to Goldman or even to bankers generally; as we saw in the prior chapter, legislation in virtually every area is written by the lobbyists dispatched by the corporations that demand it, and its passage is then ensured by politicians whose pockets are stuffed with money from those same corporations. But Goldman's dominance of political and legal institutions is particularly deep-rooted and thus offers a superb demonstration of how elites shield themselves from repercussions of their lawbreaking. Indeed, a straight line can be drawn between the government's response to the financial crisis and the record profits Goldman enjoyed literally months later. Just consider the following sequence of events.

On September 25, 2008, *ABC News* reported that Goldman and its executives and employees had spent "more than 43 million dollars on lobbying and campaign contributions to cultivate friends and buy influence in Washington, D.C. since 1989." Moreover, *ABC News* noted, "as a group, Goldman Sachs bankers have been the country's top political campaign contributors this year and have given $29.5 million in contributions since 1989." "They are almost in a class by themselves," declared Sheila Krumholz, the executive director for the Center for Responsive Politics, which compiled the data.

The same week, the *New York Times* described one of the crucial secret meetings that shaped the federal government's response to the financial crisis. Presiding over that gathering at the Federal Reserve Bank of New York was Bush treasury secretary—and former Goldman CEO—Hank Paulson. The primary topic of discussion was the imminent collapse of American International Group, the giant insurance corporation. AIG's principal government regulator was absent from the meeting, but in attendance were a small number of Wall Street executives, including Lloyd Blankfein, Paulson's successor as the CEO of Goldman Sachs. The AIG matter was of urgent concern to Blankfein because, as the *Times* put it, "a collapse of [AIG] threatened to leave a hole of as much as $20 billion in Goldman's side." The outcome of the meeting, of course, could not have been better for Goldman: "Days later, federal officials, who . . . initially balked at tossing a lifeline to A.I.G., ended up bailing out the insurer for $85 billion."

Ordinarily, when a severely distressed company such as AIG is being saved by an infusion of capital, the party providing that money has significant leverage to negotiate with the failing company's creditors. The rescuing entity can easily force those creditors to accept deep discounts on the failing company's debt as a condition of the rescue. The reason for this is obvious. The party saving the distressed company simply tells the creditors: if you refuse to settle for a partial repayment of the money you loaned, then we will not rescue the company, it will collapse, and you might collect nothing at all. The U.S. government, when bailing out AIG, was thus in the perfect position to force those companies to which AIG owed the most money—including Goldman—to agree to substantial discounts and thereby make the bailout significantly cheaper. That was particularly true since many of those same creditors (again including Goldman) were themselves vying to receive multibillion-dollar bailouts, providing added leverage for government negotiators.

But in the case of AIG and Goldman, none of that happened. Not only was the insurance firm bailed out by the federal government, but—with the U.S. government essentially in control—it ended up paying off its debts at a rate of 100 percent; not a single penny of discount was negotiated. That meant that Goldman received the full amount due from AIG, in addition to the sums received directly from the government as part of its own bailout. That decision stood in rather stark contrast to the U.S. government's dealings with the United Auto Workers in February 2009. There, the government insisted that it would only bail out the auto industry if the union agreed to massive reductions in contractually stipulated benefits.

A month after the UAW negotiations, a major controversy erupted when it was revealed that AIG executives—including many who had presided over the very transactions that had led to that firm's near demise, a demise averted only with a major infusion of taxpayer money—were to receive millions of dollars in bonuses. The Obama administration insisted that it was powerless to stop those bonuses. When asked by George Stephanopoulos of *ABC News* to defend that claim, Larry Summers, one of Obama's top economic advisers, righteously invoked noble legal principles: "We are a country of law. There are contracts. The government cannot just abrogate contracts."

Stephanopoulos notably failed to ask why that same government could force the working-class, nonculpable, politically powerless autoworkers to accept major reductions in their contractual benefits as a condition for a bailout but could not do the same for the highly culpable, extremely wealthy AIG executives. Apparently, the sanctity of contract rights shields the entitlements of financial elites but is no barrier to forcing ordinary Americans to give up vested rights upon pain of losing their jobs.

The AIG bailout was just one of the steps leading to the record Goldman profits of 2009. In October 2008, Treasury Secretary Paulson announced his choice to manage the federal government's $700 billion bailout of Wall Street: thirty-five-year-old Neel Kashkari, who had just recently come from Goldman Sachs to serve as Paulson's assistant treasury secretary. As the *Wall Street Journal* put it when the appointment was announced, "The position confers substantial power on Mr. Kashkari."

In November, Obama announced his selection of Timothy Geithner as treasury secretary. Geithner—a protégé of former Goldman CEO Robert Rubin—had served as chairman of the New York Fed for the prior five years and (as we shall soon see) had established a relationship with Wall Street that, for someone in that regulatory position, was unprecedentedly close and loyal. Shortly thereafter, Obama selected another Rubin protégé—Larry Summers—as director of the White House's National Economic Council, a position that wields as much influence as any over the nation's economic policy. Obama was certainly aware that back in the late 1990s, Summers had presided over a series of Wall Street–friendly deregulation reforms when he was Clinton's treasury secretary. What's more, according to the *Washington Post*, in the two years prior to joining the Obama administration Summers had received millions of dollars from Wall Street, including a paycheck for $135,000 from Goldman Sachs for a one-day visit in 2008.

And these appointees were not Goldman's only friends in Washington. On December 14, 2008, the *New York Times* disclosed that a central role in securing the multibillion-dollar bailout for Wall Street had been played by Democratic senator Chuck Schumer. In the weeks following the bailout, meanwhile, Schumer had addressed a gathering convened by the buyout billionaire Henry Kravis and roughly twenty other finance industry executives. The New York Democrat had assured them that "crazy, anti-business liberals" would not interfere with the legislation they wanted, and subsequently received close to $150,000 in campaign donations from the businesses in attendance. The *Times* article, headlined "A Champion of Wall Street Reaps Benefits," further detailed how Schumer, as head of the Democrats' Senate Campaign Committee, had succeeded in "raising a record $240 million while increasing donations from Wall Street by 50 percent." As the *Times* noted, that money "helped the Democrats gain power in Congress" and "elevated Mr. Schumer's standing in his party."

The banks' largesse was amply rewarded. In return for Wall Street's support, Schumer, who is often called a "liberal" Democrat, "embraced the industry's free-market, deregulatory agenda more than almost any other Democrat in Congress, backing many of the key measures blamed for contributing to the financial crisis." He took various steps "to protect industry players from government oversight and tougher rules" and "helped save financial institutions billions of dollars in higher taxes or fees." The *Times* also noted that Schumer had a long record of enabling his Wall Street patrons to engage in precisely the kinds of transactions that led to the 2008 financial crisis: he had "succeeded in limiting efforts to regulate credit-rating agencies," "sponsored legislation that cut fees paid by Wall Street firms to finance government oversight," and "pushed to allow banks to have lower capital reserves."

As the financial crisis progressed, the placement of Goldman executives in key positions continued apace. As part of the AIG bailout, for instance, the government brought in Ed Liddy to serve as the company's CEO. Liddy had previously been a Goldman executive and still owned several million dollars of Goldman shares when he was appointed to run AIG and make vital decisions affecting its debts to Goldman.

On January 27, 2009, *USA Today* reported matter-of-factly: "Treasury Secretary Timothy Geithner picked a former Goldman Sachs lobbyist as a top aide Tuesday, the same day he announced rules aimed at reducing the role of lobbyists in agency decisions. Mark Patterson will serve as Geithner's chief of staff at Treasury." One of Patterson's sterling successes as a Goldman lobbyist had come in 2007, when he had helped to defeat a Senate provision (sponsored by Obama, among others) to limit executive compensation. This state of affairs reflects what Desmond Lachman—American Enterprise Institute fellow, former chief emerging-market strategist at Salomon Smith Barney, and top IMF official; no radical he—described in the *Washington Post* as "Goldman Sachs's seeming lock on high-level U.S. Treasury jobs."

(Goldman's choice to replace Patterson as its chief lobbyist was Michael Paese, the top staffer to Democratic representative Barney Frank. Paese had spent years helping Frank carry out his duties as chairman of the House Financial Services Committee, the committee responsible for oversight of Wall Street. Now, he would put his Washington Rolodex and his substantial influence in the halls of Congress at the service of Goldman's legislative agenda.)

At roughly the same time, Reuters announced:

President Barack Obama's nominee to oversee U.S. futures markets, who has confessed he should have done more [when serving as a financial official under Clinton] to rein in exotic financial instruments that have battered global markets, was approved by the Senate Agriculture Committee on Monday. The approval of Gary Gensler, a former Goldman Sachs executive, clears the way for a Senate vote putting him in charge of the Commodity Futures Trading Commission.

Many of the Wall Street–subservient legal changes that led to the 2008 crisis had been accomplished during the late 1990s, during the second term of the Clinton administration. Incredibly, neither the key role Gensler had played in that orgy of deregulation nor his subsequent return to Goldman were any impediment to his being once again empowered to oversee the very industry he had so loyally served the first time around (and which in return had then lavishly rewarded him). And this return was part of a pattern. The catastrophic spasm of deregulation in the late 1990s had been led by the former Goldman CEO Robert Rubin and then by Larry Summers, who both served as Clinton's treasury secretary. Now, Summers, along with Gensler and fellow Rubin acolyte Tim Geithner, formed the top tier of Obama's economics team as it managed the fallout from the financial crisis. As *Rolling Stone*'s Matt Taibbi put it, "The only thing to remember is that all the ones who got us into this mess—Rubin, Summers, Goldman in general—are now being put in charge of the cleanup by a president who spent most of 18 months on the campaign trail pledging to end the influence of money in politics."

Just think about how this cycle works. People like Rubin, Summers, Patterson, and Gensler shuffle back and forth between the public and private sectors, taking turns as needed with their GOP counterparts. When in government, they ensure that laws and regulations are written to redound directly to the benefit of a handful of Wall Street firms, abolishing most regulatory safe-guards that keep those behemoths in check. When the electoral tide turns against them, they return to those very firms and col-lect millions upon millions of dollars, profits made possible by the laws and regulations they implemented (or failed to imple-ment) when they were in charge. Then, when their party returns to power, back they go into government, where they use their influence to ensure that the cycle keeps on going.

This is exactly what Simon Johnson meant when he proclaimed that "the finance industry has effectively captured our govern-ment." And it's what the economist Nouriel Roubini meant when he told the makers of the 2010 documentary *Inside Job* that Wall Street has "captured the political system" on "the Democratic and the Republican side" alike.

As time passed, the connections of Wall Street to the govern-ment officials guiding Obama's economic policy became ever clearer. In April 2009, the *New York Times* conducted a thor-ough examination of Obama's treasury secretary, Tim Geithner, during his prior job as chairman of the New York Federal Reserve from 2003 to 2008, where he had been charged with regulating Wall Street. The *Times* investigation found that during this "era of unbridled and ultimately disastrous risk-taking by the finan-cial industry," Geithner "forged unusually close relationships with executives of Wall Street's giant financial institutions." As a result, "his actions, as a regulator and later a bailout king, often aligned with the industry's interests and desires, according to interviews with financiers, regulators and analysts and a review of Federal Reserve records."

The *Times* article noted that New York Fed chairmen of the past typically avoided extensive professional reliance on—and especially social intermingling with—executives of the banking industry they were charged with overseeing. By contrast, Geithner's connections to those executives were extraordinarily close. "Mr. Geithner's reliance on bankers, hedge fund managers and others to assess the market's health—and provide guidance once it faltered—stood out," the *Times* wrote.

Examining Geithner's calendars during his years at the New York Fed, the *Times* documented extensive social interactions with virtually every leading figure whom he was charged with regulating. "He ate lunch with senior executives from Citigroup, Goldman Sachs and Morgan Stanley at the Four Seasons restaurant or in their corporate dining rooms"; "attended casual dinners at the homes of executives like Jamie Dimon, a member of the New York Fed board and the chief of JPMorgan Chase"; "was particularly close to executives of Citigroup, the largest bank under his supervision"; kept in close touch with Rubin, whom he considered his "mentor"; and "met frequently with Sanford I. Weill, one of Citi's largest individual shareholders and its former chairman, serving on the board of a charity Mr. Weill led."

This list of Geithner's friends forms a substantial portion of the top-ten Wall Street culprits responsible for the 2008 financial crisis. Predictably, these relationships did not incline Geithner to take action against their reckless ways; indeed, the opposite was true. As the *Times* delicately put it, "For all his ties to Citi, Mr. Geithner repeatedly missed or overlooked signs that the bank—along with the rest of the financial system—was falling apart." To the extent that Geithner took action at all, it was to shield those financial firms from any meaningful government oversight: "As late as 2007, Mr. Geithner advocated measures that government studies said would have allowed banks to lower their reserves. When the crisis hit, banks were vulnerable because their financial cushion was too thin to protect against large losses."

Yet despite this close collaboration with the very industry most responsible for the financial crisis—or, more likely, *because* of that collaboration—Obama chose Geithner as his treasury secretary to shepherd the country out of the crisis that his Wall Street friends had caused. Geithner's failures as a regulator at the New York Fed were well known when Obama selected him. As the *New York Times* editorial page said at the time, Geithner was clearly one of the people who "played central roles in policies that helped provoke today's financial crisis."

That Obama was not only undeterred by Geithner's close ties to Wall Street but likely motivated by them when making his selection is not particularly surprising. When running for president, Obama himself had been a major beneficiary of Wall Street's largesse. In the midst of the primary war between Obama and Hillary Clinton, the *Los Angeles Times* reported that the two Democratic candidates, "who are running for president as economic populists, are benefiting handsomely from Wall Street donations, easily surpassing Republican John McCain in campaign contributions from the troubled financial services sector." Consistent with Senator Schumer's mutually beneficial relationship with Wall Street banks, the *Los Angeles Times* noted, "It is part of a broader fundraising shift toward Democrats, compared to past campaigns when Republicans were the favorites of Wall Street."

Needless to say, large amounts of money are not lavished on political candidates out of pure-hearted generosity, but rather with an expectation that the donations will secure favorable treatment, and with an implied threat that failing to offer such preferential treatment will result in the future loss of financial support. For that reason, even in the best of times it would have been inconceivable for Obama to choose a treasury secretary who was unfriendly to Wall Street. During the financial crisis, when investment banks were vying with ordinary Americans for the federal government's finite bailout funds, it was particularly imperative that the nation's top financial official be a loyal servant of Wall Street. And in Geithner, that's precisely what they got.

The ultimate result of all these job appointments and revolving doors was a textbook case of how the law can be manipulated to protect and advance the interests of the culpable parties. In September 2008, as the financial crisis was spiraling out of control, the Federal Reserve allowed Goldman (and a few other surviving institutions) to convert from an investment bank into a "bank holding company." The *Wall Street Journal* claimed at the time that any firms that converted in this fashion would "come under the close supervision of national bank regulators, subjecting them to new capital requirements, additional oversight, and far less profitability than they have historically enjoyed." The reason for this reduced profitability is that becoming a bank holding company involves a tradeoff. Such companies are able to borrow money much less expensively than investment banks and are able to take advantage of numerous other Fed facilities that investment banks cannot access; but in return for these preferred arrangements, the Fed requires—at least in theory, under the law—that bank holding companies refrain from engaging in a wide array of high-risk, high-return transactions such as derivative trading. In essence, they are obliged to avoid the very transactions that had long generated enormous profits for Goldman and other investment banks but that also caused the financial collapse.

Goldman desperately needed access to Fed resources in order to save itself, so its conversion to a bank holding company was not unexpected. But a mere nine months later, Goldman was boasting of what the *New York Times* called "blowout profits"—so much for

the *Wall Street Journal* forecast of "less profitability." As for alleg-
edly greater regulations and capital restrictions, Goldman freely
admitted from the start that it would not be hampered. "We don't
believe we'll have to get out of any businesses," said Lucas van
Praag, a Goldman spokesman, to the *Deal*. Van Praag was right.
The July 2010 *Times* article reporting on Goldman's outsize profits noted that its high-risk transactions were continuing, and
included a concise summary of the situation from Roger Free-
man, an analyst at Barclays Capital: "It is, in many respects,
business as usual at Goldman."

Goldman thus gave up nothing by being allowed to convert
to a bank holding company, but the conversion did allow it access
to large amounts of lending from the Federal Reserve. (Since
then, the Fed has increased its balance sheet by $2 trillion while
steadfastly refusing to disclose the beneficiaries of that credit.) In
other words, the law that had always imposed a choice on all
other companies—either enjoy a lack of regulation but no access
to Fed lending as an investment bank, or enjoy Fed lending but
be constrained by large amounts of regulation as a bank holding
company—simply did not apply to Goldman. It was able to obtain
all the benefits under the law while being subjected to none of the
restrictions. No wonder, then, that Goldman booked billions of
dollars in profits within months of the start of the financial crisis, even as the rest of America struggled with the worst financial
hardship in many decades.

"BECAUSE THEN YOU'D FIND THE CULPRITS"

With these facts assembled, is it even remotely possible to envi-
sion political officials using the force of law to hold financial
elites accountable for serious wrongdoing? Such accountability is

not only exceedingly unlikely but close to impossible. And the fact that the massive corruption, plundering, and illegality that caused the financial crisis has gone almost entirely without criminal investigation, to say nothing of punishment, proves that conclusively.

In April 2009, Bill Black, currently a professor of economics and law and formerly a federal securities regulator, appeared on *Bill Moyers Journal* on PBS and spoke about the unparalleled corruption of the collusion between the goverment and Goldman Sachs.

> BLACK: The Bush administration and now the Obama administration kept secret from us what was being done with AIG. AIG was being used secretly to bail out favored banks like UBS and like Goldman Sachs.... And, you know, when he was Treasury Secretary, Paulson created a recommendation group to tell Treasury what they ought to do with AIG. And he put Goldman Sachs on it.
>
> MOYERS: Even though Goldman Sachs had a big vested stake.
>
> BLACK: Massive stake. And even though he had just been CEO of Goldman Sachs before becoming Treasury Secretary. Now, in most stages in American history, that would be a scandal of such proportions that he wouldn't be allowed in civilized society....
>
> MOYERS: So, how did he get away with it?
>
> BLACK: I don't know whether we've lost our capability of outrage. Or whether the cover up has been so successful that people just don't have the facts to react to it.

Black was even more incensed by the absence of any real investigation into what caused the financial collapse, who was

responsible, whether crimes were committed, and whether indictments and criminal prosecutions were warranted. He expressed
his incredulousness over the lack of investigations this way.

> BLACK: What would happen if after a plane crashes, we said,
> "Oh, we don't want to look in the past. We want to be for-
> ward looking." Many people might have been, you know, we
> don't want to pass blame. No. We have a nonpartisan, skilled
> inquiry. We spend lots of money on, get really bright people.
> And we find out, to the best of our ability, what caused every
> single major plane crash in America. And because of that,
> aviation has an extraordinarily good safety record. We
> ought to follow the same policies in the financial sphere. We
> have to find out what caused the disasters, or we will keep
> reliving them. . . .
>
> MOYERS: Yeah. Are you saying that Timothy Geithner, the
> Secretary of the Treasury, and others in the administration,
> with the banks, are engaged in a cover up to keep us from
> knowing what went wrong?
>
> BLACK: Absolutely.

Given the extent of the economic damage, the absence of criminal proceedings against the culprits is indeed unfathomable—
except when one considers that all the politicians who could
meaningfully make such demands are captive to the very people
who ought to be the targets. When Nouriel Roubini was asked in
Inside Job why there have been no real investigations, he replied,
"Because then you'd find the culprits."

One year after the crisis exploded into public consciousness,
a McClatchy article asked a similar question: "Why Haven't Any
Wall Street Tycoons Been Sent to the Slammer?" As the piece

put it, "Millions of Americans have seen their home values and retirement savings plunge and their jobs evaporate," but "what they haven't seen are any Wall Street tycoons forced to swap their multi-million dollar jobs and custom-made suits for dishwashing and prison stripes." Although the McClatchy reporter who wrote the article noted some Washington gossip and whispers about possible postcrisis prosecutions, he could point to none that were actually under way.

Indeed, *Columbia Journalism Review*, in assessing the McClatchy report, presciently argued that its reference to only vague, unattributed rumors of possible investigations strongly suggested that there were no real efforts to prosecute any crimes relating to the financial crisis. *CJR*'s Dean Starkman wrote: "Enough about the FBI 'looking at,' 'launching probes of,' and 'investigating' things. Let's see it make a case for a change, or at least make a formal inquiry that would require disclosure."

Starkman's skepticism on the one-year anniversary of the crisis was well founded. Another year later, nothing had changed. There were still no criminal investigations, let alone prosecutions, of Wall Street criminals for the massive fraud that had been perpetrated on the nation. In October 2010, the *New York Times* columnist Frank Rich noted this lack of legal accountability.

> No matter how much Obama talks about his "tough" new financial regulatory reforms or offers rote condemnations of Wall Street greed, few believe there's been real change. That's not just because so many have lost their jobs, their savings and their homes. It's also because so many know that the loftiest perpetrators of this national devastation got get-out-of-jail-free cards, that too-big-to-fail banks have grown bigger and that the rich are still the only Americans getting richer.

Those responsible have plundered with impunity and kept their ill-gotten gains. *Inside Job* examined numerous Wall Street executives who, as the film put it, "destroyed their own companies and plunged the world into crisis" only to "walk away from the wreckage with their fortunes intact." One of the film's chief villains is Robert Rubin, the former Clinton treasury secretary and Goldman CEO, who made hundreds of millions of dollars at Citigroup while playing a central role in spawning the crisis. Today, Rubin's riches are undiminished, and he continues to exert vast influence over America's economic policies through the placement of his acolytes in the highest financial positions in the Obama administration.

It is true that there have been occasional sporadic efforts to create the appearance of accountability. However, they are so impotent, so inconsequential, that they actually serve to underscore the full-scale immunity enjoyed by the owners of our government. The Justice Department, for example, has initiated some civil actions against a few Wall Street executives, but the resulting fines are so insignificant in the scheme of their fortunes that they barely cause a dent.

For instance, in October 2010, Angelo Mozilo, the former CEO of Countrywide, settled charges brought against him by the Securities and Exchange Commission. The SEC had alleged that, among other things, Mozilo had fraudulently concealed enormous risks in the company's subprime business from investors. While aggressively lauding the virtues of Countrywide's financial instruments to the investing public, he was privately acknowledging how dubious they were. In one e-mail about the company's subprime packages, he wrote, "In all my years in the business, I have never seen a more toxic product"; in another, he derided those products as "poison." Government officials have repeatedly pointed to the Mozilo case as proof that they are serious about cracking down on Wall Street criminals. To settle all charges, Mozilo agreed to a fine of $67 million, with almost one-third of that to be paid by Countrywide.

That may seem like a substantial amount until one considers that Mozilo collected more than half a billion dollars in the prior eight years as he presided over a massive fraud. Now, the seventy-one-year-old retired executive will not spend a day in jail, and nothing prevents him from enjoying the rest of the enormous fortune he compiled. The notion that Mozilo—one of the financial world's most egregious offenders—has been subjected to meaningful accountability does not even pass the laugh test. Yet in February 2011, the DOJ announced that it was closing its file on Mozilo without bringing any criminal charges.

A similar travesty occurred in November 2009, when the government settled a major fraud suit brought by the SEC against JPMorgan Chase. The SEC alleged that the bank had made secret payments to close friends of politicians in Jefferson County, Alabama, in the amount of 8 million dollars. In exchange for that $8 million, JPMorgan was allegedly allowed to play the primary role in providing $3 billion worth of refinancing to the county, using instruments so dubious and toxic that they eventually helped push the county to the brink of bankruptcy. Covert tape recordings of JPMorgan executives captured them talking about the local officials who would "get free money from us" and how they needed to "pay off people" who had influence in the county. Ultimately, one local politician was convicted of felonies for taking bribes and was sent to prison. But nothing of the sort happened to the principals at JPMorgan. Instead, the firm simply settled a civil suit brought by the SEC, without any admission of wrongdoing.

The JPMorgan settlement included a fine in the hefty-sounding amount of $722 million. Most of that, however, was accounted for by the firm's agreement to waive fees that the bankrupt county owed to the investment bank but likely would not have been able to pay anyway. The actual amount JPMorgan paid was $75 million, which the company can easily justify as merely the cost of doing business. It pays a fine that's tiny relative to the scale of the enterprise, admits no wrongdoing, all is forgotten, and it simply moves on to the next venture. Such was the outcome in Alabama even though the SEC had set forth multiple details to support its claim that JPMorgan executives had executed a pay-for-play scheme involving both politicians and other firms participating in the deal.

Hailed as "aggressive enforcement" by DOJ press releases, such proceedings are actually the opposite. They create the illusion of accountability while enabling scheming elites to commit crimes with impunity.

In mid-2009, this illusion was momentarily shattered when the U.S. government repeatedly tried to pressure a federal judge to approve an inexcusably lenient settlement with Bank of America. The SEC complaint charged that the Bank of America, when it was planning to acquire Merrill Lynch (with substantial bailout help from taxpayers) shortly before Merrill's failure, had failed to disclose to its shareholders the fact that BoA had agreed to give Merrill's executives billions of dollars in bonus payments. Had BoA shareholders known that their company was going to grant billions to the very people who had steered Merrill Lynch to disaster, it is quite possible that they would not have approved the acquisition. But they never had a chance to make that decision because BoA executives had simply—and illegally—omitted any mention of those bonus agreements when the acquisition was being discussed.

The SEC wanted to settle all charges for a minuscule fine of $33 million, to be paid not by the defrauding BoA executives but by the company. (Although corporate executives are typically shielded from liability when acting on behalf of their employers, they can be held personally liable for outright fraud.) In an unusual act, Judge Jed Rakoff rejected the proposed settlement as inadequate, noting that the fraudulent concealment was a matter of "justice and morality" that "suggests a rather cynical relationship between the parties." He demanded that the fines be paid by "the individuals who were responsible," and rejected the executives' claim—now common among political and financial elites when they are caught committing crimes—that they were not guilty because their lawyers had approved their act. "It would seem that all a corporate officer who has produced a false proxy statement need offer by way of defense is that he or she relied on counsel," the judge noted disapprovingly.

Only when substantially more money was added to the settlement did Judge Rakoff approve it, though he noted that he was doing so "reluctantly"; even the revised settlement, he said, was "half-baked justice at best" in light of the conduct of BoA executives. Because the new settlement met the minimal legal requirements, however, Rakoff had no choice but to sign off on it.

Judge Rakoff's action, while shining a light on how the government shields corporate criminals while pretending to hold them accountable, is exceedingly rare. He is known for being a particularly aggressive jurist in these matters. Typically, such arrangements are simply rubber-stamped by the courts, and corporate executives thereby enjoy virtually complete immunity even when they are caught engaging in the most egregious criminal acts. Notably, as Bloomberg reported, the fines collected by the SEC for the fiscal year ending 2008 were the lowest since the beginning of the decade.

EVIDENCE OF CRIMINALITY IGNORED

The immunity enjoyed by financial elites in America is particularly striking when compared to other nations' responses to financial crises. In Iceland, for instance, not only have numerous bank officials been criminally investigated and charged, but, as Jurist news service reported in September 2010, "An Icelandic parliamentary commission . . . recommended that the country's former prime minister be tried for negligence" for his role in the country's 2008 financial crisis. Indeed, the subpoena-empowered commission conducted a thorough and very public investigation into the events leading to Iceland's crisis and then published a 274-page report—which, among other things, accuses the former prime minister of having been aware of the underlying crisis but purposely refraining from taking action to stop it. Based on those findings, the commission's report urges that the former prime minister be "tried and punished" for the role he played.

There is little doubt that a corresponding culpability exists in the American political establishment. Still, holding political leaders legally accountable is virtually unimaginable in the United States today, and the same is true for financial leaders.

Criminally prosecuting Wall Street executives and firms for their role in the financial crisis would not be a simple task. At issue are complex transactions, dispersed throughout multiple

large institutions, and carried out under a deliberately vague
and permissive legal regime. Indeed, in his 2003 condemnation
of derivative instruments, Warren Buffet candidly acknowledged that the complexity of these transactions meant that neither he nor anyone else truly understood their value, impact, or
interrelationships. Real investigations would require substantial
time and resources and would encounter legitimate obstacles.

That said, large-scale criminality clearly played a major role
in engendering the crisis. Even without subpoena power and
other instruments of compulsion, many experts and commentators have compellingly documented numerous clear acts of illegality. Professor Bill Black comprehensively examined public
documents to demonstrate that only "willful blindness" among
lenders and credit ratings agencies would have led them to tout
and endorse financial instruments that were essentially worth-
less. Yet virtually none of this evidence has even been meaningfully examined by the authorities, let alone pursued by
prosecutors. As *Newsweek*'s Michael Hirsh lamented two years
after the crisis, speaking about the role played by credit agencies: "One of the most distressing things about the current
financial scandal is that there has been no . . . reckoning against
the firms that were supposed to be watching the system for the
investment public."

This "no-accountability" approach is of course just a slightly
altered variant of the mentality that led to the pardon of Nixon
and the subsequent granting of immunity to powerful political
criminals. Likewise familiar is the rationale now routinely
invoked to justify the lack of prosecutions of financial elites: given
their importance, it is vital that we not disrupt their efforts and
actions by bothering them with investigations for their crimes.
As Hirsh wrote about the prospects of prosecuting the credit

agencies: "The government is simply too afraid to let that happen. Like many of the big banks, the ratings agencies have been deemed too big or important to the system to fail."

In her book *ECONned*, Yves Smith—who spent much of her career on Wall Street, including a stint at Goldman—extensively details the fraudulent accounting practices that preceded the downfall of Lehman Brothers and other banks. As she notes, "What went on at Lehman and AIG, as well as the chicanery in the CDO [collateralized debt obligation] business, by any sensible standard is criminal." Smith points out in particular the proliferation of the kind of pay-for-play that was exposed in the JPMorgan/Jefferson County case discussed earlier in this chapter.

> Municipal finance has long been a cesspool, but blatantly corrupt behavior was, not that long ago, for the most part limited to backwaters and bucket-shop operators. Now, it isn't just Jefferson County, but pretty much every big-name financial firm is involved in multiple cases of stuffing local governments and their pension funds, with derivatives that had all sorts of tricks and traps or toxic CDOs, sometimes with the liberal applications of bribes, sometimes merely with fast talk and omission of key details. Often, these government entities hired "experts" who simply sold them out for fat fees.

Perhaps the most notable argument for clear-cut lawbreaking as the cause of the financial crisis came from a very unlikely source: the longtime Federal Reserve chairman Alan Greenspan, who spent much of his career demanding fewer and fewer regulatory restraints on Wall Street. In the wake of the economic collapse, Greenspan admitted that he had been wrong to oppose increased regulations, telling a House committee, "Those of us who have looked to the self-interest of lending institutions to protect shareholders' equity, myself included, are in a state of shocked disbelief," and acknowledging that the crisis had exposed a "flaw" in his free-market ideology. But, after spending decades insisting that fraud was not a real problem on Wall Street, Greenspan also argued that much of the problem was due not to lax regulations but to outright criminality.

> Well, first of all, remember you have to distinguish between supervision and enforcement. A lot of the problems which we had in the independent issuers of subprime and other such mortgages, the basic problem there is that, if you don't have enforcement, and a lot of that stuff was just plain fraud, you're not coming to grips with the issue.

When even a longtime Wall Street servant such as Alan Greenspan admits that a substantial cause of the financial crisis was "just plain fraud," the almost complete absence of criminal consequences is clearly an extraordinary injustice.

In December 2010, ProPublic reporter Jesse Eisinger—who covered the financial crisis from the start—protested the lack of prosecutions in the *New York Times*, noting that even on Wall Street, "everyone is wondering: Where are the investigations related to the financial crisis?" Eisinger's article summarized the shocking state of affairs:

> Nobody from Lehman, Merrill Lynch or Citigroup has been charged criminally with anything. No top executives at Bear Stearns have been indicted. All former American International Group executives are running free. No big mortgage company executive has had to face the law. . . . The world was

almost brought low by the American banking system, and we are supposed to think that no one did anything wrong? . . . As a society, we have the bankers we deserve. Sadly, it's looking as if we have the regulators and prosecutors we deserve, too.

A blue-ribbon report did get issued in January 2011 by the government's Financial Crisis Inquiry Commission. It was a typical Beltway piece of obfuscation and whitewashing, a work with little real insight and even less consequence. Although the commission found that the crisis could have been averted with greater government regulation and was largely caused by industry-wide fraud, it identified no specific culprits and failed to call for any criminal investigations. Like most panels of its kind, the FCIC did not threaten the perpetrators with any real consequences, despite some harsh language blaming the financial industry as a whole. The report's release was, in the words of Joe Nocera of the *New York Times*, "almost comical" and failed in its only real mission: to "propose a satisfying theory that explains why so many people did so many wrong, and wrong-headed, things in the years leading up to the financial crisis." As a result, it did absolutely nothing to bring any real accountability to either the financial elites responsible for the crisis or the government regulators who had allowed it to happen.

What's perhaps even more astounding than the lack of criminal prosecutions is that, years later, the original practices behind the crisis have hardly been constrained at all. In January 2010, the Treasury Department's independent watchdog over the Wall Street bailout, Neil Barofsky, issued a scathing report documenting that many of the factors behind the financial crisis are still with us, and that in some respects the situation has actually worsened. "It is hard to see how any of the fundamental problems in the system have been addressed to date," Barofsky wrote. Banks that were said to be "too big to fail" are now "even larger," and Wall Street is "more convinced than ever" that it will be saved from failure by the government, thus increasing the motivation to take enormous risks. Wall Street bonuses in the year immediately after the crisis reveal "little fundamental change" in troublesome compensation schemes, while federal efforts to support the housing market "risk reinflating that bubble." Moreover, the so-called financial regulation legislation enacted by Congress in the summer of 2010 was so diluted by lobbyists and donors from the very industry it purported to regulate that the primary causes of the crisis—including the "too-big-to-fail" quandary and unregulated derivatives markets—went almost entirely unaddressed.

Indeed, the government's ties to Wall Street are stronger than ever. In September 2010, the *Huffington Post* reviewed Geithner's calendars as treasury secretary—just as the *New York Times* had done for his calendars as New York Fed chair—and found the same pattern: Geithner still spends most of his time speaking with the very banking executives whom he's supposedly regulating.

The findings included the fact that "Geithner has met more often with Goldman Sachs CEO Lloyd Blankfein than Congressional leaders." Indeed, the *Huffington Post* noted, "Goldman CEO Lloyd Blankfein has shown up on Geithner's calendar at least 38 times through March 2010 since the Treasury Secretary took office in January 2009, three more entries than Senate Majority Leader Harry Reid, 13 more than House Speaker Nancy Pelosi, and nearly four times as many as Senate Minority Leader Mitch McConnell and House Minority Leader John Boehner combined." What's more, during his first five months in office, "Geithner met with chief executives from firms like Citigroup,

JPMorgan Chase, Morgan Stanley and BlackRock at least 76 times—more calendar entries than for the heads of the regional Federal Reserve banks, who are the top overseers of systemically-important banks like JPMorgan, Citi, Bank of America and Wells Fargo—or for top members of Congress like Reid, Pelosi, their Republican counterparts, and the heads of the Senate and House committees overseeing financial institutions and economic policy."

The political class's loyalty and subservience to Wall Street grows ever more brazen. In June 2010, Peter Orszag, one of Obama's key financial officials as the director of Office of Management and Budget, announced he was leaving the administration. After his departure, Orszag spent a few months as a *New York Times* columnist (advocating for cuts in Social Security as a means of addressing America's deficit problems), and then, in November 2010, announced he was joining Robert Rubin at Citigroup to become vice chairman of global banking. In other words, after almost two years in an administration that had propped up Wall Street and returned it to tremendous profitability while ordinary Americans continued to suffer extreme economic hardship, Orszag went to collect his rewards from one of the banks that had profited the most from that administration's policies, and which had received a multibillion-dollar bailout. Orszag's announcement was branded by the longtime *Atlantic* editor James Fallows as "damaging and shocking."

> His move illustrates something that is just wrong. The idea that someone would help plan, advocate, and carry out an economic policy that played such a crucial role in the survival of a financial institution—and then, less than two years after his Administration took office, would take a job that (a) exempli-

fies the growing disparities the Administration says it's trying to correct and (b) unavoidably will call on knowledge and contacts Orszag developed while in recent public service—this says something bad about what is taken for granted in American public life.

When we notice similar patterns in other countries—for instance, how many offspring and in-laws of senior Chinese Communist officials have become very, very rich—we are quick to draw conclusions about structural injustices. Americans may not "notice" Orszag-like migrations, in the sense of devoting big news coverage to them. But these stories pile up in the background to create a broad American sense that politics is rigged, and opportunity too.

Not even a cataclysmic Wall Street–caused crisis that imposed great suffering on millions of Americans could slow down the wholesale capture of the government by the nation's wealthiest corporations. The obliteration of the wall separating the private and public spheres continues unabated, and financial elites are now more confident than ever that things such as laws and oversight exist for them in name only.

DUSTING OFF THE TELECOM IMMUNITY PLAYBOOK

Few events better illustrate the ever-expanding lawbreaking license granted to elites than the mortgage fraud crisis of 2010. Beginning in the fall of that year, incontrovertible evidence emerged showing that the nation's largest mortgage banks were operating a system built on deceit, illegality, and fictitious legal documents, all in the service of foreclosing on the homes of millions of Americans rapidly and without resistance. The fraud here was perpetrated on both the homeowners whose property was illegally seized, and on the courts to which forged documents were routinely submitted. Yet the first instinct of the political class in the face of this sweeping criminality was to find ways to protect the mortgage industry from accountability.

Once the scandal broke, virtually every day brought new stories of banks systematically foreclosing on people's homes through the use of fake documentation and manufactured affidavits. In many cases, the banks attempted to foreclose without a valid legal claim to the houses they were trying to seize. In some instances, the homeowners being targeted with foreclosure actions were not even in default. It is not hyperbole to say that this activity constituted pervasive theft by the mortgage banking industry: misleading courts into forcibly transferring people's property to these banks when they had no legal right to it.

A frank assessment of the situation comes from Janet Tavakoli, the founder and president of Tavakoli Structured Finance. For her early warnings about the fragilities in capital markets, *BusinessWeek* dubbed Tavakoli "the Cassandra of Credit Derivatives." As the mortgage scandal was breaking, she told the *Washington Post*, "This is the biggest fraud in the history of the capital markets." And she contended that the reason it was not discovered earlier was that "banks were lying and committing fraud, and our regulators were covering for them and so a bad problem has become a hellacious one."

As the mortgage crisis unfolded, more and more horror stories from homeowners made their way into the news. But because the banks appeared to be supported by the illegitimate documents that they had systematically filed with the courts, it was often difficult, if not impossible, for homeowners of limited means to stave off even the most flagrantly baseless foreclosure actions. Ohio state attorney general Richard Cordray said in an October 2010 interview with the blog Firedoglake, "What we're seeing is very disturbing . . . a systematic fraud on the courts of Ohio." State attorneys general from around the nation expressed much the same sentiment.

In December 2010, the *New York Times* reported the story of Mimi Ash, who upon coming back to her house after a long trip "discovered that someone had broken into the home," removed all of her possessions, and changed the locks. But the culprit, Ash soon learned, "was not a burglar but her bank"—specifically Bank of America, which "had wrongfully foreclosed on her house and thrown out her belongings, without alerting Ms. Ash beforehand." Imagine if an ordinary individual had broken into her home, taken all her possessions, and then put her house up for sale without any legal entitlement: that person would be imprisoned without question. But stories like hers are now commonplace; as the *Times* put it, "Lawsuits detailing bank break-ins like the one at Ms. Ash's house keep surfacing." And nobody from the banks ever goes to jail.

Despite the magnitude of the fraud—or, more accurately, because of it—the political class quickly reacted not by attempting to impose accountability on these banks, but rather by rushing to protect them from accountability. Trumpeting the same excuse now used reflexively by the political class to justify elite immunity—it's more important to fix the problems in the future than to seek retribution—the Obama administration immediately announced that it had no intention of punishing any past transgressions, even ones involving unambiguous lawbreaking. In a stunning display, administration officials affirmed the

importance of legal accountability in one breath but then proclaimed in the next that their focus would nonetheless be elsewhere. On October 20, the *Huffington Post* reported:

> U.S. Housing and Urban Development Secretary Shaun Don-
> ovan said Wednesday that the Obama administration . . . had
> yet to find anything fundamentally flawed in how large banks
> securitized home loans or how they foreclosed on them.
>
> "Where any homeowner has been defrauded or denied the
> basic protections or rights they have under law, we will take
> actions to make sure the banks make them whole, and their
> rights will be protected and defended," Donovan said at a
> Washington press briefing. "First and foremost, we are com-
> mitted to accountability, so that everyone in the mortgage
> process—banks, mortgage servicers and other institutions—is
> following the law. If they have not followed the law, it's our
> responsibility to make sure they're held accountable."
>
> He added, however, that the administration is focused on
> ensuring future compliance, rather than on looking back to
> make sure homeowners and investors weren't harmed during
> the reckless boom years. The administration is "committed to
> forcing institutions to change the way that they conduct busi-
> ness," Obama's top housing official said, "to make sure these
> problems don't happen again."

Even the administration's claim that it had "yet to find anything fundamentally flawed" in the mortgage process was the
by-product of a deliberate see-no-evil scheme of protection.
Commentators, experts, and state officials had already assembled vast and growing amounts of evidence suggesting that the
fraud was systematic and reckless, sometimes even deliberate.

But by waiting for iron-clad proof before concluding that serious wrongdoing took place, the administration skewed the inquiry in advance to protect the banks from the rule of law.

The career Wall Street financial services expert Yves Smith, writing on her blog, gloomily reflected on the administration's efforts.

> The effect of the official "don't rattle the markets" posture is a refusal to dig too deeply, and the end result is to sanction fraud. Rewarding criminal behavior has never been the foundation of a well functioning capitalist society; indeed, Singapore was able to become an economic success against considerable odds by having a clean government and tough enforcement. But the powers that be seem determined to try this experiment, since they'd rather not rattle the power structure, no matter how rotten it might turn out to be.

But even more remarkable than the Obama administration's steadfast refusal to subject these banks to criminal proceedings is the fact that a mere month or so into the scandal, government officials began openly plotting how to vest the mortgage banks with retroactive immunity and thereby shield the industry from all liability, criminal and civil alike.

In November 2010, John Carney of CNBC reported that the lame-duck Congress "may consider measures intended to bolster the legal status of a controversial bank owned electronic mortgage registration system that contains three out of every five mortgages in the country." That system, known as MERS (Mortgage Electronic Registration Systems), administers mortgages on behalf of the largest banks. It was through MERS that the fraudulent foreclosure network at the heart of the scandal had been created. In the wake of reports that liability for MERS-related reckless foreclosure actions could run into the billions of dollars, Congress began planning—just as it did with telecoms two years earlier—to retroactively legitimize the fraudulent mortgages and immunize the industry. As Carney wrote:

> MERS is owned by all the biggest banks, and they certainly do not want it to be sunk by huge fines. Investors in mortgage-backed securities also do not want to see the value of their bonds sink because of doubts about the ownership of the underlying mortgages.
>
> So it looks like the stage may be set for Congress to pass a bill that would limit MERS exposure on the recording fee issue and perhaps retroactively legitimate mortgage transfers conducted through MERS's private database.

Indeed, politicians had been looking to protect the mortgage industry even before the public and the media became aware of the existence of the scandal, let alone its breadth and depth. More than a month before Carney's piece, and just before the election recess, Congress had passed a bill designed to make it significantly more difficult for homeowners to challenge banks that improperly approved a foreclosure. That bill, called the Interstate Recognition of Notarizations Act of 2010, would have substantially eased documentation requirements for banks planning to foreclose on people's homes. Amazingly, the Senate passed this bill without debate of any kind—it did so by unanimous consent—even in the face of growing reports of foreclosures across the country being approved by so-called bank robo-signers, which were both illegal and inherently unreliable. Not until public anger over that bill had become widespread did the White

House announce that President Obama would refuse to sign it, though White House aides signaled that he was receptive to the underlying goal of the bill's sponsors and was open to approving a revised version. Those efforts are still pending.

So the banking industry perpetrates a huge fraud on the American public and its court system, stealing people's homes in the process, and the first reaction of the Obama administration is to announce that it has no intention of criminally investigating the practice, while the first response of Congress is to draft legislation to retroactively legalize what was done and prevent any lawsuits against the bankers. There, in a nutshell, is proof of how completely unraveled the rule of law in America has become.

In November 2010, as I was writing this chapter, the Nobel Prize–winning economist Joseph Stiglitz argued that the mortgage fraud crisis exemplifies what has happened in America to the concept of equality under the law.

> The mortgage debacle in the United States has raised deep questions about "the rule of law," the universally accepted hallmark of an advanced, civilized society. The rule of law is supposed to protect the weak against the strong, and ensure that everyone is treated fairly. In America in the wake of the sub-prime mortgage crisis, it has done neither.
>
> Part of the rule of law is security of property rights—if you owe money on your house, for example, the bank can't simply take it away without following the prescribed legal process. But in recent weeks and months, Americans have seen several instances in which individuals have been dispossessed of their houses even when they have no debts. . . .
>
> To some, all of this is reminiscent of what happened in Russia, where the rule of law—bankruptcy legislation in

particular—was used as a legal mechanism to replace one group of owners with another. Courts were bought, documents forged, and the process went smoothly.

In America, the venality is at a higher level. It is not particular judges that are bought, but the laws themselves, through campaign contributions and lobbying, in what has come to be called "corruption, American-style." . . .

In today's America, the proud claim of "justice for all" is being replaced by the more modest claim of "justice for those who can afford it." And the number of people who can afford it is rapidly diminishing.

Surveying both the scandal itself and the eagerness of the political class to protect the wrongdoers, the Seton Hall law professor Frank Pasquale had a similar reaction.

Is the US becoming a third world nation? . . . We as attorneys can at least insist on a common rule of law for all. And that's what our legal system has grievously failed to provide during the foreclosure crisis. As the indisputably pro-market [corporate law professor] Jonathan Macey notes, "the banks have created significant legal exposure for themselves 'by committing fraud upon the courts.'" And yet the first thing our Congress could think to do was to endorse legal cover for them, as eagerly as it retroactively immunized warrantless wiretapping. . . . If we continue to subordinate the rule of law to the whim of banks, what former IMF Chief Economist Simon Johnson described as the "quiet coup" will be complete.

The reality, as we have seen, is that this ship sailed some time ago.

STARK CONTRAST WITH THE PAST

It has always been an undeniable fact of American political life that the wealthy and powerful enjoy substantial advantages, in the legal and political realms as elsewhere. But American history is replete with examples of elites being held accountable and even severely punished for political and financial crimes far less egregious, and far less destructive, than those that the nation has witnessed over the past decade. Examining some of those incidents highlights how much has changed. While it has always been the case that possessing large amounts of money and power is preferable to having little or none, the principle that all citizens are accountable under law was applied in the past with great force and determination. Throughout the eighteenth, nineteenth, and the early twentieth centuries, even the most influential men in America were kept in check by the legal system; and if the executive or Congress failed to do its part, an adversarial mass media served as a crucial backstop against elite lawlessness.

The prosecution of Tammany Hall and its infamous leader, William "Boss" Tweed, is a classic example of the media and elected officials combining to preserve the rule of law. The 1860s and 1870s were the peak years for Tammany Hall, the Democratic political machine that controlled New York City. As head of the machine, Boss Tweed oversaw a system of spectacular corruption. Tweed and his cronies wielded their control of city contracts to personally enrich themselves to the tune of tens of millions a year—the equivalent of billions in today's dollars.

Most newspapers in New York were also held within Tweed's grip. In his 1901 book *The History of Tammany Hall*, the historian Gustavus Myers describes the largesse the Tammany machine famously showered on the press.

One paper at the Capital received, through his efforts, a legislative appropriation of $207,900 for one year's printing, whereas
$10,000 would have overpaid it for the service rendered. The
proprietor of an Albany journal which was for many years
the Republican organ of the State, made it a practice to submit
to Tweed's personal censorship the most violently abusive
articles. On the payment of large sums, sometimes as much as
$5,000, Tweed was permitted to make such alterations as he
chose.

Unfortunately for Tweed, however, some publications were
unwilling to look the other way. Beginning in the late 1860s, the
New York Times, then a Republican newspaper, began publishing
a stream of exposés and editorials highlighting the corruption
of Tammany Hall. They were joined by the political cartoonist
Thomas Nast, whose popular caricatures in *Harper's Weekly*
lampooned Tweed as a bloated symbol of greed and corruption.
Tweed was reportedly so frightened that Nast could turn public
opinion against him that he offered the cartoonist a few hundred
thousand dollars to cease his attacks, only to be rebuffed.

Responding to evidence of rampant corruption, the Democratic state assemblyman and committed reformer Samuel Tilden bucked the interests of his fellow party members and
pursued the prosecution of Tweed, the impeachment of corrupt
judges, and the eventual breakup of his own party's machinery.
Such bold action seems unthinkable today, yet Tilden's attempts
to enforce the rule of law did not render him a pariah doomed to
spend the rest of his career advocating from the fringe. Indeed,
the outcome was quite the opposite: he became a folk hero. Tilden prevailed in having Tweed and his cronies tried and convicted, rode a wave of popular support into the governorship in

1874, and eventually won the presidential election of 1876 (only to have the presidency stolen from him by Rutherford B. Hayes).

Tweed, on the other hand, was destroyed. As recounted in Albert Bigelow Paine's 1904 biography *Thomas Nast: His Period and His Pictures*, at one point Tweed escaped custody and fled to Spain, only to be recognized due to his resemblance to the cartoon depictions of him in *Harper's Weekly* and extradited back to America. Redefining poetic justice, Tweed was literally done in by a cartoon and eventually died in prison—powerless, broke, and disgraced.

Besides wielding tremendous political power, Boss Tweed was an immensely wealthy man: one of the largest landowners in New York City, with vast holdings in a wide variety of enterprises. But he was brought down thanks to the efforts of a Republican newspaper, a political cartoonist, and a determined reformer willing to confront the misdeeds of his own political party. One cannot even imagine a modern equivalent of this coalition.

A few decades later, an aggressive new reformer put on Tilden's mantle: Theodore Roosevelt. After leaving his post as the secretary of the navy to command the "Rough Riders" cavalry regiment during the Spanish-American War, Roosevelt decided to try his hand at electoral politics. He won the governorship of New York in 1898 as a Republican and proceeded to root out corruption in his own party. Roosevelt hated injustice with a passion unrivaled by any of his contemporaries, and he was such a thorn in the side of the New York machine that in 1900, the Republican political boss Thomas Collier Platt maneuvered to place him on the incumbent president William McKinley's ticket as vice president just to get him out of the way.

Believing that the vice presidency, with its lack of any official function, would neutralize Roosevelt's aggressive reform agenda, the New York machine encountered some serious bad luck: after only six months in office, Roosevelt ascended to the presidency following McKinley's assassination. Thus empowered, Roosevelt immediately mounted a vigorous crusade against the nation's richest and most powerful business elites, leading to his famous nickname of "Trust-Buster."

The turn of the twentieth century was a high point in the annals of unchecked corporate power: monopolistic corporations were strangling competition, workers were being maimed and killed inside unsafe factories, and dangerously contaminated food products were being distributed to consumers. Roosevelt recognized that business had effectively placed itself above the law, and called for bold action. In his first inaugural address, he demanded rigorous oversight: "Great corporations exist only because they are created and safeguarded by our institutions; and it is therefore our right and our duty to see that they work in harmony with these institutions."

Roosevelt backed up his aggressive talk with vigorous activity. Despite being a member of the antiregulation Republican Party, he persuaded Congress (over the objections of the business community) to create the Department of Commerce and Labor, and signed into law the Meat Inspection and Pure Food and Drug Acts of 1906. Responding to unfair business practices uncovered by the newly formed Bureau of Corporations, Roosevelt's attorney general initiated forty-four lawsuits, targeting companies such as Standard Oil and J.P. Morgan for their violations of the previously dormant Sherman Antitrust Act of 1890.

Like the founders, Roosevelt understood that the greatest remedy against corruption is the light of day. In painfully stark contrast to the see-no-evil mentality of today, Roosevelt's inaugural address outlined the need for public scrutiny of the private sector.

> The first essential in determining how to deal with the great industrial combinations is knowledge of the facts—publicity. In the interest of the public, the government should have the right to inspect and examine the workings of the great corporations engaged in interstate business. Publicity is the only sure remedy which we can now invoke. What further remedies are needed in the way of governmental regulation, or taxation, can only be determined after publicity has been obtained, by process of law, and in the course of administration. The first requisite is knowledge, full and complete—knowledge which may be made public to the world.

For Roosevelt, trust-busting was not just about fairness and the spirit of competition; it was equally about justice and the rule of law. In a 1906 speech titled "The Man With the Muck Rake," he highlighted his disgust with power-abusing elites: "My plea is not for immunity to, but for the most unsparing exposure of, the politician who betrays his trust, of the big business man who makes or spends his fortune in illegitimate or corrupt ways. There should be a resolute effort to hunt every such man out of the position he has disgraced." Starkly reaffirming his commitment to the principles of the rule of law, Roosevelt remarked: "The eighth commandment reads, 'Thou shalt not steal.' It does not read, 'Thou shalt not steal from the rich man.' It does not read, 'Thou shalt not steal from the poor man.' It reads simply and plainly, 'Thou shalt not steal.'"

When Roosevelt assumed the presidency, businesses were

threatening to destroy the basic principle of equality under the law, just as they have done during the past decade-plus orgy of deregulation. Yet through sheer force of personality and resolute confidence in the justice of his convictions, Roosevelt persuaded the citizenry and his fellow elected officials to regulate and reduce the power of those who held the most influence. In 1903, at the height of a backlash over his efforts to target the nation's most powerful elites, he delivered his third annual message to Congress, pronouncing: "No man is above the law and no man is below it; nor do we ask any man's permission when we require him to obey it. Obedience to the law is demanded as a right; not asked as a favor."

The radically different ethos of Roosevelt's time, as compared to our own day, is also reflected in the healthy fear that financial elites had back then of public resentment over their concentrated power. John D. Rockefeller's penchant for riding down the street and handing out gold coins was motivated not by generosity of spirit but by fear of public backlash against his privileges. Today's financial elites evince no such concern, and with good reason: they have seen even the most blatantly sleazy and criminal among them escape from scandals with their fortunes and liberty untouched.

As a trivial but telling example of this new indifference, consider that in August 2009—just after Goldman's "blowout" profits had been announced, with the vast bulk of the country beset by unemployment, foreclosure, and other forms of economic suffering—the *New York Post* reported that Laura Blankfein, the wife of Goldman CEO Lloyd Blankfein, and her friend Susan Friedman, the spouse of another Goldman partner, had created an ugly public scene at a Hamptons fund-raiser, yelling in protest because they were forced to wait in line with lesser donors.

"Their behavior was obnoxious. They were screaming," said one witness. Blankfein said she wouldn't wait with "people who spend less money than me."

Another observer said the women were so impatient, it was as if they were waiting on line for a kidney transplant instead of a charitable designer clothing sale.

Friedman shouted at the event organizer, "You have lost so much money because of this. . . . Why should we be treated like the $650 donors?"

Sources said Blankfein and Friedman had bought tables with blocks of tickets going for $833 apiece, as did many of the women who were waiting patiently in line, happy to raise $3.4 million for the Ovarian Cancer Research Fund.

When today's financial elites do make gestures to appease the public, they are often so halfhearted and miserly that they achieve the opposite effect. The miniscandal caused by Blankfein and Friedman followed closely on the heels of a memo from Goldman's CEO requesting that Goldman executives temporarily refrain from public displays of opulence until public outrage at the firm died down. When leaked, that memo generated even more anger.

In September 2009, by way of responding to increasing outrage over its shocking profits so soon after the taxpayers rescued it, Goldman announced that it was putting $200 million into a charitable foundation aimed at supporting educational initiatives around the world. As virtually every press report noted, though, given the size of Goldman's quarterly profits, that was a ridiculously small amount to trumpet. Clearly, Goldman's executives were confident that their ownership of the government insulates them from any real accountability, and they simply perceived no need to give away a larger amount of money to satisfy the public. Public rage today is impotent; it has no mechanism to produce consequences.

By contrast, the commitment to equality under the law was so strong in the early twentieth century that criminal investigations proceeded even when there was a handy excuse to sweep the lawbreaking under a rug. Consider, for example, the famous Teapot Dome scandal. In 1922, a little over a decade after Theodore Roosevelt left office, President Warren Harding's secretary of the interior, Albert B. Fall, leased the U.S. Navy's petroleum reserves in Teapot Dome, Wyoming, and other locations to Sinclair Oil without soliciting any competitive bids. In return, Fall received at least $100,000 in gifts disguised as interest-free "loans."

The *Wall Street Journal* reported on this lease using information leaked from a source within the Interior Department. The very next day, Democratic senator John Kendrick introduced a resolution to investigate the matter. Initially skeptical but troubled by the allegations, the legendary Republican senator "Fighting" Bob La Follette arranged for a thorough investigation and even allowed a member of the opposition party, Democrat Thomas Walsh, to chair the panel.

Just as the investigation began to intensify, in the summer of 1923, Harding died in office. This is the point where most modern Beltway insiders would expect any inquiry into the Harding administration to quietly go away. After all, what is the point of obsessing over the past? But rather than simply moving on, Harding's successor, Calvin Coolidge, continued to pay attention to what had transpired and eventually appointed a special counsel to prosecute the wrongdoing uncovered by Walsh's investigation. Coolidge justified this as being necessary under the rule of law: "I feel the public is entitled to know that in the conduct of such action no one is shielded for any party, political or other reason."

By 1929, Fall became the first cabinet official to go to prison. Almost overnight, Harding was posthumously transformed from a popular president into a national disgrace, all through the efforts of his own party. (No wonder that, shortly before he died, Harding had reportedly remarked: "I have no trouble with my enemies. I can take care of my enemies in a fight. But my friends, my goddamned friends, they're the ones who keep me walking the floor at nights!") Compare this to today, when a Democratic president, the supposed opponent of the Republican Party, refuses to investigate and prosecute pervasive wrongdoing that occurred under his Republican predecessor, invoking instead the absurd principle of look-forward-not-back.

In 1922, a single no-bid kickback contract retroactively destroyed an administration's reputation. In the twenty-first century, this sort of brazen corruption is not even a blip on the radar. Instead, far more systematic and devastating criminality is protected—most aggressively by the very people charged with punishing it.

In June 2010, this decline was aptly summarized in a *USA Today* op-ed by the George Washington University law professor Jonathan Turley. The article's headline poignantly asked, "Do Laws Even Matter Today?" Enumerating the countless scandals of elite lawlessness that have gone entirely unpunished and even uninvestigated over the last decade, Professor Turley wrote:

> A legal system cannot demand the faith and fealty of the governed when rules are seen as arbitrary and deceptive. Our leaders have led us not to an economic crisis or an immigration crisis or an environmental crisis or a civil liberties crisis.

They have led us to a crisis of faith where citizens no longer
believe that laws have any determinant meaning. It is politics,
not the law, that appears to drive outcomes—a self-destructive
trend for a nation supposedly defined by the rule of law.

What we have allowed to take root is the living, breathing
embodiment of lawlessness. It is a full-scale rejection of what
Jefferson, in his letter to George Washington, described as "the
foundation on which all [constitutions] are built": "the denial of
every preeminence." Through their ownership of political and
legal institutions, corporations and banks have secured not only
virtually absolute immunity from the dictates and accountability of law, but also the power to shape new legislation as a tool to
advance their interests. This rancid state of affairs is everything
the founders had most urgently wanted to avoid, and is exactly
the dynamic that even the most sober legal theorists have described
for centuries as the hallmark of lawlessness and tyranny.

4

IMMUNITY BY PRESIDENTIAL DECREE

Before he was elected president, Barack Obama repeatedly accused the Bush administration of breaking the law in numerous areas. As a senator, he had opposed the confirmation of Bush's former NSA chief Michael Hayden as CIA director on the ground that Hayden was "the architect and chief defender of a program of wiretapping and collection of phone records outside of FISA oversight"; voting against Hayden, Obama argued, would "send a signal to this Administration that . . . President Bush is not above the law." As a presidential candidate, he condemned waterboarding and other interrogation practices Bush had ordered, straightforwardly describing them as "torture," the authorization of which is a criminal offense under U.S. law. To a cheering crowd, Obama vowed, "The era of Scooter Libby justice . . . will be over."

Obama placed the restoration of the rule of law at the heart of his campaign, promising to reverse the culture of lawlessness in Washington. "No more ignoring the law when it's inconvenient. That is not who we are," he pledged. "We will again set an example for the world that the law is not subject to the whims of stubborn rulers, and that justice is not arbitrary." This promise was a core feature of his candidacy. As *GQ* pointed out in December 2010, Obama positioned himself as "a constitutional scholar devoted to restoring the rule of law":

> No other issue defined Barack Obama like his promise to restore America's commitment to international law. Other items may have topped his domestic agenda, but as a symbol of what Obama's candidacy meant, of what his election signi-fied to the world, nothing conveyed his message of "change" like the pledge to repair American justice.

Georgetown law professor David Cole underscored, "Obama promised change on a variety of fronts, but the central front was the rule of law."

In April 2008, when Obama's primary battle with Hillary Clinton was at its peak, Will Bunch of the *Philadelphia Daily News* asked the candidate whether an Obama administration would "seek to prosecute officials of the former Bush adminis-tration on the revelations that they greenlighted torture, or for other potential crimes that took place in the White House." Bunch cited a recent *ABC News* report detailing that torture tech-niques were not just approved but "choreographed" by "the most senior Bush administration officials" at a series of meetings in the White House situation room. Reportedly presiding at these meetings was then–National Security Adviser Condoleezza Rice, and participating were, among others, Defense Secretary Don-ald Rumsfeld, Attorney General John Ashcroft, CIA Director George Tenet, and Secretary of State Colin Powell.

According to *ABC*, these officials agreed that detainees could be "slapped, pushed, deprived of sleep or subjected to simulated drowning, called waterboarding." They also "approved interrogations that combined different methods, pushing the limits of international law and even the Justice Department's own legal approval." The torture policies being discussed were so extreme that even Ashcroft—who had demonized critics of Bush's post-9/11 policies as aiders and abettors of terrorism—felt moved to observe: "Why are we talking about this in the White House? History will not judge this kindly."

Taking up Bunch's question, Obama responded, "What I would want to do is to have my Justice Department and my Attorney General immediately review the information that's already there and to find out are there inquiries that need to be pursued." On the matter of prosecutions, Obama rightly noted, "I can't prejudge that because we don't have access to all the material right now." Still, he repeated his commitment to discovering the truth: "I would want to find out directly from my Attorney General—having pursued, having looked at what's out there right now—are there possibilities of genuine crimes?"

Obama did nod toward the precepts of elite immunity familiar since Ford pardoned Nixon, saying that he "would not want [his] first term consumed by what was perceived on the part of Republicans as a partisan witch hunt" and that "one of the things we've got to figure out in our political culture generally is distinguishing between really dumb policies and policies that rise to the level of criminal activity." But Obama emphasized that, those considerations notwithstanding, he was a believer in the rule of law.

> If crimes have been committed, they should be investigated. . . .
> If I found out that there were high officials who knowingly, consciously broke existing laws, engaged in coverups of those crimes with knowledge forefront, then I think a basic principle

of our Constitution is nobody is above the law—and I think
that's roughly how I would look at it.

Sensibly enough, Bunch concluded, "Obama sent a clear signal that . . . he is at the least open to the possibility of investigating potential high crimes in the Bush White House."

Such investigations started to seem all the more likely when
Obama, shortly after winning the election, chose Eric Holder as
his attorney general. In a June 2008 speech to the American
Constitution Society, Holder had denounced the "disrespect of
the rule of law" shown by Bush officials, going so far as to explicitly accuse them of having committed numerous crimes.

> Our government authorized the use of torture, approved of
> secret electronic surveillance of American citizens, secretly
> detained American citizens without due process of law, denied
> the writ of habeas corpus to hundreds of accused enemy com-
> batants, and authorized the use of procedures that both violate
> international law and the United States Constitution.

Most notable was Holder's insistence that the "patriotism of
those responsible for these policies . . . does nothing to mitigate the
fact that these steps were wrong when they were initiated and they
are wrong today." In what was widely understood to be a demand
for accountability, Holder declared, "We owe the American people
a reckoning." What was at stake was the soul of the nation.

> Unfortunately in the last few years, we have quite frankly lost
> our way with respect to this commitment to the Constitution
> and to the rule of law. The rule of law is not, as some have seen
> it, an obstacle to be overcome, but the very foundations of our

nation. It is the rule of law that has held us together despite our differences while other nations have descended into strife. It is the rule of law that has made the United States a beacon to the world—a nation that others aspire to emulate.

Top Democrats in Congress, too, pledged throughout 2008 to conduct formal investigations into a wide array of Bush-era crimes. Bush officials had spent two years brazenly refusing to comply with an array of congressional subpoenas. With Bush out of the White House, Democrats promised, this stonewalling would end.

But almost immediately after winning the election—indeed, before he was even inaugurated—Obama beat a quick retreat, abandoning and even renouncing his prior righteous rhetoric about the rule of law. Instead, he passionately devoted himself to blocking and suppressing all investigations of the Bush administration, whether carried out by the DOJ or by Congress, by U.S. courts or by judges overseas. Thus began Obama's crusade as a champion of elite immunity—of the very "Scooter Libby justice" he had vowed to end.

In fact, Obama went beyond the Nixon pardon, telecom immunity, and even the failure to investigate rampant Wall Street illegality. Those measures were indeed lawless, but there was at least some legal pretext for them: the Constitution gives presidents the power of granting pardons; retroactive telecom immunity was bestowed through an act of Congress; and the DOJ can hide behind claims of prosecutorial discretion when it refuses to hold financial elites accountable. But Obama's wholesale protection of Bush-era criminals enjoyed none of those excuses. Instead, his administration, in the course of obstructing investigations, explicitly disregarded numerous legal dictates and thus profoundly violated both the president's specific constitutional duty to "take Care that the Laws be faithfully executed" and the general principle of equality under the law.

A QUICK RETREAT

Nine days before Obama's inauguration, the *New York Times* published an article headlined "Obama Reluctant to Look Into Bush Programs." It compiled a series of unmistakable signals from Obama and his closest aides that the campaign vow to examine Bush crimes was being tossed overboard. On Capitol Hill, the article reported, there "has been a growing sense that Mr. Obama was not inclined to pursue these matters."

The most significant of those preinauguration signals was an interview that the president-elect gave to *ABC News* on January 11, 2009. *ABC News* had invited viewers to vote on the questions that they most wanted to hear Obama answer, and Obama's own Web site, change.gov, had done the same. The interviewer, George Stephanopoulos, noted that the most popular question on Obama's site was: "Will you appoint a special prosecutor, ideally Patrick Fitzgerald, to independently investigate the greatest crimes of the Bush administration, including torture and warrantless wiretapping?"

Obama began his response by paying lip service to the core principle of the American founding: "We're going to be looking at past practices and I don't believe that anybody is above the law." But he devoted the bulk of his answer to laying the foundation for his future opposition to investigations of any kind.

> On the other hand I also have a belief that we need to look forward as opposed to looking backwards. And part of my job

is to make sure that for example at the CIA, you've got extraordinarily talented people who are working very hard to keep
Americans safe. I don't want them to suddenly feel like they've
got to spend all their time looking over their shoulders and
lawyering up.

Obama's insistence that "we need to look forward as opposed
to looking backwards" echoed similar phrasing from Gerald
Ford, George H. W. Bush, and Bill Clinton. And given that "looking backwards" is, by definition, what any investigation entails, it
was a motto of pure lawlessness.

Stephanopoulos then asked Obama whether he would at
least approve a 9/11-type "commission with independent subpoena power" in order to bring Bush-era crimes to light. Obama
was no more receptive to that suggestion. While again including
the cursory caveat that this "doesn't mean that if somebody has
blatantly broken the law, that they are above the law," he immediately negated that principle by reaffirming his disinclination
to look into what Bush officials had done: "My instinct is for us
to focus on how do we make sure that moving forward we are
doing the right thing. . . . My orientation's going to be to move
forward." Stephanopoulos asked him once more whether he was
"ruling out prosecution," and Obama—while noting that ultimately prosecutions are decided by the attorney general—again
underscored his own obvious opposition: "My general belief is
that when it comes to national security, what we have to focus on
is getting things right in the future, as opposed to looking at
what we got wrong in the past."

"Look forward, not backward" became the mantra that
Obama and his top aides would endlessly repeat to justify their
active suppression of all forms of accountability for crimes

committed by the Bush administration. A particularly illustrative example of this mentality arose less than three months into Obama's presidency. On April 16, 2009, Obama declassified and publicly released four Bush-era Justice Department memos that described in detail the brutal and patently illegal torture techniques that America's highest political leaders had ordered over the prior eight years. At the same time, however, Obama announced that there would be no prosecutions of the government officials who had ordered or implemented the methods discussed. "This is a time for reflection, not retribution," he intoned.

> At a time of great challenges and disturbing disunity, nothing will be gained by spending our time and energy laying blame for the past. Our national greatness is embedded in America's ability to right its course in concert with our core values, and to move forward with confidence. That is why we must resist the forces that divide us, and instead come together on behalf of our common future.

Behold the language of elite immunity. Punishing political leaders for well-documented crimes is scorned as "retribution" and "laying blame for the past." Those who believe that the rule of law should be applied to all are dismissed as "the forces that divide us." The bottomless corruption of letting elites break the law without suffering any consequences is sanctified as "mov[ing] forward" and "com[ing] together on behalf of our common future."

Obama's attitude was all the more remarkable because the crimes described in the memos involved not a mere break-in targeting an opposing party's office or the covert provision of weapons to a foreign regime that the United States wished to influence. Rather, the declassified DOJ memos constituted compelling evidence that the U.S. government had authorized and carried out brutal torture—one of the most serious and heavily sanctioned crimes under U.S. domestic law, and a war crime that carries the death penalty in international law. As Bush's own attorney general, Michael Mukasey, unequivocally told the *Wall Street Journal* three days before Obama's inauguration, "Torture is a crime."

Indeed, the exact same interrogation tactics that the Bush administration authorized had been prosecuted in the past as felonies and war crimes. In 2007, the federal judge Evan Wallach had reminded *Washington Post* readers that in previous decades the U.S. government had "not only condemned the use of water torture but had severely punished those who applied it." Wallach noted that at the end of the World War II the United States had organized war crimes tribunals against Japanese soldiers, several of whom were convicted of torture: "The principal proof upon which their torture convictions were based was conduct that we would now call waterboarding." And Attorney General Holder himself, five days prior to Obama's inauguration, pointed out that "we prosecuted our own soldiers for using it in Vietnam. . . . Waterboarding is torture."

Rendering Obama's reluctance to prosecute yet more problematic is that the United States is legally required to investigate allegations of torture and to bring the torturers to justice. Not doing so is itself a criminal act. The Third Geneva Convention, which was enacted in the wake of severe detainee abuse during World War II, obliges each participating country to "search for persons alleged to have committed, or to have ordered to be committed, such grave breaches, and . . . bring such persons, regardless of their nationality, before its own courts."

Some have disputed the applicability of the Geneva Conventions to "war on terror" detainees, on the ground that they are not actually prisoners of war. But even if the Geneva Conventions do not apply, there is no such dispute about the Convention Against Torture, a treaty negotiated and signed by President Ronald Reagan, and ratified by the U.S. Senate in 1994. Article 4 of that treaty requires each country to "ensure that all acts of torture are offences under its criminal law," and Article 5 dictates that "each State Party shall likewise take such measures as may be necessary to establish its jurisdiction over such offences in cases where the alleged offender is present in any territory under its jurisdiction." Most significantly, Article 7 makes it mandatory for each signatory country to investigate allegations of torture and "submit the case to its competent authorities for the purpose of prosecution."

The Convention Against Torture explicitly bars considerations of national security or fears of terrorism from being offered as an excuse for perpetrating torture or refusing to prosecute the torturers. Nor is taking orders from one's commanders considered a valid defense. Article 2 of the treaty states unambiguously:

> No exceptional circumstances whatsoever, whether a state of war or a threat of war, internal political instability or any other public emergency, may be invoked as a justification of torture.
>
> An order from a superior officer or a public authority may not be invoked as a justification of torture.

The Convention permits the exercise of some prosecutorial discretion in deciding whether a case should proceed, but specifies that authorities must investigate each case with potential prosecution in mind. There is no doubt, then, that a policy of blanket immunity for torturers—a presidential decree that nobody shall be prosecuted—constitutes a blatant violation of America's obligations under the Convention. On that critical point the law is clear, and clearly understood. When President Reagan transmitted the treaty to the Senate and urged its ratification, he underscored that its intent was to enforce an absolute legal bar on all acts of torture. The Convention, he said,

> marks a significant step in the development during this century of international measures against torture and other inhuman treatment or punishment. Ratification of the Convention by the United States will clearly express United States opposition to torture, an abhorrent practice unfortunately still prevalent in the world today.

The requirements imposed by the treaty are so clear that even Bush himself felt obliged to pay lip service to the law. Speaking in 2004 on the UN Day to Support Torture Victims, he emphasized the country's legal duty to hold torturers accountable.

> The United States has joined 135 other nations in ratifying the Convention Against Torture and Other Cruel, Inhuman or Degrading Treatment or Punishment. America stands against and will not tolerate torture. We will investigate and prosecute all acts of torture and undertake to prevent other cruel and unusual punishment in all territory under our jurisdiction. American personnel are required to comply with all U.S. laws, including the United States Constitution, Federal statutes, including statutes prohibiting torture, and our treaty obligations

with respect to the treatment of all detainees.... Torture is wrong no matter where it occurs, and the United States will continue to lead the fight to eliminate it everywhere.

The UN likewise regards the treaty as unambiguously requiring that torturers be prosecuted. Indeed, upon Obama's inauguration in January 2009, Manfred Nowak, the UN special rapporteur on torture, announced, "Judicially speaking, the United States has a clear obligation to bring proceedings against top government officials who authorized techniques that under international law are considered torture." A few months later, Nowak warned that Obama's no-investigations posture violated international law and America's treaty obligations. I interviewed Nowak shortly after that warning, and he elaborated.

If under the direct jurisdiction of the United States of America, a government official—whether it's a high official or a low official or a police officer or military officer, doesn't matter—whoever practices torture shall be brought before an independent criminal court and be held accountable. That is, the torturer, him or herself, but also those who are ordering torture practices, or in any other way participating in the practice of torture. This is a general obligation, and it applies to everybody; there are no exceptions in the Convention.

A criminal investigation of torture allegations is thus mandatory under both the Geneva Conventions and the Convention Against Torture. Refusing to carry out such an investigation is in itself a crime, a new violation of the law separate from the original acts of torture.

As we saw in the run-up to the Iraq war, the political class tends to regard with contempt the notion that American leaders (as opposed to the rulers of other countries) should be constrained in any way by things like international conventions and the pronouncements of UN officials. But compliance with treaties is not just merely a matter of respect for international agreements. As Article VI of the U.S. Constitution states, "All treaties made, or which shall be made, under the authority of the United States, shall be the supreme law of the land; and the judges in every state shall be bound thereby, anything in the Constitution or laws of any State to the contrary notwithstanding." Compliance with the Convention Against Torture—including its mandate that torturers be brought to justice—is not a matter of heeding Manfred Nowak or other UN officials; it is required by the dictates of America's own supreme law.

THE DARKEST CRIMES

Entire books have been written documenting the severity of the Bush torture regime, most notably Jane Mayer's *The Dark Side*. For our purposes, it suffices to consider just a sliver of that evidence to demonstrate how clear it is that the Bush administration's practices should have triggered obligations to prosecute. Consider, for instance, the admission reported by the *Washington Post* on January 14, 2009.

> The top Bush administration official in charge of deciding whether to bring Guantánamo Bay detainees to trial has concluded that the U.S. military tortured a Saudi national who allegedly planned to participate in the Sept. 11, 2001, attacks,

interrogating him with techniques that included sustained isolation, sleep deprivation, nudity and prolonged exposure to cold, leaving him in a "life-threatening condition."

"We tortured [Mohammed al-]Qahtani," said Susan J. Crawford, in her first interview since being named convening authority of military commissions by Defense Secretary Robert M. Gates in February 2007. "His treatment met the legal definition of torture. And that's why I did not refer the case" for prosecution.

An equally damning statement came from the retired four-star general Antonio Taguba after he was appointed to formally investigate the abuse at Abu Ghraib prison. (Taguba's inquiry was not a criminal proceeding and had no power to impose any punishment on the perpetrators; it was thus a far cry from the kind of prosecution that's required by the Convention Against Torture.) Taguba's findings were included in a McClatchy article from June 18, 2008.

The Army general who led the investigation into prisoner abuse at Iraq's Abu Ghraib prison accused the Bush administration Wednesday of committing "war crimes" and called for those responsible to be held to account.

The remarks by Maj. Gen. Antonio Taguba, who's now retired, came in a new report that found that U.S. personnel tortured and abused detainees in Iraq, Afghanistan and Guantánamo Bay, Cuba, using beatings, electrical shocks, sexual humiliation and other cruel practices.

"After years of disclosures by government investigations, media accounts and reports from human rights organizations, there is no longer any doubt as to whether the current administration has committed war crimes," Taguba wrote. "The only question that remains to be answered is whether those who ordered the use of torture will be held to account."

Notably, these accusations that high-level Bush officials authorized torture and committed serious war crimes come not from Democratic politicians or the ACLU but from a high-level American military officer and from Bush's own top official on detainee policy. A leaked confidential report prepared in 2007 by the International Red Cross came to the same conclusion: "The allegations of ill treatment of the detainees indicate that, in many cases, the ill treatment to which they were subjected while held in the C.I.A. program, either singly or in combination, constituted torture."

But the most damning evidence came from the four memos that had been prepared by lawyers at the Office of Legal Counsel inside the Bush DOJ between 2002 and 2005 and released by the Obama administration in April 2009. Written in response to the desire of the White House and the CIA to employ a variety of torture methods, those memos had predictably told Bush officials what they wanted to hear: that such methods would be legal under domestic and international law. But in the process of reaching that strained conclusion, the memos detailed some of the techniques under consideration, and their brutality is undeniable.

One forty-six-page memo from OLC chief Steven Bradbury, dated May 10, 2005, authorized the following acts to be performed on "high-value detainees": forced nudity, "dietary manipulation" involving "minimum caloric intake," "corrective techniques" such as facial and abdominal slapping, water dousing, stress positions designed to "induce muscle fatigue and the attendant discomfort," and sleep deprivation. Bradbury also approved various degrading acts that might be used against the detainees. He was of the opinion, for example, that a detainee undergoing sleep deprivation could legally be made to wear diapers, "because releasing a detainee from the shackles would present a security problem and would interfere with the effectiveness of the technique."

An August 1, 2002, memo by then OLC lawyer (and now federal judge) Jay Bybee, meanwhile, describes waterboarding in excruciating detail, matter-of-factly noting that "the subject's body responds as if the subject were drowning." Amazingly, while the OLC lawyers admitted that "the use of waterboarding constitutes a threat of imminent death," they claimed that the procedure was permissible because it does not result in "prolonged mental harm"—an exception found nowhere in the Convention Against Torture. They did tell the White House to perform "no more than two sessions" of waterboarding in "any 24-hour period," even though, as the legal analyst Marcy Wheeler of Firedoglake pointed out, the same document mentions that "Khalid Sheikh Mohammed was waterboarded 183 times in March 2003 and Abu Zubaydah was waterboarded 83 times in August 2002."

Similar brutality permeates Bybee's descriptions of various other techniques to be used against Zubaydah, who was shot three times during his capture and was still suffering from those wounds at the time of his interrogation. These techniques included "walling," "cramped confinement," and "insects placed in a confinement box." "Walling" was slamming someone into a wall. "Cramped confinement" meant, as the memo put it, "placement of the individual in a confined space" that "is usually dark . . . the dimensions of which restrict the individual's movements—in other words, a coffin-like space." And here is how "insects placed in a confinement box" was supposed to play out.

You would like to place Zubaydah in a cramped confinement box with an insect. You have informed us that he appears to have a fear of insects. In particular, you would like to tell Zubaydah that you intend to place a stinging insect into the box with him. You would, however, place a harmless insect in the box.

Notably, these memos explicitly recognized that the United States had long considered the very techniques these lawyers were approving to be criminal and to constitute torture—when committed by other nations. As the Bradbury memo explained:

Each year, in the State Department's Country Reports on Human Rights Practices, the United States condemns coercive interrogation techniques and other practices employed by other countries. Certain of the techniques the United States has condemned bear some resemblance to some of the CIA interrogation techniques. In their discussion of Indonesia, for example, the reports list as "[p]sychological torture" conduct that involves "food and sleep deprivation," but give no specific information as to what these techniques involve. In their discussion of Egypt, the reports list as "methods of torture" "stripping and blindfolding victims; suspending victims from a ceiling or doorframe with feet just touching the floor; beating victims [with various objects]; . . . and dousing victims with cold water."

See also, e.g. Algeria (describing the "chiffon" method, which involves "placing a rag drenched in dirty water in someone's mouth"); Iran (counting sleep deprivation as either torture or severe prisoner abuse); Syria (discussing sleep deprivation and "having cold water thrown on" detainees as either torture or "ill-treatment"). The State Department's inclusion of nudity, water dousing, sleep deprivation, and food deprivation among the conduct it condemns is significant and provides some indication of an executive foreign relations tradition condemning the use of these techniques.

Although the Bush lawyers attempted to dismiss these prior State Department reports as lacking the force of law, they clearly knew that they were approving the practice of torture. By their own acknowledgment, they were authorizing precisely the techniques that the U.S. government had condemned when practiced by other nations—specifically nations the United States had long denounced as the world's most oppressive, such as Iran, Syria, Egypt, and Algeria.

Besides publishing the OLC memos, in August 2009 Obama released a report by the CIA's inspector general, compiled in 2004 and devoted to discussing the agency's interrogation tactics. This document detailed the use of multiple practices long condemned by the United States as criminal and inhumane, including: threatening to kill the detainees and their families, threats to rape a detainee's female relatives in front of him, "buttstroking" prisoners with rifles and knee kicks, hanging detainees by their arms until interrogators thought their shoulders might dislocate, stepping on their ankle shackles to cause severe bruising and pain, and putting them in diapers and leaving them doused with water on concrete floors in cold temperatures in order to induce hypothermia. The CIA report discussed numerous deaths of detainees in U.S. custody, including several caused directly by abusive treatment.

From a legal standpoint, torture is unlawful no matter whom it is applied to. But the CIA report added an extra layer of moral horror to the situation by noting that many of the detainees were tortured pursuant to "assessments that were unsupported by credible intelligence"—meaning there was no actual reason to think they had done anything wrong. Obama's release of this report thus confirmed what had been suspected for quite some time: that many of the people whom the United States had detained without charges and brutalized in captivity were completely innocent.

This fact had long been obscured because for years the detainees were not allowed any access to the court system—first as a matter of Bush administration policy and then by the 2006 Military Commissions Act, which expressly prohibited courts from dealing with detainees' claims of wrongful imprisonment. Only in 2008, after the Supreme Court struck down that provision of the act as a violation of the constitutional right of habeas corpus review, did Guantánamo detainees—some of whom had by then been imprisoned for seven years—gain the chance to have their claims of innocence reviewed by a court of law. Since then, the results have been striking. Of the fifty-nine detainees who so far have had their habeas cases heard in federal court, thirty-eight of them have won. In other words, in almost two-thirds of the cases reviewed, the courts ruled that there was no credible evidence to justify the detention.

For the Bush administration, keeping innocent people imprisoned was a deliberate policy. In 2009, Colonel Lawrence Wilkerson, chief of staff to Colin Powell, said that top Bush officials realized early on that "many of the detainees were innocent of any substantial wrongdoing, had little intelligence value, and should be immediately released." Nonetheless, they persisted in assuring the country that Guantánamo held only "the worst of the worst." Bush officials refused to liberate detainees who had been seized by mistake out of concern that once freed they would publicize the abuse to which they had been subjected. In 2010, Colonel Wilkerson signed an affidavit attesting under oath that "George W. Bush, Dick Cheney and Donald Rumsfeld covered up that hundreds of innocent men were sent to the Guantánamo Bay prison camp because they feared that releasing them would harm the push for war in Iraq and the broader War on Terror."

Not all "war on terror" detainees lived to see the 2008 Supreme Court decision reaffirming the principle of habeas corpus. Many of them died in U.S. custody— and not from natural causes. As General Barry McCaffrey put it in a 2009 interview calling for investigations, "We tortured people unmercifully. We probably murdered dozens of them during the course of that, both the armed forces and the C.I.A." The Human Rights Watch researcher John Sifton has documented that "approximately 100 detainees, including CIA-held detainees, have died during U.S. interrogations, and some are known to have been tortured to death."

These are the plainly criminal acts whose perpetrators the Obama administration has steadfastly shielded from any and all accountability. And to do so, Obama officials have engaged in some rather legally dubious conduct of their own.

POLITICIZED JUSTICE PRODUCES IMMUNITY

The April 2009 release of the OLC torture memos revitalized the debate over accountability for Bush-era war crimes and led to fresh demands from many Obama supporters for criminal investigations. But within a few days, Obama's chief of staff,

Rahm Emanuel, appeared on *ABC News* and all but ordered the Justice Department to refrain from looking into the issue. When asked whether Obama "believe[s] that the officials who devised the policies should be immune from prosecution," Emanuel replied: "He believes that people in good faith were operating with the guidance they were provided. They shouldn't be prosecuted."

Emanuel's phrasing momentarily obscured the distinction between two separate groups responsible for the torture regime: those who had crafted and authorized the torture policies (the president, his highest aides, and OLC lawyers) and those who had physically carried out the torture (CIA agents and military personnel). Emanuel was asked specifically about those in the former group, but his answer addressed those in the latter category. When the interviewer asked again whether the no-prosecution policy included those "who devised the policy"—meaning Bush and his top aides and lawyers—Emanuel said that it did: Obama "believes that they . . . should not be prosecuted either, and that's not the place that we go." And in a familiar rhetorical flourish, Emanuel added, "It's not a time to use our energy and our time in looking back and any sense of anger and retribution."

The following day, White House press secretary Robert Gibbs echoed these sentiments when asked why Obama had determined that there should be no accountability: "The president is focused on looking forward, that's why." The line had been drawn, Gibbs said: "Those that followed the legal advice [in the OLC memos] and acted in good faith on that legal advice shouldn't be prosecuted."

To start with the obvious: the very idea of having political officials in the White House—or even the president himself—announce that there should be no prosecutions of a set of criminal suspects is improper in the extreme. One of the central principles of the American justice system is supposed to be that specific decisions about Justice Department prosecutions are to be made by that department itself, independent of all political considerations.

That principle is so sacrosanct that its violation, or even suspected violation, has in the past been treated as a political scandal. One of Nixon's most criticized acts—the trigger for what became known as the Saturday Night Massacre—involved the resignation of Attorney General Elliot Richardson due to his refusal to follow Nixon's order to fire Watergate Special Prosecutor Archibald Cox. In the 1990s, Attorney General Janet Reno was frequently attacked by the American right for her purported lack of independence in refusing to appoint independent prosecutors to investigate every last one of the Clinton White House's alleged improprieties. During the Bush years, Attorney General Alberto Gonzales's habit of collaborating with the White House and making decisions about prosecutions on the basis of political rather than legal considerations was a recurring source of controversy and ultimately helped to drive Gonzales out of office.

Given the importance of the torture debate, it's perhaps unreasonable to argue that the president should have kept his thoughts on the matter completely hidden. But the line of propriety can easily be crossed, and the proclamations from Emanuel and Gibbs, all but decreeing that there would be no prosecutions of Bush officials, definitely crossed it. Even a former official in Bush's State Department, Philip Zelikow—who, unsurprisingly, opposed criminal investigations of the administration in which he had served—was appalled at the efforts of the White House to pressure the DOJ. As he put it in a radio interview, "I really don't think the president should have opinions on who should or should not be prosecuted—full stop."

DOJ lawyers (at least the honest ones) tend to safeguard their political independence, and according to various reports there was considerable anger in the department at the notion that decisions about criminal investigations would be dictated to them by political officials, up to and including the president. In response to increasing suggestions that the White House was acting improperly, Obama held a press conference, emphasizing that the decision whether to prosecute Bush officials who authorized torture was one for the attorney general to make, and that Obama did not want to "prejudge" that question.

But by then the damage, as intended, was done. Obama had spent months publicly and privately signaling that he did not want investigations. Subsequent coverage by the *New Yorker*'s Jane Mayer, the *New York Times*'s Charlie Savage, and other journalists detailed the substantial infighting between Emanuel and Holder over the White House's belief that the attorney general was politically harming the president by insisting on some degree of adherence to Obama's campaign rhetoric about the rule of law. Mayer reports that when the White House heard that Holder and the DOJ were considering torture investigations, Emanuel yelled at an intermediary, "Didn't he get the memo that we're not relitigating the past?"

Just to be extra certain that Holder would not initiate criminal proceedings against Bush officials, the White House continued to pressure the attorney general even after Obama had publicly acknowledged that such pressure was inappropriate. On August 20, just days before Holder was expected to announce his official decision about whether any investigations would take place,

Robert Gibbs declared from his podium: "The administration has been very clear. A hefty litigation looking backward is not what we believe is in the country's best interest."

Such relentless political pressure from the president is not easy to resist, and as one would expect, Holder eventually snapped into line. He announced that all Bush officials who had acted within the confines of the OLC memos by ordering interrogators to use techniques sanctioned by DOJ lawyers would be safe from prosecution. The only individuals subject to possible investigation would be low-level personnel who had gone beyond the memos' remit—by, say, waterboarding a detainee more times than the DOJ lawyers had discussed or beating someone harder than the memos specified. Holder's decision ensured that only the politically powerless could face criminal charges for Bush's torture regime—a perfect expression of the culture of elite immunity that Washington has established for itself. Holder's announcement left no doubt that, as the *Washingt Post* put it, "the actions of higher-level Bush policymakers are not under consideration for possible investigation."

Targeting low-level interrogators while shielding high-level policy makers from prosecution was essentially the worst of all worlds—arguably worse than no prosecutions at all. That approach replicated the disgraceful whitewashing of the Abu Ghraib prosecutions, where only privates such as Lynndie England were punished while top White House officials (who, as the Senate Intelligence Committee found, had written the policies that led to those abuses) suffered no consequences.

What's more, Holder's decision bolstered a key weapon of presidential lawlessness: the notion that because Bush officials were able to find some DOJ functionaries to sign off on the torture the president wanted to order, it was, by definition, "legal," no matter what the law actually said. Under this theory, the president is free to commit whatever crimes he wants with total impunity as long as he can find some DOJ underlings to opine in advance that he has the legal authority to do so, something that every president—who always commands vast hordes of dutiful partisans and ideological loyalists—would be able to do in every instance. As the blogger Digby wrote about Holder's DOJ "permission slip" premise:

> If it is the case that the president can designate an Office of Legal Counsel functionary to immunize government officials and employees against criminal behavior, then it is true, to all intents and purposes, that "if the president does it it's not illegal." . . .
>
> Ever since Nixon, the political class has reaffirmed the idea that anything the president does as a political leader or in his official capacity is unpunishable. And more recently we've seen that anyone who carries out his orders is also immune, which wasn't always the case. Nixon's people did do time.

Illegal behavior does not and cannot be converted into legal behavior merely because political appointees in the Justice Department declare it to be such. Basic constitutional doctrine is that Congress makes our laws and the judiciary decides what they mean. The executive branch exists to carry out those laws—not to act as a unilateral tribunal dictating what the law does and does not allow.

In fact, legal memos that "authorize" criminal conduct such as torture are, as many have argued, themselves criminal. They are written not to explain the law but to evade it. They perform a similar function to the getaway driver in a bank robbery, shielding the perpetrators from accountability and allowing them to commit crimes with impunity. To venerate lawyer opinions as though they constitute law—or, worse, to acquiesce to the claim that government lawyers can vest their bosses with immunity in advance—is to attack the rule of law itself.

What's particularly striking about the decision not to investigate the architects of Bush's torture regime is that it was manifestly driven by political considerations, not legal ones—precisely the accusation Democrats had lobbed at Alberto Gonzales and the Bush DOJ. Holder himself was remarkably candid about the reasoning behind the White House dictates. As he told *GQ* in November 2010:

> You only want to look back at a previous administration if you feel you really have to. . . . Because it has a potential chilling effect. If people who work in this administration today think that four years from now, or eight years from now, the decisions they make are going to be examined by a successor administration, you don't want that to happen. So that's a political consideration.

To make decisions about who should and should not be prosecuted based on "political considerations" is to convert the Justice Department from an independent law enforcement agency into a political arm of the White House.

Holder's specific rationale for blocking torture investigations—that allowing them would risk subjecting the current president and his aides to possible future investigations—confirms that elite immunity is essentially self-serving. By protecting their pre-decessors, politicians preserve and strengthen a culture in which illegal activity by the powerful goes unpunished, thus ensuring that they too can commit crimes with impunity while in office.

Perversely, some opponents of torture investigations claimed that only in corrupt countries are criminal charges ever filed against former political leaders. In April 2009, for example, John McCain said on the CBS network that advocates of investiga-tions wanted to create a "banana republic" that would "prosecute people for actions they didn't agree with under previous admin-istrations." But the truth is exactly the opposite. As the Western world has been arguing for decades, the surest sign of an under-developed, tyrannical society is just what the United States has now embraced: a setup where political elites are free to break the law with impunity and never suffer the consequences that ordi-nary citizens do. Unequal treatment, not legal accountability, is the defining feature of a "banana republic."

INVESTIGATIONS QUASHED WHEREVER THEY ARISE

Barack Obama's commitment to shielding Bush appointees from investigation was by no means confined to pressuring the DOJ. From the start of his presidency, Obama repeatedly stepped for-ward to impede investigative proceedings no matter where they emerged: in Congress, in American courts, or in other countries.

In April 2009, the *New York Times* published an article head-lined "Obama Resisting Push for Interrogation Panel." The piece described efforts by White House officials to forestall any for-mal inquiry into Bush's torture regime that might be carried out by a congressional committee. Nor did they want to see Congress create a separate commission armed with subpoena power: "The White House and the Democratic leadership in the Senate signaled on Thursday that they would block for now any effort to establish an independent commission to investigate the Bush administration's approval of harsh interrogation techniques."

As the *Times* article reported, Obama had gone to Capitol Hill to tell Democratic leaders that "a special inquiry would steal time and energy from his policy agenda, and could mushroom into a wider distraction." The *Times* also quoted Democratic Majority Leader Harry Reid, whose incoherent argument—"I think it would be very unwise, from my perspective, to start having commissions, boards, tribunals, until we find out what the facts are"—missed the obvious point that finding out "what the facts are" could only be done through precisely such investigations. And, as usual, the White House had Robert Gibbs chime in with his now-clichéd mantra: "we're all best suited looking forward."

But if Obama was intent on shielding American torturers from accountability, other countries were not so accommodating and initiated their own proceedings. Several nations, including those whose citizens were among the victims of America's torture regime, concluded that they were obligated by their treaty commitments to pursue American torturers—especially given that the U.S. government was doing nothing of the sort.

In April 2009, Scott Horton of *Harper's* reported that in Spain, "prosecutors have decided to press forward with a criminal investigation targeting former U.S. Attorney General Alberto Gonzales and five top associates [John Yoo, Jay Bybee, David Addington, Doug Feith, and William Haynes] over their role in the torture of five Spanish citizens held at Guantánamo." Moreover, Spanish authorities "advised the Americans that they would suspend their investigation if at any point the United States were to undertake an investigation of its own into these matters."

In an interview with *CNN Español*, Obama immediately spoke up against the Spanish efforts: "I'm a strong believer that it's important to look forward and not backwards, and to remind ourselves that we do have very real security threats out there." And numerous diplomatic cables released by WikiLeaks show that in April 2009, Obama's State Department warned Spanish authorities that any efforts to hold Bush torturers accountable would, as one cable put it, "not be understood or accepted in the US and would have an enormous impact on the bilateral relationship." Those threats eventually resulted in the Spanish government blocking its own courts from proceeding with investigations. As David Corn of *Mother Jones* reported:

> During an April 14, 2009, White House briefing, I asked press secretary Robert Gibbs if the Obama administration would cooperate with any request from the Spaniards for information and documents related to the Bush Six. He said, "I don't want to get involved in hypotheticals." What he didn't disclose was that the Obama administration, working with Republicans, was actively pressuring the Spaniards to drop the investigation. Those efforts apparently paid off, and, as this WikiLeaks-released cable shows, Gonzales, Haynes, Feith, Bybee, Addington, and Yoo owed Obama and Secretary of State Hillary Clinton thank-you notes.

The release of the WikiLeaks cable prompted the *Philadelphia Daily News*'s Will Bunch to write a scathing column titled "The Day That Barack Obama Lied to Me." Recalling his interview with the candidate who had committed to look into Bush crimes, Bunch wrote: "The breakdown of justice in this country is far from exceptional. In fact, it's contemptible. And the lie that Barack Obama told . . . is a big part of that."

Other nations were also stymied in their efforts to enforce accountability. In November 2009, a court in Italy found twenty-two CIA agents guilty of the 2003 kidnapping of an Islamic cleric, Hassan Mustafa Osama Nasr, off the street in Milan. After the kidnapping, the agency had "rendered" Nasr (also known as Abu Omar) to Egypt to be tortured. With the support of the U.S. government, the CIA agents refused to submit to the juris-diction of the Italian court and were thus convicted in absentia. One of the defendants, the former CIA station chief in Milan, who had traveled to Egypt to take part in the interrogation, was sentenced to an eight-year prison term.

Obviously, Italy has a legitimate interest in not permitting its residents to be abducted off its streets and sent off to be tortured—imagine the uproar if a foreign nation did the same to an American citizen on U.S. soil. But as soon as the Italian court announced the verdict, the Obama administration emphatically denounced it. "We are disappointed by the verdicts against the Americans and Italians charged in Milan for their alleged involvement in the case involving Egyptian cleric Abu Omar," State Department spokesman Ian Kelly said, according to Reuters. Despite the findings of criminal guilt, the administra-tion has actively protected these CIA agents from any extradi-tion attempts by the Italian authorities.

The Obama administration also undertook extraordinary efforts to prevent courts in Britain from investigating claims of torture by Binyam Mohamed, a British resident who was incar-cerated at Guantánamo for six years without charges. Mohamed has persistently sought justice for what was done to him: torture and abuse that included, among other things, cutting of his genitals. But his tormentors have been continuously protected, and Mohamed's quest for a day in court repeatedly thwarted.

In 2008, while he was being held in Guantánamo, Mohamed filed a petition with a British court asking for his lawyers to be provided with vital documents in the possession of British intelligence agencies: specifically, notes taken by British agents during discussions with CIA agents who detailed to the Brits what they were doing to Mohamed. A British High Court ruled in his favor, finding that Mohamed was entitled to obtain the documents to prove that he had been tortured in American custody. As part of its ruling, the British High Court prepared a summary of the notes in question. But as that ruling was about to be released—and the world about to learn the details of Mohamed's abuse at the hands of his American captors—the British government warned the court that British national security would be severely jeopardized if these details were disclosed.

Specifically, the British government said, the Obama administration had issued a threat: if the British court disclosed the facts of Mohamed's torture, U.S. intelligence agencies would no longer pass on to Britain any information about terrorist plots aimed at British citizens. In April 2009, I interviewed the British international law expert Clive Stafford Smith, who was representing Mohamed in the British proceedings. In his view, the Obama administration's extraordinary effort to force British courts to conceal evidence of torture was in itself probably a criminal act.

It is clear that there has now been a threat, and indeed the judges say eight times in the latest opinion, that the British government was threatened with sanctions if they were to release evidence of torture. And this needs to be put into perspective. Actually covering up evidence of torture is a criminal offense for which you can go to prison here in Britain, and I imagine in the US but I'm not quite sure about that. And the idea that the British government would conspire with the US or be threatened by the US to do this is again an independent violation of the law.

Smith likewise told the *Washington Times* that the American threats violated British law, specifically the International Criminal Court Act of 2001. "The U.S. is committing a criminal offense in Britain by seeking to conceal this information," he said. "What the Obama administration did is not just ill-advised, it is illegal."

In May 2009, British government lawyers filed with the High Court a letter documenting that the United States was continuing to make these threats. The British judges could hardly contain their shock. As they put it, it was "difficult to conceive that a democratically elected and accountable government could possibly have any rational objection to placing into the public domain such a summary of what its own officials reported as to how a detainee was treated by them and which made no disclosure of sensitive intelligence matters." They went on to strongly denounce the American cover-up attempt.

We did not consider that a democracy governed by the rule of law would expect a court in another democracy to suppress a summary of the evidence contained in reports by its own officials or officials of another State where the evidence was relevant to allegations of torture and cruel, inhuman or degrading treatment, politically embarrassing though it might be.

The manifest mistake of the British court was in assuming that the United States is a democracy "governed by the rule of law." It may be so in theory, but plainly not in practice.

The British judges' indignant protests did not in the end save them from having to bow to American pressure. Reversing its earlier stance, the High Court ruled that it would, after all, keep the seven paragraphs detailing Mohamed's torture concealed, explaining:

> The United States Government's position is that, if the redacted paragraphs are made public, then the United States will re-evaluate its intelligence-sharing relationship with the United Kingdom with the real risk that it would reduce the intelligence it provided . . . [and] there is a real risk, if we restored the redacted paragraphs, the United States Government, by its review of the shared intelligence arrangements, could inflict on the citizens of the United Kingdom a very considerable increase in the dangers they face at a time when a serious terrorist threat still pertains.

Of course it's certainly possible that the British government was not so much a victim of U.S. threats as a willing partner, colluding with the American intelligence agencies to pressure the British courts into suppressing the torture details. But whatever the case, the Obama administration had once again succeeded in shielding the torturers from accountability.

Obama has been every bit as aggressive—often more so—in

blocking America's own judiciary from examining allegations that the Bush torture regime broke the law. Binyam Mohamed's experience is a case in point. Aside from his legal proceedings in Britain, Mohamed had filed a lawsuit in an American court against Jeppesen, a subsidiary of Boeing which the CIA had regularly hired to fly its detainees to faraway lands to be tortured as part of the Bush "rendition" program. Before his incarceration at Guantánamo, Mohamed had been stripped, blindfolded, shackled, and flown by Jeppesen to Morocco, where he was secretly detained for eighteen months and tortured by Moroccan intelligence services. But in February 2009, Obama's DOJ demanded that Mohamed's lawsuit be dismissed, invoking the "state secrets privilege" and arguing that U.S. security would be harmed if the case came to trial.

The "state secrets" privilege has a sordid history. It was first created by the Supreme Court in 1953 in the case of *United States v. Reynolds,* a lawsuit brought against the U.S. government by the widows of three air force pilots who died when their military jet crashed during a training mission. The widows contended that the air force had been negligent in maintaining the jets and that this negligence resulted in their husbands' deaths. To prove their case, they sought to obtain the maintenance records for the jet their husbands had flown.

The government, however, told the court that disclosing these records would jeopardize national security, as it risked letting America's enemies learn the secret design of the aircraft. The Supreme Court agreed and ruled that, notwithstanding their obvious relevance, the government could keep these sensitive documents hidden. It was only in 2000, when the maintenance records were obtained via a Freedom of Information Act request filed by one of the pilots' family members, that it was revealed that the government had blatantly lied to the court. The records in question contained no military secrets at all but were full of information showing that there had indeed been gross negligence in how the plane's engines had been maintained by the air force.

Under Bush, the state secrets privilege was wildly expanded in scope. Rather than merely asking to have specific documents excluded from court proceedings (the way that other privileges, such as attorney-client or doctor-patient privilege, are used), the Bush DOJ began applying the doctrine to lawsuits themselves, arguing that the entire subject matter of some particular suits was so secretive that no court could safely hear the case. Bush's lawyers repeatedly used this claim to prevent courts from ruling on the legality of their actions in almost every realm relating to national security, including eavesdropping, torture, and renditions, among others. In other words, while Bush officials publicly insisted their conduct was lawful, they did everything in their power to prevent their victims from obtaining judicial rulings on that question. Thus did they convert the "state secrets" doctrine from a narrow evidentiary privilege into one vesting high-level officials with full-scale legal immunity.

The Bush DOJ's continuous use of the state secrets privilege as a way to shield its conduct from judicial review was a constant source of Democratic grievance. Numerous senators, including Joe Biden and Hillary Clinton, cosponsored legislation to severely curtail use of this doctrine on the ground that it was being abused. And throughout the 2008 campaign, the Obama/Biden Web site prominently displayed the phrase "Plan to Change Washington," under which one found the following: "THE PROBLEM: Secrecy Dominates Government: The Bush administration . . . has invoked a legal tool known as 'the state secrets privilege' more than any other administration to get cases thrown out of civil court."

Yet from the very start of his presidency, Obama has used this privilege as aggressively as Bush, and in the same radical form. In Mohamed's suit against Jeppesen, the DOJ argued that the entire subject matter of the lawsuit—Bush's torture and rendition program—was a "state secret" beyond the reach of courts. Based on this theory, the DOJ succeeded in having the case dismissed.

The following month, Obama invoked the same state secrets privilege to deal with the latest round of lawsuits brought against the government in the aftermath of the NSA wiretapping scandal. These new lawsuits had been explicitly invited by the Democrats back in 2008, after the retroactive immunity granted to the telecoms had caused intense anger among their supporters. To mitigate the backlash, leading Democratic senators had insisted that architects of the warrantless eavesdropping program could still be held accountable: instead of suing the telecoms, people could sue the government directly, notwithstanding the Bush DOJ claim that the wiretapping program was a state secret. As Jay Rockefeller, one of the main proponents of telecom immunity, wrote in an op-ed in the *Washington Post*: "Lawsuits against the government can go forward. There is little doubt that the government was operating in, at best, a legal gray area. If administration officials abused their power or improperly violated the privacy of innocent people, they must be held accountable."

The Electronic Frontier Foundation took the Democrats at their word, commencing a lawsuit against the government and the Bush officials who had been responsible for the illegal spying. Yet Obama, who as a candidate had loudly denounced the warrantless wiretapping as a crime, now embraced the Bush arguments. The entire NSA program, he declared, was a vital state secret and could not be examined by the courts.

In addition, the Obama DOJ invented a brand-new claim of immunity to shield the Bush officials. Responding to the EFF lawsuit, Obama's lawyers argued that government officials can never be held accountable for warrantless spying—even when the spying is *knowingly* illegal—unless those officials "willfully disclose" what they learn. Not even the Bush DOJ had ever made such a claim. As a headline from the EFF put it: "Obama DOJ's New Arguments Are Worse Than Bush's."

All of these events led the liberal Web site Talking Points Memo to issue a strong condemnation of the Obama administration for "mimicking its predecessor on issues of secrecy and the war on terror."

> Does [the administration's behavior] represent a continuation of the Bushies' obsession with putting secrecy and executive power above basic constitutional rights? Is it a sweeping power grab by the executive branch, that sets a broad and dangerous precedent for future cases by asserting that the government has the right to get lawsuits dismissed merely by claiming that state secrets are at stake, without giving judges any discretion whatsoever?
>
> In a word, yes.

When a president's illegal acts, conducted in secret, are shielded from judicial review, we are far indeed from *Marbury v. Madison*.

The Obama administration has not even shied away from explicitly asserting that executive branch officials are beyond the reach of the law. In 2009, Jose Padilla—an American citizen who was imprisoned for years without charges and tortured during his detention—sued the Bush OLC lawyer John Yoo for having authorized the torture regime. The Obama DOJ vigorously defended Yoo, demanding dismissal of the lawsuit at the outset on the grounds that even if the allegations were true, Yoo could not be held legally accountable for his acts because he was a government official who had acted in "good faith." This position prompted what one Bloomberg report described as "surprise" from the Bush 43–appointed federal judge, who reminded the DOJ lawyer: "The allegation is that Professor Yoo knew what the law was, knew that he was not following the law, knew he was not following constitutional precedent, and intentionally gave incorrect information to give cover for illegal activity." As the judge noted, since Yoo is alleged to have "set in motion a series of events that resulted in the deprivation of Padilla's constitutional rights," it is imperative that he be required to answer for his actions in court like any other citizen. The case is now pending before the Supreme Court.

The Obama DOJ's most egregious defense of lawlessness was yet to come. In January 2010, it was revealed that Obama had claimed the right to have American citizens assassinated if he thought that they were "terrorists"—even if those citizens were far from any actual battlefield and had never been charged with any crime. The *Washington Post*'s Dana Priest reported that at least three Americans were on the president's hit list. On April 7, 2010, both the *New York Times* and *Washington Post* confirmed that, as the *Times* put it, "the Obama administration has taken the extraordinary step of authorizing the targeted killing of an American citizen, the radical Muslim cleric Anwar al-Awlaki."

As a result of these reports, Awlaki's father brought suit against the Obama administration in a U.S. federal court, arguing that the planned assassination of his son was unconstitutional and asking the court to order it stopped. In response, the administration raised the state secrets privilege, proclaiming that the court was barred from even hearing the Awlaki case. In other words, according to the Obama DOJ, not only does the president have the right to sentence Americans to death with no due process or charges of any kind, but his decisions on who will be killed and why he wants them dead are state secrets that no court may review or even know about. The president thus asserts the power to be judge, jury, and executioner. (In the Awlaki case, a federal judge eventually dismissed the suit on the ground that Awlaki's father had no standing to sue on behalf of his son, and on the further ground that courts should not intervene in military decisions of the president.)

There is seemingly no limit to the willingness of the Obama administration to protect itself and fellow political elites from legal consequences. When I began writing this book, I was certain that one particular case would offer a serious counterexample to my thesis that the politically powerful are exempt from legal accountability. In January 2008, it was revealed that after various detainees had spoken about being tortured, the CIA had deliberately destroyed numerous videotapes of their interrogations. The CIA officials got rid of these videos despite numerous court orders, and an express directive from the 9/11 Commission, to preserve all such evidence. When they learned of the CIA's act, the two very sober and rhetorically restrained cochairmen of the commission, Lee Hamilton and Thomas Kean, wrote an indignant op-ed in the *New York Times* accusing the CIA of "obstruction." Later, the *New York Times* reported that the destruction of the videos had been undertaken with the knowledge, and possibly at the direction, of several key Bush White House officials.

The criminality here seemed so glaring and obvious—it's the dictionary definition of *obstruction of justice*—that I expected there to be at least some indictments. I believed this would be, as the cliché goes, the exception that proved the rule. Even our political class, I thought, couldn't allow lawbreaking this brazen to go entirely unpunished. But I was wrong. Clearly, there is no such thing in today's Washington as cynicism that is too extreme, nor elite criminality too egregious to enjoy a shield of immunity. In November 2010, the Obama DOJ announced that it was closing its investigation of the matter without bringing charges against anyone involved.

It's instructive to compare how victims of the American "war on terror" have been treated in the U.S. judicial system with their treatment in foreign venues. Maher Arar—an innocent Canadian citizen who was abducted by the United States in 2002 at JFK Airport and sent to Syria to be tortured for ten months—had his case dismissed by American courts without a trial under the state secrets privilege. By contrast, the Canadian prime minister publicly apologized to Arar and announced that Arar would be paid $8.9 million in compensation for Canada's role in what happened to him.

Binyam Mohamed—the British resident who was rendered to Morocco and then brutally tortured at Guantánamo—suffered the same fate in American courts as Arar: the DOJ deprived him of a hearing by insisting that what was done to him was a state secret. On the other hand, British courts repeatedly ruled in Mohamed's favor, and in November 2010 it was announced that the British government would pay him, along with fifteen other Guantánamo detainees, several million dollars in damages. Similarly, in January 2011 an Australian citizen, Mamdouh Habib, reached a monetary settlement with the Australian government after winning the right to sue Australian officials in that nation's court system for their collusion in his torture at Guantánamo and other locations. Numerous countries in both eastern and western Europe have probed their governments' role in colluding with the United States in abusing human rights over the last decade; the U.S. government, which led the way in creating this torture and detention system, stands alone in steadfastly blocking all such investigations. Indeed, the American political class barely bothers any longer with even the pretense of legal accountability and, with increasing frequency, is being quite blatant about its repudiation of it.

THE WATCHDOG PRESS OPPOSES ACCOUNTABILITY

It was not just President Obama, many leading Democratic officials, and virtually all GOP politicians who opposed investigating Bush-era crimes. Joining them were the denizens of the establishment media, who rose up, as they always do, to echo the consensus of the most powerful political figures. With few exceptions, these self-proclaimed crusaders for disclosure and accountability marched in lockstep, demanding that when it came to pervasive criminality in the Bush administration there should be no disclosure or accountability of any kind.

The journalists' coddling of politicians both reflected and bolstered the culture of impunity. One of their favorite tactics was to argue—often falsely—that the public opposes any investigations of political misdeeds. Frequently, media figures asserted that looking into allegations of Bush wrongdoing would doom the Democrats, even when polls revealed exactly the opposite.

To take just one example: On March 25, 2007, MSNBC's Chris Matthews gathered together four journalists to discuss whether Democrats should attempt to compel the top Bush White House aide Karl Rove to respond to congressional subpoenas. Those subpoenas had been issued as part of an investigation into the firings of eight U.S. attorneys, after evidence had emerged that these prosecutors were terminated either because of their refusal to go after Democratic officials targeted by the White House or because they had dared to probe the potential law-breaking of GOP officials. In other words, the core allegation of this scandal was that the Bush White House had converted the DOJ into its own political arm and was firing honest prosecutors who refused to advance that agenda. Rove had raised dubious arguments, grounded in sweeping claims of executive privilege, as to why he was not obligated to comply with the subpoenas.

Matthews and his guests—*Time* managing editor Rick Stengel, MSNBC's Norah O'Donnell, Gloria Borger of *U.S. News & World Report*, and Patrick Healy of the *New York Times*—spent four straight minutes scoffing at the idea that Rove or other White House aides should be investigated to determine whether they had played any role in the firings. The well-documented allegations that powerful executive branch officials were subverting the core mission of the Justice Department could not have been less interesting to the journalists.

Instead, what angered them—the only thing that angered them—was the prospect that Democrats would pursue the investigation. As they so often do, these TV personalities insisted that they were merely speaking for the ordinary American people.

Time's Stengel said: "I am so uninterested in the Democrats want-ing Karl Rove, because it is so bad for them. Because it shows busi-ness as usual, tit for tat, vengeance. That's not what voters want to see." Matthews warned that trying to figure out the truth behind the dismissals would be perceived as "politics" and would backfire on Democrats. O'Donnell agreed, adding, "The Democrats have to be very careful that they look like they're not the party of investi-gation rather than legislation in trying to change things."

In fact, exactly the opposite was true. Immediately before the 2006 midterm election that gave Democrats control of Con-gress, a CNN poll had asked voters this question: "Do you think it would be good for the country or bad for the country if the Democrats in Congress were able to conduct official investiga-tions into what the Bush administration has done in the past six years?" Fifty-seven percent of the respondents—a distinct majority—believed it would be good if such investigations could be conducted, while only 41 percent believed it would be bad.

Even worse for the journalists' anti-investigation claims was a substantial set of polling data from *USA Today*. Released literally days before Matthews and his guests made their confident asser-tions about the public's desires, the poll touched on precisely the question they addressed. It revealed overwhelming majorities demanding that the U.S. attorneys investigation be pursued and that Rove be forced to testify.

14. Do you think Congress should—or should not—investigate the involvement of White House officials in this matter?
Yes, should—72%; No, should not—21%

15. If Congress investigates these dismissals, in your view, should President Bush and his aides invoke "executive privilege" to

protect the White House decision making process or should they drop the claim of executive privilege and answer all questions being investigated?

Invoke executive privilege—26%; Answer all questions—68%

16. In this matter, do you think Congress should or should not issue subpoenas to force White House officials to testify under oath about this matter?

Yes, should—68%; No, should not—24%

Americans are inculcated from childhood with the proposition that nobody is above the law, that in this country the most powerful political official will be punished for breaking the law in the same way as the least powerful citizen. That was why there was such intense opposition to Ford's pardon of Nixon even when the political and media classes overwhelmingly endorsed it, and that disparity has persisted. Polls constantly show substantial portions of the public demanding investigations of politicians' wrongdoing, even while the public's self-anointed spokespeople in the media falsely claim that most oppose such accountability.

The same dynamic arose in relation to the torture investigations. It was conventional wisdom among journalists that Americans view the world through the prism of Jack Bauer and therefore wanted our government to torture. And so, they insisted, Americans did not want, and indeed would not tolerate, criminal investigations into what had been done by Bush officials.

Polls quickly and clearly revealed those claims to be false. A *Washington Post/ABC News* poll in January 2009 found that by a wide margin—58 percent to 40 percent—Americans said that torture should never be used, no matter the circumstances.

More to the point, a full 50 percent of Americans said that the Obama administration should investigate whether the Bush administration's treatment of detainees was illegal. And a distinct majority (52 percent to 42 percent) opposed the idea of Bush issuing pardons to those "who carried out his administration's policy on the treatment of terrorism suspects."

Other polls found even greater majorities in favor of the rule of law. On February 12, 2009, *USA Today* reported that "close to two-thirds of those surveyed said there should be investigations into allegations that the Bush team used torture to interrogate terrorism suspects and its program of wiretapping U.S. citizens without getting warrants." A Gallup poll the same month detailed very similar findings: 71 percent favored either criminal or congressional investigations into whether the Bush White House had attempted to use the DOJ for political purposes (41 percent favored criminal investigations); 63 percent favored either criminal or congressional investigations into whether the Bush administration's wiretapping of telephones without warrants was illegal (38 percent favored criminal investigations); and 62 percent favored either criminal or congressional investigations into torture (38 percent favored criminal investigations). In essence, it was only hard-core Republican partisans—a minority of the country—who wanted to sweep this systematic wrongdoing under the rug.

All of that polling data was released at the same time that the *Washington Post*'s David Ignatius was denouncing those who favored investigations as nothing more than "liberal score-settlers." Senator Lindsey Graham was featured in *Politico* stating without contradiction that "only the hard left" favors investigations. *Newsweek*'s John Barry insisted that there should be no investigations because they were about nothing more than a desire for "vengeance, pure and simple." On January 22, 2009, the *Washington Post* reporter Lois Romano was asked about investigations and prosecutions and likewise claimed that the public was against them.

> I think right now, President Obama wants to follow the concerns of most Americans—which are the economy and health care. Starting a partisan fight—even if it is legal—would be a major distraction for him and likely not sit well with millions of Americans who are out of work and losing their homes.

It's remarkable that large pro-investigation majorities were seen in the January and February 2009 polls even though few members of the media or leaders of either party were promoting that viewpoint. As it gradually became clear that not only Republicans but also President Obama and the Democratic leadership opposed any inquiries into Bush-era lawbreaking, the polls did begin shifting against the idea of investigations. That's not surprising: once both political parties agree on a position, it becomes unchallenged consensus and is rarely even debated or contested again. But before Obama's anti-investigation posture became clear, large portions of the public clearly had been eager for inquiries into Bush's policies—exactly the opposite of what so many prominent journalists repeatedly claimed.

Whether majorities favor criminal investigations and prosecutions is, of course, irrelevant to the question whether they should occur. Decisions about equality under the law and accountability for crimes should be driven by legal principles, not majoritarian sentiment. But the polls do expose the fact that establishment journalists are not representing the public but rather competing to see who can most dutifully repeat the administration's self-justification.

On April 19, 2009, in the wake of the release of the OLC torture memos, *Meet the Press* convened a panel to discuss what should be done about the crimes those documents reflected. The panel was moderated by David Gregory and included five exceedingly typical Beltway insiders: the *Washington Post*'s Steven Pearlstein, *Fortune*'s Nina Easton, *Time*'s Rick Stengel, former GOP House majority leader Dick Armey, and former conservative Democratic Representative Harold Ford Jr. Exactly as one would expect, they were all in full and complete agreement that there must be no investigations or prosecutions of any kind. Not a syllable was uttered to suggest that political officials should be treated the same as ordinary Americans when they got caught breaking the law. Instead, all the panel members recited the same Washington gospel that is always hauled out to justify elite immunity.

ARMEY: Forget about—why are you talking, smacking George
   Bush around now? Look for the future.
STENGEL: [Obama] is very Mandela-like in the sense that he's
   saying let the past be the past and let us move into the future.
FORD: Look, I think the president said it best. . . . He said look,
   the past is the past, let's move forward.
EASTON: I was just going to say that he clearly *wanted* to put
   this behind him, or behind the country, by releasing them.

What a characteristically vibrant, spirited, and diverse media debate that was. The way in which the entire gathering harmoniously repeated the same White House refrain was disturbing indeed. Needless to say, this profound sense of leniency and forgiveness is exclusively reserved for Washington and financial elites. Such sentiments are almost never heard from the media when it comes time to mete out some punishment to ordinary Americans. (The next time you're pulled over by a police officer for speeding, try quoting Barack Obama and his media defenders: "This is a time for reflection, not retribution." See if that works. If not, perhaps this will do: "It's time to focus on the future, not look to the past." Still no luck?)

As time went on, the establishment media came up with ever more contorted defenses for the political elites. *Newsweek*'s intelligence community reporter John Barry scorned investigations as "the politics of vengeance" and urged Obama "to avoid the blame game" regarding what he euphemistically called "Bush's security failings." As a journalist, Barry is supposed to serve as an adversarial check on wrongdoing in the intelligence community, yet he immediately positioned himself as one of the most aggressive and loyal spokesmen for the agencies he covers, demanding that their actions be shielded and forgotten rather than examined and judged.

Then there was *Time*'s Joe Klein, who was more explicit than most in defending the right of political officials to break the law with impunity. In arguing against any action that might lead to accountability for the torture regime, he enumerated what he saw as the dangers for Obama in alienating CIA officials: morale will drop; they'll all retire at the time he needs them most for Afghanistan and Pakistan; investigations might spark a "rebellion in the clandestine service." Apparently, we must let CIA personnel break the law lest they become demoralized. Klein also offered the deeply Orwellian observation that "some operators" are required "to behave extra-legally for the greater good of the nation." Note that Klein was not merely arguing against investigating Bush-era activities but also insisting that criminal behavior is actually vital for the country's well-being and must be protected.

Finally we come to Ruth Marcus, whose December 2008 column in the *Washington Post* unwittingly displayed the utter incoherence that lies at the crux of the case for elite immunity. Marcus began by reviewing the life of Mark Felt, the number two FBI official under J. Edgar Hoover, who had just died that week. Felt was most famous for having been Bob Woodward's "Deep Throat" source in the Watergate investigation, but Marcus focused on a different part of his life: the 1980 criminal trial in which Felt was convicted of having ordered illegal, warrantless searches of the homes of 1960s radicals and their friends and relatives.

Less than twenty-four hours after Felt's 1980 conviction, he (along with an FBI codefendant) was pardoned by Ronald Reagan. Reagan justified his pardon with these following words, obviously relevant to the contemporary debate about possible prosecution of Bush officials.

> [The men's convictions] grew out of their good-faith belief that their actions were necessary to preserve the security interests of our country. The record demonstrates that they acted not with criminal intent, but in the belief that they had grants of authority reaching to the highest levels of government.

To give the other side its due, Marcus quoted Felt's special prosecutor, John Nields, who angrily protested the Reagan pardon by pointing out that even the highest levels of government are supposed to be constrained by the Constitution and the rule of law. But like the good, representative establishment media figure that she is, Marcus concluded that in the modern-day controversy over whether Bush officials should be investigated and prosecuted for their crimes, she felt more at home "in the camp of Reagan than Nields." Her reasoning was a perfect distillation of conventional Washington wisdom on this topic.

> I understand—I even share—Nields's anger over the insult to the rule of law. Yet I'm coming to the conclusion that what's most crucial here is ensuring that these mistakes are not repeated. In the end, that may be more important than punishing those who acted wrongly in pursuit of what they thought was right.

Leave aside Marcus's revealing and now-common description of government crimes as mere "mistakes." Further leave aside the implicit premise that punishment is unwarranted when crimes are committed by those who acted "in pursuit of what they thought was right," an excuse that would set free many (perhaps most) convicted criminals. What is particularly striking about Marcus's argument—that what matters is preventing future criminality, not punishing past transgressions—is how utterly, blatantly self-contradictory it is.

Aside from a desire for just retribution, the principal reason we impose penalties on those who commit crimes is deterrence. The punishments are there to provide an incentive for potential lawbreakers to refrain from breaking our laws, to outweigh whatever benefits they might derive from criminal activity, rather than deciding that it is beneficial to do so. Though there is legitimate debate about how best to prevent crime and how effective jail terms ultimately are, deterrence of future crimes has always been, and remains, a core purpose of the criminal justice system. That is about as basic as it gets.

Punishment for lawbreaking is precisely how we try to ensure that crimes "never happen again." If instead, as Marcus and so many of her media colleagues suggest, we hold political leaders as harmless when they break the law, if we exempt them from judicial punishment, what possible reason would they have to refrain from breaking the law in the future? The important thing, Marcus says, is "ensuring that these mistakes are not repeated." But by telling political leaders that they will not be punished when they break the law, we achieve exactly the opposite. As Hamilton warned in *Federalist 15:*

> It is essential to the idea of a law, that it be attended with a sanction; or, in other words, a penalty or punishment for disobedience. If there be no penalty annexed to disobedience, the resolutions or commands which pretend to be laws will, in fact, amount to nothing more than advice or recommendation.

Marcus rightly observed that the controversies that arose over Bush lawbreaking are not new; indeed, they seem to arise over and over again. And why is that? Because our political leaders keep breaking the law, chronically and deliberately. And why do they keep doing that? Because there is no punishment— hence no deterrent. Every time we immunize political leaders in the name of ensuring that lawbreaking never happens again, we guarantee that it will. Immunity only breeds more immunity: Richard Nixon is pardoned, J. Edgar Hoover's lawbreakers are protected, the Iran-Contra criminals are set free and put back into government, Lewis Libby is spared having to serve even a single day in prison despite multiple felony convictions.

And now we have even let go unpunished those who spied on Americans and tortured detainees in violation of numerous treaties, domestic laws, and the most basic precepts of civilized Western justice.

The effect of this leniency is to signal to current and future political leaders that they, too, can break the law without suffering consequences. Indeed, the rehabilitation of the last decade's war criminals is so complete that their war crimes haven't even damaged their careers. Not only are the nation's torturers, criminal eavesdroppers, and other chronic lawbreakers not in prison, but—just like the Iran-Contra criminals before them—they are thriving, with their platforms undiminished and their reputations as honorable public servants fully intact.

Several Bush officials with direct involvement in the torture regime now enjoy high-level positions in Obama's administration. General Stanley McChrystal became Obama's top military commander in the war in Afghanistan despite ample evidence that detainee abuse was rampant under his command. (He was later dismissed in the aftermath of a controversial *Rolling Stone* interview.) The Bush-era CIA official John Brennan is Obama's top terrorism adviser despite his multiple statements endorsing rendition and "enhanced interrogation tactics" other than waterboarding. William Lietzau became Obama's deputy assistant secretary for detainee affairs even though during the Bush years he had been a key aide to Jim Haynes, the top Pentagon lawyer who gave legal sanction to the torture regime.

The message all this sends to America's political class has been heard loud and clear. High-level political officials are now well aware of the immunity they enjoy and make little attempt to hide it. In February 2010, Dick Cheney went on *ABC News* and openly boasted of the role he had played in ordering the waterboarding of detainees, insisting that what he authorized was the right thing to do and all but taunting the Justice Department to do something about it.

A handful of commentators pointed out that Cheney's statements were tantamount to a guilty plea to serious felonies. The *Atlantic*'s Andrew Sullivan accurately described Cheney's statement as a "confession of committing a war crime on national television." Scott Horton of *Harper's*, an international human rights lawyer, pointed out the specific criminal statutes Cheney had admitted violating, made clear that there is no possible doubt regarding the criminality of waterboarding under U.S. and international law, and then asked, "What prosecutor can look away when a perpetrator mocks the law itself and revels in his role in violating it?" But on the whole, major media outlets competed to offer Cheney a platform and treated him with the respect reserved for honored statesmen.

In general, people who commit felonies avoid publicly confessing to having done so, and they especially avoid mocking the authorities who failed to lock them up. Cheney is certainly not stupid, and yet he was doing exactly that. Indeed, throughout 2010, he gradually escalated his boasting about having authorized illegal policies. Why? Because he knows there will never be any repercussions, that he will never be prosecuted no matter how openly he talks about his serious crimes. And can anyone doubt that Cheney's assessment is right?

That same year, George W. Bush released his memoirs to great media fanfare. His being feted by virtually every media outlet was in no way impeded by the fact that in his book, the forty-third president followed Cheney's lead—not merely acknowledging, but proudly boasting about, his decision to order waterboarding. ("Damn right," he eloquently wrote.) The week after his book's publication, the *Washington Post* editorial board furrowed its brow, scratched its chin, and wondered—as the *Post*'s headline put it—"Why George W. Bush Can Confess to Approving Torture," even though, "waterboarding . . . had been considered a crime by the U.S. government for at least 90 years." The *Post* editors came up with the following answer.

> Mr. Bush feels free to confess to authorizing its use against three al-Qaeda leaders. That's because senior lawyers in his administration—most of them political appointees—provided him with secret memos declaring waterboarding and other standard torture tactics legal.

Actually, the fact that Bush got his own lawyers to write permission slips for him to break the law and torture people is only one reason that he feels free to publicize a book confessing to war crimes. Another reason is that America's media class is filled with people like the *Washington Post*'s own editorial page editor Fred Hiatt, who just the year before had urged that there be no criminal investigations or prosecutions.

> On the one hand, this is a nation of laws. If torture violates U.S. law—and it does—and if Americans engaged in torture—and they did—that cannot be ignored, forgotten, swept away. When other nations violate human rights, the United States objects and insists on some accounting. It can't ask less of itself.
>
> Yet this is also a nation where two political parties compete civilly and alternate power peacefully. Regimes do not seek vengeance, through the courts or otherwise, as they succeed each other. Were Obama to criminally investigate his predecessor for

what George W. Bush believed to be decisions made in the national interest, it could trigger a debilitating, unending cycle.

In lieu of criminal investigations, Hiatt proposed an alternative. He suggested setting up what he called "a fair-minded commission," to be led by two old Washington hands—for instance, Sandra Day O'Connor and David Souter. As Hiatt imagined it, the commission would have no punishment power of any kind but would merely "examine the choices made in the wake of Sept. 11, 2001, and their consequences." It was a puzzling proposal. Aside from the fact that the Obama administration had already refused the possibility of an independent commission, how could this O'Connor-Souter panel possibly compel people never to torture again?

Sure, Hiatt acknowledged with a yawn, we're "a nation of laws" and we can't simply forget when our most powerful political officials commit the most serious war crimes, et cetera, et cetera. But criminal investigations are so terribly messy, uncivil, uncouth, distracting, and disruptive. Criminal prosecutions are for the dirty rabble on the street, not for our upstanding, serious political leaders. When *they* commit grievous crimes, we should have an impotent commission of other upstanding, serious political leaders politely look at what happened, issue a pretty embossed report, and then call it a day.

The reason that George W. Bush and Dick Cheney feel so free to run around beating their chests and boasting of their war crimes is ultimately the same reason that future leaders will undoubtedly violate the law boldly and without fear: because Fred Hiatt and his media comrades, masquerading as watchdogs over the politically powerful, have created a climate where such crimes can be not only committed, but publicly confessed and heralded, with total impunity.

ACCOUNTABILITY FOR OTHERS

The dangers and injustice of elite immunity are not unknown to America's politicians and journalists. They're fully aware of the risks. That is evident by how frequently they lecture other nations about the need to uphold the rule of law by imposing accountability on their most powerful leaders.

In March 2010, President Obama gave an interview to an Indonesian television station. Two years earlier, Indonesia had empowered a national commission to investigate human rights abuses committed by its own government under the U.S.-backed Suharto regime in an attempt to bring the perpetrators to justice. Asked about the commission, Obama stressed the importance of acknowledging past human rights abuses. In a complete reversal of his administration's usual motto, he told the Indonesians, "We can't go forward without looking backwards."

In July 2009 Obama gave a similar speech in Ghana, calling on all Africans to apply "the rule of law" by punishing their nations' past leaders for corruption. As *CBS News* reported, Obama insisted that only such punishment could ensure "the equal administration of justice," and vowed that "we will stand behind efforts to hold war criminals accountable"—meaning, of course, only African war criminals.

In August 2009, Obama's secretary of state, Hillary Clinton, visited Kenya and delivered yet another rule-of-law sermon. A *New York Times* account of that visit mentioned "the pressure

America has put on Kenya to set up a special tribunal to try the perpetrators of the election-driven bloodshed last year, in which more than 1,000 people were killed." Asked by the Nairobi press about the Kenyan government's rejection of that proposal on the ground that such efforts would be politically divisive, Clinton said, "We are waiting; we are disappointed." In response to suggestions that the International Criminal Court in The Hague, rather than Kenya, might investigate and prosecute the perpetrators, Clinton recalled Kenyans to their task: it is "far preferable that prosecutors, judges and law enforcement officials step up to their responsibility."

In November 2010, Secretary Clinton visited Cambodia and, according to the *New York Times*, urged that nation to promptly hold trials of the former regime's surviving leaders in order to "confront its past." According to the *Times* article, the secretary of state insisted that "a country that is able to confront its past is a country that can overcome it," and warned: "Countries that are held prisoner to their past can never break those chains and build the kind of future that their children deserve. Although I am well aware the work of the tribunal is painful, it is necessary to ensure a lasting peace."

Similar pieties were commonplace during the Bush administration as well. In December 2008, U.S. prosecutors asked a federal judge for a sentence of 147 years in prison for Charles Emmanuel, the son of former Liberian president Charles Taylor, who had just been convicted in an American court of having tortured people when he was chief of a paramilitary unit during his father's reign. Emmanuel was the first person convicted under a 1994 law that—implementing the obligations of the Convention Against Torture—allowed prosecution in the United States for acts of torture committed overseas. As part of their request for such a harsh sentence, Bush DOJ prosecutors filed a brief that shamelessly proclaimed that government-ordered torture "undermines respect for and trust in authority, government and a rule of law." And weeks later, Bush's attorney general, Michael Mukasey, gave a speech at the Holocaust Museum in which he praised the Bush administration's prosecution of Emmanuel as an exemplary instance of America's devotion to the rule of law.

> [Emmanuel's] conviction—the first in history under our criminal anti-torture statute—provides a measure of justice to those who were victimized by his reprehensible acts, and it sends a powerful message to human rights violators around the world that, when we can, we will hold them accountable for their crimes.

More amazingly still, a 2006 report from the Bush State Department condemned the Russian government for failing to comply with its own laws on domestic eavesdropping, and for refusing to impose accountability on the government leaders who were responsible. The report noted that "the law [in Russia] permits the government to monitor correspondence, telephone conversations, and other means of communication only with judicial permission," and lamented that surveillance had been carried out without the warrants required by law. Worse, the State Department complained, "there were no reports of government action against officials who violated these safeguards." Behold Russian tyranny as condemned by the U.S. State Department: the Russians not only spy on their own citizens without the warrants required by law, but then fail to prosecute those who do so.

Media accounts frequently participate in the sermonizing.

Thus the *New York Times* article on Clinton's trip to Kenya included a reference to that nation's "culture of impunity." That same phrase pops up in another recent *Times* article, this time applied to Iraq's failure to prosecute the politically powerful who had committed crimes. Iraq's "culture of impunity" is "so widespread that it has become one of the main obstacles to stability and progress in Iraq, according to Iraqi and American officials," warned the paper of record. "Among the barriers, the officials say, are laws that give ministers the right to pardon offenders, as well as partisan and sectarian interference, pressure, infighting." A search through the archives reveals that the phrase "culture of impunity" has almost never been applied by the paper or any of its sources to the United States. Apparently, such a terrible dynamic is confined to places such as Iraq and Kenya.

The issue here goes far beyond hypocrisy. The willingness to impose on other nations precepts of international law from which the United States flamboyantly exempts itself is also a form of lawlessness. In the same way that most Americans are bound by statutes that do not constrain political and financial elites, so, too, does the United States immunize itself from the very standards to which it demands other nations adhere. Abused in this way, law becomes a tool—both domestically and internationally—by which the powerful can coerce and control the powerless, rather than a system for ensuring that all are subjected to common rules.

Nowhere is this more evident than in the principles that Western nations, led by the United States, enshrined at the Nuremberg trials—principles which the American political class explicitly now claims the right to violate. The purpose of the Nuremberg proceedings was not only to punish Nazi war criminals but also to promulgate legal codes to which all civilized nations in the future would be bound. As the lead prosecutor (and former U.S. attorney general) Robert Jackson explained in his opening statement:

> What makes this inquest significant is that these prisoners represent sinister influences that will lurk in the world long after their bodies have returned to dust. . . . And let me make clear that while this law is first applied against German aggressors, the law includes, and if it is to serve a useful purpose it must condemn, aggression by any other nations, including those which sit here now in judgment.

Central to the Nuremberg principles was the imperative that crimes be punished regardless of the status, motives, or excuses of those who perpetrated them. War crimes, Jackson observed, are such that "civilization cannot tolerate their being ignored, because it cannot survive their being repeated." And contrary to the self-protective claims of contemporary Washington elites, Jackson pointed out that the only way to ensure such crimes don't happen again is through accountability and punishment: "The common sense of mankind demands that law shall not stop with the punishment of petty crimes by little people. It must also reach men who possess themselves of great power."

Despite the esteem in which the Nuremberg principles are held in theory, anyone arguing today that they should actually be applied to American leaders is quickly dismissed as frivolous. This is particularly true when it comes to what Jackson called "the greatest menace of our times" and "the central crime in this pattern of crimes, the kingpin which holds them all together": "the plot for aggressive wars." Jackson firmly declared that "no political, military, economic, or other considerations shall serve as an excuse or justification for such actions [except] exercise of the right of legitimate self-defense."

There is no doubt that the 2003 attack on Iraq by the United States was an "aggressive war" by every measure, and certainly by the standard codified at Nuremberg. Moreover, that attack resulted in the deaths of hundreds of thousands of civilians, the displacement of millions more, and the total devastation of a nation of 26 million people. But the very idea that American leaders responsible for it should be held legally accountable under the Nuremberg principles, or condemned as having done anything criminal, is violently rejected by the Washington consensus whenever the idea is brought up at all. Jackson's warning that the Nuremberg proceedings would be meaningful only if their principles bound all nations in the future, including the nations that had convened the trial, has simply been brushed aside.

The Nuremberg trials also have relevance to a key claim repeatedly made by opponents of torture prosecutions, those in the media and the political class who oppose prosecutions for torture sanctioned by the Bush administration: namely, that it would be terribly unfair to punish people for having done something that DOJ lawyers had told them they could. That claim, of course, is quite similar to the central argument of the Nuremberg defendants, who said that they were only following instructions from official government authorities. However, Article 8 of the Nuremberg rules rejected that defense in advance: "The fact that the Defendant acted pursuant to order of his Government or of a superior shall not free him from responsibility, but may be considered in mitigation of punishment if the Tribunal determines that justice so requires." And that principle was further codified in Article 2 of the later Convention Against Torture: "An order from a superior officer or a public authority may not be invoked as a justification of torture."

Given the clarity of this law and its multiple reiterations, what can explain the resolve of the political and media class to ignore it? Why do ostensibly adverse factions leap to one another's defense even in cases of egregious criminality, with Democrats shielding Republicans, media figures demanding no transparency or accountability for political officials, self-proclaimed populist politicians devoting themselves to the protection of Wall Street? One easy answer is that those factions are not really adversaries, at least not in any way that counts. All their members belong to the same class—the powerful and the elite—and thus are motivated, as discussed, to defend an immunity that they might one day need themselves.

But the unanimous support for Bush-era war criminals is motivated by more than just shared self-interest; it has at least as much to do with shared guilt. Bush officials did not commit their crimes by themselves. Virtually the entire Washington establishment supported or at least enabled the lawbreaking.

Leading members of the Democratic Party were implicated in various ways. In July 2008, the reporter Jane Mayer was asked in a *Harper's* interview why there was so little push by Democrats— the "opposition party"—for investigations into Bush programs of torture, warrantless eavesdropping, and the like. She pointed out that one "complicating factor is that key members of Congress sanctioned [these activities], so many of those who might ordinarily be counted on to lead the charge are themselves compromised."

Indeed, key congressional Democrats were contemporaneously briefed on what the Bush administration was doing, albeit often in vague and unspecific ways. The fact that they did nothing to stop the illegal plans, and often explicitly approved of them, obviously gives leading Democratic officials an incentive to block any investigations or judicial proceedings. In December 2007, the *Washington Post* reported that back in 2002 the CIA had briefed a bipartisan group of congresspeople on its use of waterboarding and other torture tactics. That group included the ranking members of both the Senate and House intelligence committees: Jay Rockefeller and Nancy Pelosi. Yet, reported the *Post*, "no objections were raised. Instead, at least two lawmakers in the room asked the CIA to push harder."

Similarly, several leading Democrats, including Rockefeller and Representative Jane Harman, were told that the Bush administration was eavesdropping on Americans without warrants. Rockefeller did nothing to stop it, and Harman actually became the administration's leading defender: after the illegal program was revealed by the *New York Times*, she publicly stated that the wiretapping was "both necessary and legal." Two years after he coauthored the story revealing the Bush NSA program, *New York Times* reporter Eric Lichtblau revealed that Harman had attempted to convince him not to write about the program on the ground that it was so vital. Appearing on MSNBC in June 2009, the law professor Jonathan Turley pointed out the logical result of this bipartisan support for the crimes.

There's no question in my mind that there is an obvious level of collusion here. We now know that the Democratic leadership knew about the illegal surveillance program almost from its inception. Even when they were campaigning about fighting for civil liberties, they were aware of an unlawful surveillance program as well as a torture program. And ever since that came out, the Democrats have been silently trying to kill any effort to hold anyone accountable because that list could very well include some of their own members.

As Mayer put it, "Figures in both parties would find it very hard at this point to point the finger at the White House, without also implicating themselves."

The opinion-making elites were similarly implicated. Very few media figures with any significant platform can point to anything they did or said to oppose the lawbreaking—and they know that. Indeed, some of the nation's most prominent so-called liberal commentators vocally supported Bush's policies. It was *Newsweek*'s Jonathan Alter who became the first establishment media figure to openly advocate torturing prisoners: his November 5, 2001, *Newsweek* column (headlined "Time to Think About Torture") began by proclaiming that "in this autumn of anger, even a liberal can find his thoughts turning to . . . torture" and went on to suggest "transferring some suspects to our less squeamish allies." It was Alan Dershowitz who argued for the creation of "torture warrants," proposing for cases such as the proverbial "ticking time bomb" that "judicially monitored physical measures designed to cause excruciating pain" should be made "part of our legal system." It was the writers of the *Washington Post* editorial page who hailed the Military Commission Act—the single most repressive law enacted during the Bush era, crucial parts of which the Supreme Court ultimately struck down as unconstitutional—as a "remarkably good bill" that "balances profound and difficult interests thoughtfully and with considerable respect both for the uniqueness of the current conflict and for the American tradition of fair trials and due process."

When it comes to media figures who cheered on Bush's lawlessness and then self-servingly demanded that there be no investigations, the *Washington Post*'s David Broder is a particularly illustrative case. In April 2009, he wrote a column dramatically denouncing the Bush presidency as "one of the darkest chapters of American history, when certain terrorist suspects were whisked off to secret prisons and subjected to waterboarding and other forms of painful coercion in hopes of extracting information about threats to the United States." Despite this acknowledgment, Broder in the same column opposed any criminal investigations of the Bush torture regime, proclaiming Obama "right to declare that there should be no prosecution of those who carried out what had been the policy of the United States government."

Given Broder's acknowledgment of how horrific Bush's presidency had been, what explains his simultaneous opposition to investigations? The answer is clear. Like most of his journalistic colleagues, the dean of the Washington press corps never sounded the alarm while this lawlessness was taking place, when it mattered. He did the opposite, repeatedly mocking those who warned of how radical and dangerous the Bush administration was. As torture went on, he continuously defended what Bush officials were doing as perfectly normal and well within the bounds of legitimate policy.

After the 2004 election, for example, Broder dismissed those who were arguing that Bush and Cheney had succeeded in entrenching presidential lawlessness. "Checks and balances are still there," he insisted. "The nation does not face 'another dark age,' unless you consider politics with all its tradeoffs and bargaining a black art." In 2006, he derided those who warned that the "war on terror" had ushered in an era of extreme lawlessness by sarcastically proclaiming, "I'd like to assure you that Washington is calm and quiet this morning, and democracy still lives here," and then denouncing Bush critics "who get carried away by their own rhetoric." Broder's 2009 recognition that the Bush presidency was "one of the darkest chapters of American history" came, of course, with no acknowledgment of his 2004 declaration that "the nation does not face 'another dark age.'"

So when these media and political elites are defending Bush officials, minimizing their crimes, and arguing that no one should be held accountable, they're actually defending themselves as well. Just as Jane Harman and Jay Rockefeller can't possibly demand investigations for actions in which they were complicit, media stars can't possibly condemn acts that they supported or toward which, at the very best, they turned a blissfully blind eye. Bush officials must be exonerated, or at least have their crimes forgotten—look to the future and ignore the past, the journalists all chime in unison—so that their own involvement might also be overlooked.

In this world, it is perfectly fine to say that a president is inept or even somewhat corrupt. A titillating, tawdry sex scandal, such as the Bill Clinton brouhaha, can be fun, even desirable as a way of keeping entertainment levels high. Such revelations are all just part of the political cycle. But to acknowledge that our highest political officials are felons (which is what people are, by definition, who break our laws) or war criminals (which is what people are, by definition, who violate the laws of war) is to threaten the system of power, and that is unthinkable. Above all else, media figures are desperate to maintain the current power structure, as it is their role within it that provides them with prominence, wealth, and self-esteem. Their prime mandate then becomes protecting and defending Washington, which means attacking anyone who would dare suggest that the government has been criminal at its core.

The members of the political and media establishment do not join forces against the investigations and prosecutions because they believe that nothing bad was done. On the contrary, they resist accountability precisely because they know there was serious wrongdoing—and they know they bear part of the culpability for it. The consensus mantra that the only thing that matters is to "make sure it never happens again" is simply the standard cry of every criminal desperate for escape: I promise not to do it again if you don't punish me this time. And the Beltway battle-cry of "look to the future, not the past!" is what all political power systems tell their subjects to do when they want to flush their own crimes down the memory hole.

In the long run, immunity from legal accountability ensures that criminality and corruption will continue. Vesting the powerful with license to break the law guarantees high-level lawbreaking; indeed, it encourages such behavior. One need only look at what's happened in the United States over the last decade to see the proof.

5

AMERICAN JUSTICE'S SECOND TIER

When ordinary Americans come in contact with the justice system, everything changes. The world we have been examining reverses. In the United States, the lack of accountability for elites goes hand-in-hand with a lack of mercy for everyone else. As our politicians increasingly claim the right to commit crimes with impunity, they simultaneously escalate the severity of punishments imposed on ordinary Americans who have broken even minor laws.

As a result, precisely what the founders most feared has come to exist: a two-tiered system of justice in which outcomes are determined not by the law itself but by the status, wealth, and power of the lawbreaker. And these days, the people advocating for elite immunity are often the same ones who emphatically insist upon rigid, unyielding enforcement of the rules for the rest of us. Indeed, when it comes to crime and punishment, the trends for powerful and ordinary Americans have been heading in completely divergent directions. During the same four-decade period in which the nation's political class has expanded legal immunity for political and financial elites, it has imposed ever-harsher prison terms on more and more of the nation's citizens.

Permissiveness for elites, by itself, is unjust enough. But at least if that leniency were available on an equal basis to everyone, it might arguably be fair, and certainly less injurious to basic precepts of justice. It is the elites' insistence on treating all others in precisely the opposite fashion from the way they treat themselves that is so pernicious.

The United States now imprisons more of its citizens than any other nation in the world, both per capita and in absolute terms. The numbers are staggering. The United States has only 5 percent of the world's population, yet nearly 25 percent of all prisoners in the world are on American soil. "Simply put, we have become a nation of jailers," writes the Brown University professor Glenn Loury. "The American prison system has grown into a leviathan unmatched in human history."

According to the King's College International Centre for Prison Studies, at the end of 2008 the United States was incarcerating more than 2.2 million of its citizens in federal and state prisons and local jails around the nation. In July 2010, the *Economist* similarly put the number at "between 2.3 and 2.4 million." The nation with the next-largest prison population, China, has 1.6 million people in prison—which means that the United States, a nation of 300 million, imprisons 700,000 more of its citizens than a country whose population is 1.3 billion. And that number is continuing to increase. As a 2007 report from the JFA Institute described it, "If you put them all together in one place, the incarcerated population [of the United States] in just five years will outnumber the residents of Atlanta, Baltimore and Denver combined."

The United States also has the highest rate of imprisonment of any nation in the world, with 756 people in prison per 100,000 citizens. The next-highest rates belong to Russia (629) and Rwanda

(604). The rates in most of the world are far lower. The median imprisonment rate for South American countries is 154; for western Europe, 95; and for western African countries, 35. On a per capita basis, the United States is practically in a league by itself.

America's overall "correctional population"—which includes not just those in prison but also people on probation and on supervised parole—is even more enormous and continues to grow. According to Justice Department statistics, at the end of 2008 over 7.3 million people—one in every thirty-one U.S. adults—were on probation, in jail or prison, or on parole. And that's not even counting the nation's 4.3 million ex-convicts who have fulfilled their parole obligations.

Worse, American criminal justice policy has been trending in only one direction: toward ever more prosecutions, convictions, and imprisonments. Over the last forty years, the growth in America's prison state has been unremitting. (The total adult correctional population decreased very slightly in 2009 after decades of uninterrupted growth, but the reduction was so small that it was most likely a statistical aberration rather than the result of any policy changes.) In 1970, fewer than 190,000 people were incarcerated in the United States; since then, we have seen more than a tenfold increase. In 2008, when Pew released a comprehensive report on America's prison state, it reported that "for the first time in history more than one in every 100 adults in America are in jail or prison." The increase in probation and parole numbers has been similarly dramatic.

These trends have continued right through periods of rising crime and falling crime, prosperity and economic hardship, war and peace, Democratic and Republican rule. In 2007, the JFA Institute noted that "prison populations have been growing

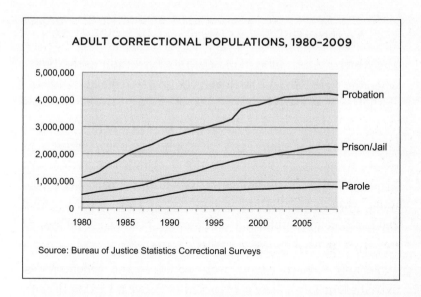

ADULT CORRECTIONAL POPULATIONS, 1980–2009

Source: Bureau of Justice Statistics Correctional Surveys

steadily for a generation, although the crime rate is today about what it was in 1973 when the prison boom started." Indeed, as the institute put it, "most scientific evidence suggests that there is little if any relationship between fluctuations in crime rates and incarceration rates. In many cases, crime rates have risen or declined independent of imprisonment rates."

Clearly, the growth in prison populations is not a response to national circumstances. What it represents, rather, is a deliberate choice by the political class to lock up more and more people for longer periods and for ever more trivial offenses. While wealthy and powerful Americans are increasingly able to avoid suffering any consequences for their lawbreaking, ordinary Americans have had little means to resist the punitive onslaught.

"LAW-AND-ORDER" EXTREMISM GOES BIPARTISAN

The American prison system began its expansion in the 1960s, when the right wing of the Republican Party, led by presidential candidate Barry Goldwater, vowed to make "the abuse of law and order in this country" a central issue. In Republican parlance, this meant more aggressive policing, longer prison sentences, stricter criteria for parole and probation, and less leniency in general. Social unrest in the 1960s—the civil rights movement, antiwar protests, assassinations, and urban race riots— further increased the appeal of a law-and-order platform. Ronald Reagan rode that sentiment to the California governorship in 1966, and Richard Nixon, who would be the beneficiary of extreme leniency a mere six years later, drove it hard to become president in 1968.

Conservative politicians often used appeals to law and order to mask their opposition to social welfare programs, such as Lyndon Johnson's Great Society. Goldwater, for example, repeatedly blamed the welfare state for what he insisted (without much evidence) was America's growing crime problem.

> If it is entirely proper for the government to take away from some to give to others, then won't some be led to believe that they can rightfully take from anyone who has more than they? No wonder law and order has broken down, mob violence has engulfed great American cities, and our wives feel unsafe in the streets.

Johnson, for his part, attempted to sell his sweeping social programs to America's middle class by packaging them as a law-and-order solution. Poverty was the root cause of lawbreaking, he argued, and consequently alleviating it would reduce crime.

From the outset, issues of race as well as class pervaded discussions of criminality. With the civil rights movement rendering overt expressions of racial prejudice less acceptable, opponents of racial equality channeled their animus into law-and-order rhetoric. In 1966, Nixon blamed societal decline on the civil disobedience of Martin Luther King Jr. and other civil rights leaders, arguing that "the deterioration of respect for the rule of law can be traced directly to the spread of the corrosive doctrine that every citizen possesses an inherent right to decide for himself which laws to obey and when to disobey them." Meanwhile, focusing on the root causes of crime was derided by the Republicans as a destructive liberal delusion. Gerald Ford, the House minority leader at the time, demanded to know, "How long are we going to abdicate law and order in favor of a soft social theory that the man who heaves a brick through your window or tosses a firebomb into your car is simply the misunderstood and underprivileged product of a broken home?"

Over the following decades, the law-and-order mentality of the 1960s became one of the most influential forces in American political culture, consistently targeting the poorest, most marginalized, and most powerless Americans. In the 1970s, Nixon regularly maligned the Warren Court as one of society's prime villains. Its sin: recognizing a slew of constitutional rights and establishing various safeguards for criminal defendants, including the right to have improperly obtained evidence or coerced confessions excluded from trial (*Mapp v. Ohio* and *Escobedo v. Illinois*), the right of indigent defendants to have counsel provided for them (*Gideon v. Wainright*), and the right to be told about one's rights upon being taken into custody (*Miranda v. Arizona*). Scapegoating judicial and political liberalism as the prime cause of crime, Nixon dramatically increased the power and scope of federal law enforcement agencies—most notably with the 1973 creation of the Drug Enforcement Agency. He also made adherence to law-and-order ideology the primary consideration in his judicial selections, including the appointment of conservatives Warren Burger and William Rehnquist to the Supreme Court.

Notably, Ford's pardon of Nixon in 1974 did little to stem the rising tide of law-and-order enthusiasm. By the time Reagan was elected president in 1980, appeals to law and order were a constant refrain in American politics. Reagan made attacks on excessive "leniency" a vital part of his campaign against Jimmy Carter. And once in office, he replaced the Warren Court with a new scapegoat: the Cadillac-driving welfare queen, a caricature meant to represent a scheming and dishonest underclass. As the criminology scholars Katherine Beckett and Theodore Sasson document in their book *The Politics of Injustice*, within the first year of Reagan's presidency his attorney general, William French Smith, slashed resources devoted to prosecuting white-collar crimes and domestic violence and "began to pressure federal law enforcement agencies to shift their focus . . . to street crime."

Most significant for the growth of America's penal state was the federal government's increased emphasis on the "war on drugs." "The drug problem has become so widespread that the FBI must assume a larger role in attacking the problem," declared FBI director William Webster in 1981. The DEA grew very rapidly in the 1980s, relocating from a modest downtown Washington building into a sprawling northern Virginia complex. Strident warnings about the drug trade, particularly the melodramatic 1980s media jeremiads about the "crack epidemic," further fueled the law-and-order movement. Multiple new laws, including the Anti-Drug Abuse acts of 1986 and 1988, imposed draconian minimum sentence requirements on those convicted of trafficking in illicit substances or even merely possessing relatively small amounts of them.

But it was the 1988 presidential election that cemented law and order as American orthodoxy. A prime cause for the defeat of Democratic candidate Michael Dukakis was the George Bush campaign's vilification of the Massachusetts governor as "soft on crime," which it accomplished through the infamous television ad featuring Willie Horton. Horton, a menacing-looking African American convicted murderer, had received a weekend furlough from prison as part of a program supported by Dukakis, and while on furlough had raped a white woman in front of her husband. In the *Washington Post*, the reporter Sidney Blumenthal quoted a Bush campaign aide exulting over the Horton episode as "a wonderful mix of liberalism and a big black rapist." Further cementing Dukakis's "soft-on-crime" image was a presidential debate in which CNN's Bernard Shaw asked the candidate whether he would continue to oppose the death penalty if his own wife were raped and murdered. The uncharismatic Democrat responded by dispassionately enumerating the policy flaws of the death penalty, a stoic reaction which led to widespread accusations that he lacked "manly emotions."

The Dukakis fiasco doomed any efforts to curb law-and-order extremism. There was little to gain, and much to lose, for any politician advocating moderation in criminal punishment of the marginalized.

Bill Clinton left no doubt that he had learned the lesson. Branding himself a "New Democrat" during the 1992 presidential campaign, he touted his unflinching belief in "tough-on-crime" measures, declaring that Democrats "should no longer feel guilty about protecting the innocent." To underscore the point, the Arkansas governor left the campaign trail to preside over the execution of Ricky Ray Rector, an African American convicted murderer who was functionally retarded and entirely incapable of understanding what was taking place. Clinton's carefully crafted crime-warrior image protected him against the racially charged attacks that destroyed Dukakis and was an important factor in his victory over the incumbent, President Bush.

True to his campaign rhetoric, Clinton's presidency ushered in a series of policies that ensured a rising prison population. In the process, he converted the law-and-order mind-set from a GOP attack strategy into a bipartisan policy consensus. Like all policies enjoying bipartisan consensus, being tough on crime was thus removed from the realm of the debatable.

The right's efforts to exploit crime to undermine Clinton were continuously thwarted by his willingness to adopt the right-wing approach to penal issues. In 1994, for instance, the GOP's "Contract with America" included a section titled "The Taking Back Our Streets Act," which demanded, among other things, more severe criminal punishments, longer prison sentences, mandatory sentencing requirements, and more prisons.

> The bill embodies the Republican approach to fighting crime: making punishments severe enough to deter criminals from committing crimes. . . . The bill sets mandatory sentences for crimes involving the use of firearms, authorizes $10.5 billion for state prison construction grants, establishes truth-in-sentencing guidelines, reforms the habeas corpus appeals process [by making it more difficult for prisoners to file them], allows police officers who in good faith seized incriminating evidence in violation of the "exclusionary rule" to use the evidence in court, requires that convicted criminals make resti-

tution to their victims, and authorizes $10 billion for local law enforcement spending.

The following year, Clinton signed into law an "anticrime" bill that largely incorporated these demands. The only real "concession" Clinton extracted from the Republicans was the inclusion in the bill of an assault weapons ban. But when he stood for reelection in 1996, Clinton heralded the bill as one of the crown jewels of his presidency, repeatedly boasting that his increased "law enforcement spending" had added 100,000 police officers to the street.

The bipartisan emphasis on law and order led to a shift in priorities across the board. Government programs were no longer focused on creating opportunities for the poor; instead, the focus was on locking them up. From Reagan's presidency through the Clinton years, the steep rise in state spending on police and corrections was accompanied by a precipitous decline in spending on the poor.

Today, it is commonplace for politicians in both parties at the federal, state, and local levels to compete with one another over who can advocate the most draconian punishments for ordinary Americans. During the Democrats' protracted 2008 primary fight, Hillary Clinton attacked Barack Obama by claiming that he was too liberal to win the election. Asked for specifics, her campaign pointed to a 2004 statement in which Obama had advocated the abolition of mandatory minimum sentences for federal crimes.

As president, Obama himself has demonstrated a readiness to follow his predecessors and position himself as a law-and-order politician. In April 2010, he gave an interview about "judicial activism"—that is, courts acting beyond their

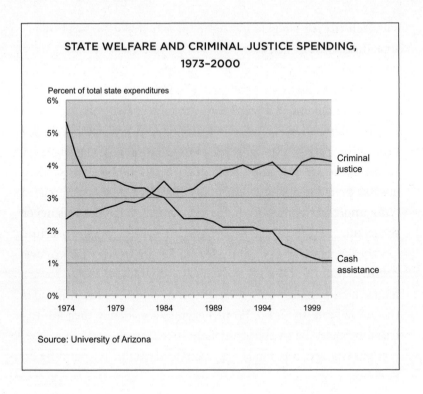

STATE WELFARE AND CRIMINAL JUSTICE SPENDING,
1973–2000

Percent of total state expenditures

Source: University of Arizona

authority—which echoed Nixonian complaints about the Warren Court. As the *New York Times* put it, "President Obama has spoken disparagingly about liberal victories" such as *Miranda* rights and the guarantee of legal representation for indigent defendants.

Here's another way to think of all this history. The man who initially enshrined law and order as the foundation of the nation's federal justice system—Richard Nixon—committed serious felonies but did not spend a day in prison. The man who most popularized the no-mercy mentality—Ronald Reagan—not only spared from prison Mark Felt, an FBI official convicted of illegally spying on Americans, but himself presided over a criminal effort to fund Nicaraguan terrorists. That all ended satisfactorily for Reagan: virtually all of his top aides, and therefore Reagan himself, were shielded from accountability by his handpicked successor, George H. W. Bush, who pardoned six key conspirators who were either about to go on trial or who had already pleaded guilty or been convicted.

The man who converted the tough-on-crime crusade into bipartisan orthodoxy—Bill Clinton—abandoned his call for investigations into past political crimes as soon as he was safely elected president. In addition, of course, Clinton admitted to lying under oath during a deposition in a civil suit but was never prosecuted. He was followed by the equally tough-on-crime George W. Bush, whose entire presidency was a spree of law-breaking. And Bush was succeeded by Barack Obama, who has engaged in Herculean efforts to shield Bush and his top aides from any investigation, and has done the same for plundering, fraud-perpetrating Wall Street elites.

THE WESTERN WORLD'S ROGUE JUSTICE STATE

There is little question that this decades-long law-and-order movement is a major cause of America's ever-expanding prison population. Numerous new laws enacted at the federal, state, and local levels have been moving the United States in the direction of longer prison terms, less leniency, and less sentencing discretion available to judges. Nationwide, politicians in both parties have established their tough-on-crime bona fides by supporting—and demanding ever-greater application of—a slew of prison-populating policies, such as "three-strikes-and-you're-out" laws and abolition of parole.

Beyond laws deliberately intended to incarcerate people for longer periods, prison has become the punishment for an ever-broader array of transgressions, including many that, according to the JFA Institute, "pose little if any danger or harm to our society." In fact, the United States routinely imprisons its citizens even for nonviolent crimes for which no other Western nation imposes jail terms, from petty drug offenses to writing bad checks. In April 2008, the *New York Times* reporter Adam Liptak compared the contemporary American approach to criminal justice with that of the rest of the world and found an "enormous and growing" gap: "Americans are locked up for crimes . . . that would rarely produce prison sentences in other countries." For Vivien Stern, a research fellow at the prison studies center in London quoted by Liptak, the United States has become "a rogue state, a country that has made a decision not to follow what is a normal Western approach."

The scope of criminal law has expanded so rapidly, and now includes such minor offenses, that Alex Kozinski, who is the chief judge of the Ninth Circuit Court of Appeals, and the lawyer Misha Tseytlin titled a 2009 essay, with only a little irony, "You're (Probably) a Federal Criminal." As they put it, "Most Americans are criminals, and don't know it, or suspect that they are but believe they'll never get prosecuted. . . . Violations are so common that any attempt to go after all criminals would sweep up untold millions of people."

As Kozinski and Tseytlin note, anyone who has ever misfiled their taxes (even inadvertently), or consumed any illegal drugs (including marijuana), or bet on a sporting event with a bookie, or lied to a government bureaucrat, or even just performed their job poorly (if it's an occupation regulated by the federal government) has committed a federal offense for which they could be sent to prison—and for which many of their fellow citizens are now actually imprisoned. Similarly, the criminologists Beckett and Sasson report that "in 2000, police arrested more than 2 million individuals for such 'consensual' or 'victimless' crimes as curfew violations, prostitution, gambling, drug possession, vagrancy, and public drunkenness. Fewer than one in five of all arrests in that year involved people accused of the more serious 'index' crimes" such as assault, larceny, rape, or homicide. It should hardly be controversial that a system of criminal law that theoretically renders a substantial portion—if not an outright majority—of the citizenry subject to long prison terms is both excessive and unjust.

It is not merely the proliferation of criminal statutes that has turned America into the world's largest prison state, but also the severity of punishment. The law professor Michael Tonry, a leading authority on crime policy, writes in his *Handbook of Crime and Punishment* that American prison sentences are "vastly harsher than in any other country to which the United States would ordinarily be compared." According to the 2007 JFA report, "For the same crimes, American prisoners receive sentences twice as long as English prisoners, three times as long as Canadian prisoners, four times as long as Dutch prisoners, five to 10 times as long as French prisoners, and five times as long as Swedish prisoners." Notably, these more severe punishments produce little benefit for the United States. The rates of violent crime in all those countries are lower than America's, and their rates of property crime are comparable.

One of the most disturbing aspects of the American approach to crime is the embrace of mandatory minimum sentencing schemes, which eliminate mercy and flexibility by denying judges the ability to adjust sentences when circumstances merit. These laws force the courts to subject all convicted defendants to unyielding harshness, even when doing so produces gross injustice. The advocacy group Families Against Mandatory Minimums has documented numerous travesties resulting from these mandatory sentencing rules, such as cases where young adults convicted of petty drug offenses were sentenced to decades in prison.

Almost every new wave of law-and-order enthusiasm has exacerbated the problem. Currently, in California alone, there are roughly 8,700 inmates serving life sentences under the "three-strikes-and-you're-out" law; almost 3,700 of them are imprisoned under that punishment scheme despite having committed non-violent third-offenses, such as petty theft. Close to half the states in the country have enacted some version of a "three-strikes" law. In 2003, a 5 to 4 majority of the U.S. Supreme Court rejected the claim that such mandatory life imprisonment constitutes "cruel and unusual punishment," and thus upheld it as constitutional.

Even worse, these specific measures have given rise to a generalized mind-set of ruthlessness that pervades the entire legal system. Leniency and mercy, once the hallmarks of civilized rule, to say nothing of the great Western religions, have come to be scornfully equated with coddling, weakness, and liberalism. Particularly at the state level, where judges are elected rather than (as in the federal system) appointed for life, the political calculus—in which harsher punishments equal more votes—pushes the courts to ever-lower depths of punitive retribution. Some judges are now so eager to prove their chops, reports the *Economist*, that they "appear in campaign advertisements waving guns and bragging about how tough they are."

One could write an entire book chronicling cases of excessive punishments that would strike any decent person as unconscionable. But to demonstrate the merciless nature of American law when it's applied to the powerless, a few examples will suffice.

In mid-2006, Jessica Hall, a twenty-five-year-old African

American unemployed mother of three, was driving on Interstate 95 through Virginia with her three children in the back and her pregnant sister—who was experiencing early contractions—sitting next to her. Traffic ground to a halt, and when it began moving again another vehicle cut Hall off. In frustration, she tossed a large McDonald's cup filled with ice into the other car. As Eliza Fowle, a passenger in that car, described it to the *Washington Post* in February 2007: Hall "chuck[ed] a big, supersized McDonald's cup at us. It was gross and sticky and got all over me and the front of our car, the dashboard and the windshield."

Hall had no prior criminal record. Nobody was injured in the incident. But as the *Post* reported, Hall "was charged and convicted by a Stafford County jury of maliciously throwing a missile into an occupied vehicle, a felony in Virginia." The jury instructions stated that "any physical object can be considered a missile. A missile can be propelled by any force, including throwing." By the time of her trial, Hall had spent more than a month in jail, leaving her small children without a parent to care for them: Hall's husband, a marine, was serving in Iraq. The jury sentenced Hall to two years in prison, the minimum penalty allowed under the law. The *Post* article describes the aftermath.

> [Hall] never fathomed that it would land her in jail for the first time in her life, wearing a standard-issue jumpsuit frayed up both legs and learning to curl her hair using toilet paper. . . . "I passed out when they said guilty, two years," she added. "I became a convicted felon."
>
> "I think that this is way too much of a punishment for her actions. This is just to me absolutely ridiculous," Fowle said. Community service would have made more sense, she said. Hall said she has cried every day she has spent locked up and

wakes most days to find clumps of hair on her pillow from the stress. She shares a cell with two other women and spends 19 hours a day in the cell, she said.

After the case received substantial local media attention and Hall had spent seven weeks in prison, the judge suspended her sentence on the condition of five years of good behavior. She told reporters that she had planned to go to nursing school but now believed her status as a convicted felon would preclude that. Even the "victim" was so horrified by what happened to Hall that she said she would be reluctant to report a crime in the future.

Hall's case is not the only appalling story to come out recently from Virginia. In 2007, Elisa Kelly and her then-husband, George Robinson, threw a birthday party at their southern Virginia home for Kelly's sixteen-year-old son and his friends of the same age. The couple provided beer and wine for the party, and Kelly collected keys from all guests when they arrived to ensure that they could not drive until the next morning. None of the teens left the party and nobody was injured, but a neighbor called the police and reported underage drinking.

Kelly and Robinson were convicted of nine misdemeanor counts of contributing to the delinquency of a minor (one count for each minor who drank at the party) and were each sentenced to eight years in prison. On appeal, the sentences were reduced to twenty-seven months, but no further. The Virginia Supreme Court refused to hear the case, and the couple began serving their prison terms that June.

Moving a little farther south, we find the case of Roy Brown, a fifty-four-year-old African American homeless man who lived on the street in Shreveport, Louisiana. In December 2007, Brown walked into a Capital One bank branch, put his finger inside his jacket, pointed it at a teller, and told her that this was a robbery. She handed him three stacks of bills, but he took only a single one-hundred-dollar bill and gave the rest back to her.

The next day, feeling remorseful, Brown turned himself in to the local police. According to a local Shreveport newspaper, he "told the police he needed the money to stay at the detox center and had no other place to stay and was hungry." He pled guilty in a Caddo County district court to a single count of first-degree robbery and was sentenced to fifteen years in prison—fifteen years, for the unarmed theft of a single one-hundred-dollar bill.

Some episodes make it particularly clear that such lack of mercy has little to do with notions of deterrence or justice but is simply driven by a desire to punish. In 2005, Genarlow Wilson, a seventeen-year-old African American boy in Atlanta—an honor student and homecoming king—was arrested for having engaged in consensual oral sex (but not intercourse) with a girl two years younger than he. Under Georgia law, a fifteen-year-old is underage, and neither her consent nor the minimal age difference between the perpetrator and victim could be taken into account. Wilson repeatedly refused to plead guilty and accept a five-year prison term. When the case went to trial, he was convicted of aggravated child molestation—"aggravated" because oral sex was involved, not because of any coercion—and sentenced to ten years in prison. As a convicted sex offender, he was ineligible for parole. Moreover, the sex offender status carried with it lifelong penalties, including registry requirements and a ban on contact with his younger sister.

Wilson insisted that he had done nothing wrong and vowed

to appeal his conviction and sentence. Twice, the Georgia Supreme Court refused to hear his appeal, leaving him in prison. In 2007, after Wilson's sentencing, the Georgia state legislature changed the state's molestation law so that any minor convicted of molestation would be guilty only of a misdemeanor and subject to just a one-year sentence. But with Wilson in mind, the legislature explicitly included a provision stating that the change would not be retroactive.

Despite that provision, the new law did prompt a state court judge to grant Wilson's habeas corpus petition. By a 4–3 vote, the Georgia Supreme Court held that in light of the revised law Wilson's sentence constituted "cruel and unusual punishment," and ordered him released. Only a single vote of the court spared Wilson from another eight years in prison.

THE SECOND TIER

So why do Americans tolerate such a draconian legal system, one which imprisons exceptionally large numbers of people for no good reason? The answer is clear: because most people believe—correctly—that they themselves are unlikely to be sucked into its vortex. They are right to believe this because the two-tiered justice system that separates elites from ordinary Americans intensifies as one moves down the rungs of power and privilege. The rich and powerful are able to commit crimes with impunity far more easily than middle-class Americans; but similarly, middle-class criminals are far more likely to escape unpunished than the poorest among us. This is how the JFA Institute report put it.

> A significant number of Americans cheat on their taxes, steal from their employers, receive stolen goods, purchase illegal

cable boxes, illegally download music, use illegal drugs, or participate in many other illegal acts. . . .

The most prestigious Wall Street firms have engaged in large-scale illegal trading practices. . . . Policemen are filmed using excessive use of force on citizens, make arrests based on racial stereotypes, deal in drugs, plant evidence on innocent people, and lie under oath. Sports figures are accused of rape, assault and taking steroids. . . .

But given that most of us commit some type of crimes in our lifetimes, the most severe punishments are targeted toward lower class citizens. It is this class of people we are willing to punish disproportionately to their criminal acts.

By imposing the brunt of criminal punishment on the most powerless and marginalized groups, the legal system ensures that people who suffer the most from its injustices are the ones least able to subvert it. Many Americans acquiesce to the prison state because neither they nor their families nor their friends are at risk. That's what allows the population to largely tolerate and even cheer for a system that imposes extreme punishments for the pettiest offenses. Only a person with little power, money, or status is likely to feel the full brunt of America's harshest laws. Indeed, given the severity of its provisions, the contemporary American criminal justice system would be unsustainable if it were applied with equity across the population.

One of the ugliest and most toxic aspects of the multi-tiered approach to justice is that those who suffer the most from it are, in extreme disproportion, racial minorities. In 1997, the government's Bureau of Justice Statistics found that "about 9% of the black population in the U.S. was under some form of correctional supervision compared to 2% of the white

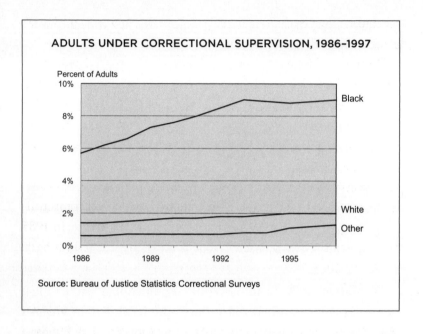

ADULTS UNDER CORRECTIONAL SUPERVISION, 1986–1997

Percent of Adults

Black

White
Other

1986   1989   1992   1995

Source: Bureau of Justice Statistics Correctional Surveys

population and over 1% of other races." This represented a 42 percent increase for whites and 57 percent for blacks since 1986. Tracking the period beginning with the middle of the Reagan presidency and ending in the middle of Clinton's, the accompanying chart from the Bureau of Justice Statistics starkly highlights the disparate growth in the correctional population.

And that trend has continued through the recent years. The JFA Institute's 2007 report details that incarceration rates for blacks and Latinos are now more than six times higher than for whites; as a result, 60 percent of America's prison population is either African American or Latino. One out of every twelve working-age African American males languishes in prison; 21 percent of those between twenty-five and forty-four years old have been imprisoned at some point. At current rates, one in seventeen white males, one in six Latino males, and one-third of all black males will go to prison during their lifetimes.

Putting someone in prison for a prolonged period, even when justified, devastates not only that person's life but also the lives of their families, especially their children. Growing up with a parent in prison is itself a predictor of later criminality. In other words, the very policies America has been implementing in the name of fighting crime—ever-longer and more unyielding prison sentences—play a leading role in perpetuating the cycle of crime. And here, too, the burden falls particularly severely on communities of color. As Radley Balko noted in *Reason* magazine, in 1985 "one in every 125 American children had a parent behind bars. Today [in 2008] it's one in 28. For black children, it's one in nine, a fourfold increase during the last 25 years."

Multiple, complex factors contribute to this racial disparity, but it is clear that America's harsh laws and the unequal enforcement of them play a large role. And at the heart of the racial inequality lies America's failed "war on drugs."

Overall, the growth in drug-related incarcerations has been astronomical. In 1980, 19,000 people were under the jurisdiction of state correctional authorities for drug offenses; by 2006, the number was 265,800—a fourteenfold increase in just twenty-six years. By contrast, for the same period, the number of violent offenders increased only threefold. American jails and prisons are bulging in large part because of the vast number of people incarcerated for nonviolent drug offenses. Beckett and Sasson summarize the grim reality as follows:

> Our prisons and jails house many people whose most serious violation is the possession or sale of illicit drugs. In state prisons in 2001, 21% of inmates were serving time for a nonviolent drug

offense, up from 9% in 1985. In the smaller federal system, 57% of inmates are serving time on drug charges. Most of those imprisoned for drug offenses are convicted of possession—rather than distribution—of drugs.

The government's own chart (below) highlights the steep and continuous climb in drug-related arrests.

But it is the racial aspect of the drug war—the undeniable fact that minorities are arrested, prosecuted, and imprisoned at far greater rates than white offenders—that ought to be the greatest source of national shame. America's drug policy is one of the most profound betrayals of the founding principle of equality before the law. Government statistics compiled by the law professor Ilya Somin show that, as of 2008, "over 62% of incarcerated nonviolent drug offenders are black (most of them poor black

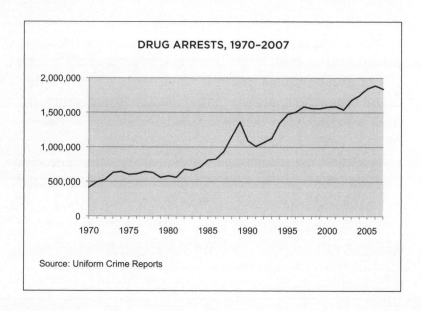

Source: Uniform Crime Reports

males)." And there's no question that this disparity is the result of drug laws and enforcement that are implicitly—and sometimes overtly—race-based.

Different sentences for possession of identical amounts of cocaine—dictated by whether the drug is in the form of crack or powder cocaine—have been among the most significant contributors to the racially imbalanced incarceration rate. In the 1980s, crack was a drug used disproportionately by racial minorities and the very poor, for the simple reason that it was cheap. Cocaine in powder form, far more expensive, was the choice of America's middle-class, young white suburbanites and budding Wall Street tycoons. Even though both substances are forms of the same drug, both the 1986 and 1988 versions of the Anti-Drug Abuse Act imposed drastically higher punishments for dealing and possession of crack than of powder cocaine—an unequal penalty scheme which provoked little objection from those with a public platform.

According to the Sentencing Project, the mandatory penalties for possession of crack cocaine were "the harshest ever adopted for low level drug offenses." The trigger point for severe sentences for powder cocaine possession, by contrast, was a hundred times higher.

> Defendants convicted with just five grams of crack cocaine, the weight of less than two sugar packets and a quantity that yields about 10 to 50 doses, were subject to a five-year mandatory minimum sentence. The same five-year penalty was triggered for the sale of powder cocaine only when an offense involved 500 grams, 100 times the minimum quantity for crack, which yields between 2,500 and 5,000 doses.

Predictably, the vastly harsher sentencing rules for crack resulted in vastly higher rates of incarceration for minority drug users and dealers than for their white counterparts. In 2010, Congress finally reduced the crack/powder cocaine sentencing disparity, changing the 100:1 ratio to 18:1. Even the new sentencing rules are a far cry from eliminating the difference entirely, however. What's more, the new statute prohibits retroactive application, which means that all accused crack offenders whose cases were pending when the law was enacted will still be subject to the 100:1 disparity and oppressive, mandatory prison terms.

The racially discriminatory impact of America's drug war is also due to variations in the way that drug laws are enforced. Government data demonstrate that overall drug usage rates are similar among all racial and ethnic groups. Even with the relative popularity of crack among blacks, two-thirds of crack cocaine users in the United States are white or Hispanic. Yet according to the U.S. Sentencing Commission, over 80 percent of defendants accused of crack-related crimes—possession or dealing—in 2006 were African American. The Sentencing Project describes the effect that this has on prison populations.

> African American drug defendants have a 20 percent greater chance of being sentenced to prison than white drug defendants. Between 1994 and 2003, the average time served by African Americans for drug offenses increased by 62 percent, compared to an increase of 17 percent for white drug offenders. Moreover, African Americans now serve virtually as much time in prison for a drug offense (58.7 months) as whites do for a violent offense (61.7 months).

Race-based enforcement of drug laws is not confined to cocaine alone. A report released in October 2010 by the Marijuana Arrest Research Project for the Drug Policy Alliance and the NAACP documented that "in the last 20 years, California made 850,000 arrests for possession of small amounts of marijuana, and half-a-million arrests in the last 10 years. The people arrested were disproportionately African-Americans and Latinos, overwhelmingly young people, especially young men." Los Angeles in particular "arrested blacks for marijuana possession at seven times the rate of whites."

If marijuana usage rates were substantially higher among African Americans and Latinos than whites, these statistics would be less shameful. But precisely the opposite is true in California and across the nation. As the *New York Times* columnist Charles Blow notes, "Young white people consistently report higher marijuana use than blacks or Hispanics." Indeed, among whites nationwide, 44 percent have used marijuana, compared to 38 percent for blacks and 27 percent for Latinos. Nevertheless, as the Drug Policy Alliance report documented, "police in 25 of California's major cities arrested blacks at four, five, six, seven, and even 12 times the rate of whites," while "major cities in California arrested and prosecuted Latinos for marijuana possession at double to nearly triple the rate of whites." This disturbing finding gives rise to an obvious question: what is the cause of such race-biased patterns of arrest? Based on the data in that report, the answer is clear: young police officers assigned to low-income black and Hispanic neighborhoods aggressively use stop-and-frisk tactics, which commonly result in discovery of marijuana. White citizens—especially those in neighborhoods that are middle-class and above—are generally not subjected to such searches and thus are by and large free to commit the same crimes with impunity.

The repercussions of marijuana-possession convictions extend far beyond penal sanctions; especially for America's poor, they can be life destroying. In 1998, Bill Clinton signed into law a statute barring people with drug convictions from being granted financial aid—either temporarily or permanently, depending on how many drug-related offenses a person has. While such oppressive and cruel law-and-order measures are usually thought to be the province of the GOP, the reality is that these efforts are wholly bipartisan. Democrats under Obama, for instance, worked hard to sink a 2010 California referendum that would have legalized marijuana. They also acted to increase funding for such 1980s war-on-drugs initiatives as the Byrne Formula Grant program, which helps state and local forces make more drug arrests. Such programs, argues the Ohio State University law professor Michelle Alexander in her book *The New Jim Crow*, are being used to create a permanent undercaste—"a lower caste of individuals who are permanently barred by law and custom from mainstream society." In the *New York Times*, Charles Blow denounced such efforts as "outrageous and immoral," concluding that "the Democrats' complicity is unconscionable, particularly for a party that likes to promote its social justice bona fides."

(One Democrat who, to his credit, has been stalwart in vocally protesting America's race-biased justice system, often at great political risk, is the former Reagan official and current Virginia senator Jim Webb. In 2009, when proposing to form a commission to recommend how the nation should overhaul its criminal justice system, Webb took to the Senate floor and drew attention to what he called "the elephant in the room": the transparent racism of America's prison state and specifically the drug war. He pointed out that although African Americans have about the same rates of drug use as the rest of the population, "they end up being 37% of those arrested on drug charges, 59% of those convicted, and 74% of those sentenced to prison." Overall, Webb said, "America's criminal justice system has deteriorated to the point that it is a national disgrace." Unfortunately, his views are rarely heard in most mainstream political precincts, and in 2010 the Democratic-led Congress failed to act on his proposal.)

Unequal treatment in the American justice system is dictated by class as well as race. Anyone who has ever interacted with the courts in the United States—whether as a lawyer, an accused criminal, or a plaintiff, whether in criminal proceedings or a civil suit—knows that the outcomes are determined at least as much by the wealth of the parties as by the merits of their positions. In criminal court, wealthy defendants can amass large teams of lawyers who will devote themselves for months or even years to winning an acquittal. The indigent, on the other hand, are assigned public defenders who are almost always so overworked and stretched so thin that a full-on defense is impossible, resulting—at best—in substantial pressure placed on even the most innocent to plead guilty and accept long prison terms.

In civil suits, meanwhile, poor parties are often unable to obtain counsel at all, forced to navigate the complexities of the judicial system pro se, often against wealthy corporations with multiple lawyers. Proceeding without counsel is usually a ticket to being marginalized, patronized, and defeated, regardless of the merits of one's claims. Indeed, even most middle-class Americans cannot afford to hire high-quality lawyers for protracted litigation, enabling the legal interests of the wealthiest and most powerful factions in America to prevail more or less by default.

The wealthy, of course, have long enjoyed advantages in the

justice system. But just as America's wealth inequality in general has recently seen dramatic increases, so too the dispensation of justice is now more bifurcated than ever before.

In 2010, the World Justice Project published a "Rule of Law Index," which compiled "indicators on the rule of law from the perspective of the ordinary person" in nations around the world. In terms of access to legal counsel for civil proceedings, the United States ranked twentieth out of the thirty-five nations surveyed, below countries such as Mexico, Croatia, and the Dominican Republic. The WJP study showed that America's disparate treatment of rich and poor is highly atypical.

> Only 40% of low-income respondents who used the court system in the past three years reported that the process was fair, compared to 71% of wealthy respondents. This 31% gap between poor and rich litigants in the USA is the widest among all developed countries sampled. In France this gap is only 5%, in South Korea it is 4% and in Spain it is nonexistent.

Those depressing findings are consistent with those documented by the Legal Services Corporation, the inadequately funded entity created by Congress to provide legal representation to low-income civil defendants. LSC is required by law to issue reports on the ability of America's poor to access the justice system. Its 2009 report documented the bleak reality of America's unequal justice.

> Studies show that the vast majority of people who appear without representation are unable to afford an attorney, and a large percentage of them are low-income people who qualify for legal aid. A growing body of research indicates that out-

comes for unrepresented litigants are often less favorable than those for represented litigants.

The severity of this problem was underlined by an October 2010 *New York Times* editorial aptly titled "Need a Lawyer? Good Luck." Across the nation, the article noted, programs designed to provide legal services to the poor "are so cash-strapped that they are turning away numbers of people." Even people with the most pressing legal needs—say, those trying to stave off fraudulent home foreclosures or obtain protection from domestic violence— "often navigate the judicial system on their own or give up." The political class's strident demands for budget cuts and austerity measures are almost always targeted at America's minorities and the poor; government-provided legal services are thus certain to decline further even as the need for them continues to increase.

America's indigent class is so severely bereft of access to anything resembling justice that even the U.S. government has been forced to acknowledge the problem, though it has merely pretended to address the issue. In February 2010, President Obama announced that he was appointing his former law professor, Laurence Tribe of Harvard, as a DOJ adviser charged with "increasing legal access for the poor." But in April, just two months after Tribe's appointment, the *New York Times* reported that his position had been downgraded. Tribe, stated the *Times*, "has a small staff, a limited budget, little concrete authority and a portfolio far less sweeping than the one he told friends he had hoped to take on in Washington." Moreover, he was "largely invisible," as the Justice Department was "not allowing him to give interviews, apparently in part because of nervousness in the administration that his unabashedly liberal views might draw criticism."

Small wonder, then, that when he gave a speech that June to

the National Institute of Justice, Tribe lamented how little was being done to facilitate basic justice for the poor. He delivered shocking statistics: public defender caseloads were "often 5 to 6 times that of the ceiling" recommended by attorney monitoring groups, and "some defenders in New Orleans averaged 19,000 cases a year, allowing an average of just seven minutes per case—a mere seven minutes to talk to a lawyer about a life-altering decision." Tribe explained that "the situation is no less dire in civil cases, including those that involve life-altering matters like deportation, loss of child custody, and eviction," and noted that "no one doubts that those who cannot afford counsel in proceedings touching such momentous matters are at a potentially ruinous disadvantage."

All of that led Tribe to declare: "The truth is that, as a nation, we face nothing short of a justice crisis. It is a crisis both acute and chronic, affecting not just the poor but the middle class. The situation we face is unconscionable." There is no disputing that *unconscionable* is indeed the right word for the refusal of one of the world's wealthiest nations to provide even basic legal representation to the majority of its citizens.

The point about the middle class not being exempt from the justice system's crisis was reinforced just a few months later, when the mortgage fraud scandal erupted and numerous stories emerged of homeowners who were the victims of illegal foreclosure actions. Many of them were simply incapable of battling the armies of lawyers employed by banks and mortgage companies, and their homes were lost because they lacked the means to demonstrate the fraud and defects at the heart of the banks' case.

In the November 2010 issue of *Rolling Stone*, Matt Taibbi reported on the special courts established around the country for the express purpose of streamlining and accelerating foreclosure actions. Presided over by retired judges who were unfamiliar with the complexities involved in the mortgage fraud, these courts were not set up "to decide right and wrong, but to clear cases and blast human beings out of their homes with ultimate velocity." The whole process was designed to transfer the property of ordinary citizens to the nation's largest banks regardless of entitlement. As Taibbi wrote:

> The judges, in fact, openly admit that their primary mission is not justice but speed. One Jacksonville [Florida] judge, the Honorable A. C. Soud, even told a local newspaper that his goal is to resolve 25 cases *per hour*. Given the way the system is rigged, that means His Honor could well be throwing one ass on the street every 2.4 minutes.

The following month, the *Washington Post* reported that similar courts in Virginia were "making it easier for lenders to defend themselves when accused of giving homeowners too little warning of impending foreclosures." Indeed, "the process moves so quickly in Virginia . . . that homeowners can receive less than two weeks' notice that their house is about to be sold on the courthouse steps." The design of the courts guaranteed that even banks with no legal foreclosure entitlement had an almost insurmountable advantage. In the very short time they were accorded, homeowners seeking to stop foreclosure had to "gather evidence, file a lawsuit and potentially post a bond with the court that could total thousands of dollars." These arduous requirements, combined with the near-impossible deadlines, meant that many borrowers simply ran out of time when trying to fight invalid foreclosure proceedings.

It is hard to imagine a purer expression of two-tiered justice than special courts created for the sole purpose of helping large banks take people's homes more expeditiously. Such courts show that the legal system not only fails to protect Americans from societal injustice and inequality, but also serves as a tool of injustice and inequality in its own right.

PRISONS FOR PROFIT

When it comes to the way money shapes American justice, nothing competes with the impact of the privatized prison lobby. Imprisoning criminals, once exclusively a government responsibility, has—like most government functions—been increasingly privatized. All over the United States, more and more prisons are managed not by government agencies but by for-profit private corporations such as Geo Group and Corrections Corporation of America. (In 2008, private prisons housed 7.5 percent of all inmates nationwide.) Those same companies accrue substantial revenues by providing contracting services to government-run prisons. They quite naturally view prisoners as their basic stock in trade and earn a profit for each one they incarcerate.

Like all private companies, the prison industry has an insatiable appetite for more business, and thus it agitates in favor of greater demand for its services—demand created through longer prison sentences, fewer opportunities for parole, and constant increases in the number of transgressions deemed prison-worthy. In other words, the private prison industry profits from precisely the draconian approach to penal policies implemented over the past several decades. This perverse dynamic was perfectly captured by the headline for a November 2008 *Wall Street Journal* article: "Larger Inmate Population Is Boon to Private Prisons."

And the article itself made it clear that the prison companies don't expect the tide to turn anytime soon.

> Corrections Corp., the largest private-prison operator in the U.S., with 64 facilities, has built two prisons this year and expanded nine facilities, and it plans to finish two more in 2009. The Nashville, Tenn., company put 1,680 new prison beds into service in its third quarter, helping boost net income 14% to $37.9 million. "There is going to be a larger opportunity for us in the future," said Damon Hininger, Corrections Corp.'s president and chief operations officer, in a recent interview.... Geo Group, of Boca Raton, Fla., the second-largest prison company, has built or expanded eight facilities this year in Georgia, Texas, Mississippi and other states, and it plans seven more expansions or new prisons by 2010.

Simply put, incarceration is now big business in the United States. According to the Pew, "Total national spending on corrections has jumped to more than $60 billion from just $9 billion in 1980, even as recidivism rates have barely changed." Indeed, "prisons are the fourth-largest state budget item behind health, education and transportation." Government at every level continues to spend more on incarceration and other phases of the correction process with every passing year. The DOJ's own statistics are striking (see chart on next page).

Private prison corporations are receiving an increasing share of this spending, and the industry appears to be recession-proof. In early 2009, as most of the nation suffered from the financial crisis, CorpWatch noted that Geo Group "reported impressive quarterly earnings of $20 million ... along with an

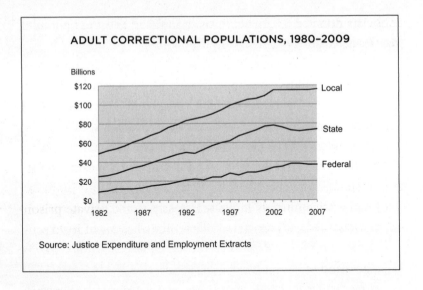

ADULT CORRECTIONAL POPULATIONS, 1980–2009

Source: Justice Expenditure and Employment Extracts

annual income of $61 million for 2008—up from $38 million the year before."

Like all profitable industries—especially those that rely on the government for business—private prison corporations dedicate substantial amounts of money to shaping laws that will maximize their revenue. Indeed, the increasing role played by these private corporations in performing what had traditionally been a government function is another manifestation of the public/private merger: the for-profit prison companies have, in essence, established themselves as part of the government, and laws are written by them and for their benefit. In the case of the prison industry, that's particularly perverse, as their interest is best served by ever-harsher punishment schemes for ordinary Americans. A 2004 report from the National Institute on Money in State Politics revealed that for the 2002 and 2004 election cycles, these companies and their directors, executives, and lobbyists donated $3.3 million to candidates and state political parties across forty-four states.

In a comprehensive article in *In These Times* documenting the success of the private prison industry in shaping America's penal laws, Silja J. A. Talvi noted that "private prison companies strongly favor giving to states with the toughest sentencing laws—in essence, the ones that are more likely to come up with the bodies to fill prison beds." And, of course, one finds countless instances of "revolving door" transfers, in which public criminal justice officials move seamlessly to the private prison industry while that industry in turn sends hordes of its executives into the very government positions that dole out prison contracts and implement penal policies.

A particularly repellent consequence of the public/private prison industry merger was exposed in a December 2008 investigative report from the *Boston Phoenix*, which showed that the prison companies have been expending vast resources to combat drug policy reform. The corporations fear an end to their greatest source of income: the incarceration of hundreds of thousands of citizens for nonviolent drug offenses. Such reform strikes at the heart of the industry's capacity for future growth, and private prison operators have thus made it a priority not only to preserve current punishment schemes but to advocate for even harsher ones. Accordingly, the *Phoenix* revealed, the industry "regularly lobb[ies] against criminal-punishment reforms, and for the creation of new criminal statutes and overly harsh prison sentences. While these efforts are cloaked as calls for public safety, they are essentially creating more business for themselves."

The report noted that significant sums of money were at stake.

The country's largest private prison provider, the Corrections
Corporation of America (CCA), spent more than $2.7 million
from 2006 through September 2008 on lobbying for stricter
laws. Last year alone, the company, listed on the New York
Stock Exchange, generated $133 million in net income.

Since there is no well-funded lobby advocating for penal
reform or promoting the interests of prisoners, the prison lobby
goes virtually unchallenged and can buy the ability to shape per-
tinent laws at bargain basement prices.

Even worse than the corruption is the perverse incentive that
these for-profit corporations have to operate increasingly inhumane facilities. By forcing prisoners into severely overcrowded
quarters and depriving them of the supervision necessary to
prevent rape and other forms of abuse, corporations can reduce
costs and thus increase their profits. As Senator Webb put it, the
levels of violence and sexual victimization in this country's prisons are completely "off the charts."

The American justice system has become a weapon to control, exploit, and profit off vast numbers of American citizens.
That the victims of this exploitation are disproportionately the
poor and the powerless makes it all the more repugnant.

BELOW THE SECOND TIER

America's war on drugs set in motion some of the most brazen,
systematic attacks on equality under the law in the modern era.
But the "war on terror" has taken those attacks to new depths of
injustice.

As we have seen, President Obama has gone to extreme
lengths to shield high-level Bush officials and Wall Street plun-

derers from the consequences of even the most egregious crimes, based on his oft-stated view that "it's important to look forward and not backwards." The American justice system relentlessly "looks backward," however, to seek out and punish the crimes of ordinary Americans, and Obama has done nothing to retard the booming growth of America's prison state.

Another remarkable disparity has been the wildly divergent treatment of elite criminals as opposed to "whistle-blowers"— those who reveal government and corporate secrets in order to expose high-level corruption and criminality. While immunizing high-level lawbreakers, the Obama administration not only has failed to extend the protective shield of immunity to America's whistle-blowers but has pursued them with uncommon vigor. In other words, powerful criminals are protected, while those who expose their crimes are persecuted.

To be sure, protecting high-level criminals while prosecuting those who expose them is not entirely Obama's invention; that approach certainly had currency during the Bush administration. In May 2006, for example, Attorney General Alberto Gonzales appeared on *ABC News* and declared it a "possibility" that the *New York Times* reporters who wrote about Bush's illegal warrantless eavesdropping program would be prosecuted. (The government officials who had committed crimes by ordering the illegal eavesdropping, on the other hand, were of course in no such danger.)

But the Bush administration had merely suggested that it *might* prosecute whistle-blowers. The Obama administration, by contrast, has actually carried through on those threats, repeatedly and aggressively. In April 2010, the Obama DOJ announced it had obtained an indictment against the NSA whistle-blower Thomas Drake, who had exposed serious waste, abuse, and possible illegality at the agency. In May, the DOJ reissued an abandoned Bush-era subpoena to James Risen of the *New York Times*, demanding that he identify the source who had told him of the extremely inept CIA effort to infiltrate the Iranian nuclear program. (The DOJ has now indicted a former CIA official who it claims was the source in question.) The next month, the Obama DOJ targeted Shamai Leibowitz, an FBI linguist who had leaked what he believed to be evidence of lawbreaking, though what exactly it was has never been revealed. As *Politico*'s Josh Gerstein reported, Leibowitz's sentence of twenty months in prison is "likely to become the longest ever served by a government employee accused of passing national security secrets to a member of the media," and it was imposed even though the sentencing judge admitted that he had no knowledge of what the linguist had leaked or how it damaged national security.

In June 2010, the *New York Times* noted that "the Obama administration is proving more aggressive than the Bush administration in seeking to punish unauthorized leaks." Through such prosecutions, of course, the Obama DOJ also intimidates and deters potential future whistle-blowers, thus further blocking one of the very few remaining paths Americans have to breach the virtually impenetrable wall of secrecy surrounding the surveillance and national security state. As we saw in the previous chapter, the Obama administration has relentlessly fortified that wall, making promiscuous use of state secrets and immunity claims to ensure that high-level criminality and other forms of corruption can take place free of all accountability.

Perhaps nothing better illustrates the reprehensible double standard than the Obama administration's actions against the whistle-blowing site WikiLeaks. Throughout 2010, WikiLeaks published thousands of documents relating to U.S. wars in Iraq and Afghanistan, which revealed shocking abuses and outright criminality on the part of the American occupiers. The files showed American soldiers firing on unarmed civilians and journalists, covering up multiple killings of civilians, and adopting a formal policy of turning a blind eye to systematic human rights abuses perpetrated by Iraqi forces right under the Americans' noses. Needless to say, none of these revelations resulted in any criminal investigations from the Obama administration.

In December, WikiLeaks released another trove of information: numerous diplomatic cables that had been sent from U.S. embassies around the world. Like the war documents, these cables revealed numerous instances of wrongdoing. They made it clear, for example, that the U.S. government had lied about its involvement in Obama-approved civilian-killing air strikes in Yemen; that the Obama State Department had pressured Spain not to criminally investigate the torture of Spanish citizens by the United States; that the British government had secretly promised to protect Bush officials from "embarrassment" as part of its purported investigation into the Iraq war; and that U.S. and British officials had colluded to allow the United States to keep cluster bombs on British soil even though Britain had signed a treaty banning such weapons.

Obama's administration, once again, showed no interest in holding the perpetrators of these outrages responsible. Instead, the administration did something else entirely: it launched an all-out war on WikiLeaks itself. Numerous reports quickly surfaced that the Obama DOJ was actively attempting to indict WikiLeaks founder Julian Assange, an Australian citizen, under the Espionage Act of 1917—which, if successful, would be the first time in U.S. history that a nongovernment employee was convicted of espionage for publishing classified material. Meanwhile, a very sophisticated cyberattack temporarily drove WikiLeaks offline. Overt pressure from American government officials resulted in Australia threatening to revoke Assange's passport. Joe Lieberman, chairman of the Senate Homeland Security Committee, publicly warned companies not to associate with WikiLeaks in any way, after which the assets of WikiLeaks were frozen and the organization's accounts with MasterCard, Visa, PayPal, and Bank of America were terminated, impeding the group's ability to raise funds. What's more, when a handful of teenage hackers targeted a few of these companies with some trivial "denial of service" attacks, Attorney General Holder announced that the DOJ was criminally investigating those attacks—but not the far more sophisticated and damaging cyber-attacks that had caused WikiLeaks to lose its Internet home.

To recap "Obama justice," then: if you create a worldwide torture regime, illegally spy on Americans without warrants, abduct people with no legal authority, or invade and destroy another country based on false claims, then you are fully protected. But if you expose any of these lawless actions by publishing the truth about what was done, then you are a criminal who deserves the harshest possible prosecution.

It's true, of course, that leaking classified information is a crime. That's what makes whistle-blowers and leakers so courageous. And if all wrongdoing, including that of the politically powerful, were always fully punished according to the law, one could accept whistle-blower prosecutions. But that's not the situation that prevails. Instead, there are no prosecutions in sight for years of war crimes, torture, and illegal spying, as well as the greatest financial theft in American history. There, we are told to "look forward, not backward." But when anyone dares to expose the overweening corruption and illegality of the national security state, the full weight of the "justice system" is brought mercilessly crashing down upon that person.

And the assault on whistle-blowers is not even the worst of the ongoing abuses of the legal system. Since September 2001, the "war on terror" has opened up an entire dimension in which the rule of law simply vanishes. For those who are accused of being "terrorists"—even if they are never charged with any crime—there is now a limbo world in which there exists not even the pretense of due process, let alone equality. Those who have the misfortune to find themselves there are not merely unequal but essentially *nonpersons* as far as the American legal system is concerned. Anything and everything are fair game.

With terrorism as its rationale, the United States has proclaimed the power to detain people indefinitely without a trial—a power that extends equally to Americans arrested on U.S. soil and foreign citizens seized anywhere in the world. Thousands of people have been imprisoned by the U.S. government over the last decade without any legal recourse, all based exclusively on the executive branch's unilateral, unreviewable accusation that the prisoner is a terrorist. And brand-new "military commissions" have been established which deprive the defendants of crucial rights that they are supposed to possess under American law.

That the majority of the detainees subjected to this newly concocted system have been imprisoned without any credible evidence against them has had little effect on its proliferation. As detailed in the prior chapter, the U.S. government has lost 65 percent of the habeas corpus cases brought by Guantánamo detainees. Colin Powell's former chief of staff, Colonel Lawrence Wilkerson, has openly acknowledged that many Guantánamo detainees were innocent and that the Bush administration knew they were innocent. Yet the Obama administration not only has left Guantánamo open but has aggressively sought to expand its ability to keep people imprisoned without any due process.

Indeed, while as a candidate Obama had lavishly praised the Supreme Court's 2008 *Boumediene* ruling, which established that Guantánamo detainees are entitled to habeas review, the Obama DOJ has argued that detainees who are shipped to a "war zone"—such as the U.S. prison in Bagram, Afghanistan—have no rights of any kind. Although this theory was rejected by a district court judge, it has been accepted by an appellate court, which means that the habeas right established by *Boumediene* can be nullified through the simple expedient of substituting Bagram for Guantánamo. And let's not forget Obama's claimed right to target American citizens far from any battlefield for assassination, based solely on the president's unilateral, unchallengeable decree that the individual is a terrorist. What could be more lawless than that?

Perhaps most perversely, the Obama administration has now resorted to making up rules as it goes along, based solely on its assessment about what is most likely to ensure victory for the government. In November 2009, Attorney General Holder announced that five Guantánamo detainees, including the alleged 9/11 mastermind Khalid Sheikh Mohammed, would be granted civilian trials in a real American court. Others, however—such as the detainee accused of staging the 2000 attack on the USS *Cole*, as well as the first "child soldier" to be tried for war crimes in American history—would be sent to military tribunals at Guantánamo.

And still others, Holder later made clear, will be denied all due process and simply held indefinitely.

Thus, in Obama's multitiered justice system, only certain detainees are entitled to real trials: namely, those whom the government is sure it can convict. Others, for whom conviction is less certain, will be accorded fewer rights and tried by military commission. And those whom the government believes it can't convict in either forum will simply be held indefinitely with no charges, a power the Obama administration announced it intends to preserve. (Echoing legal theories adopted by Bush/ Cheney, Obama's lawyers argue that this boundless detention is permitted by "the laws of war," and that the president's role as commander in chief of the armed forces entitles him to make such decisions unilaterally and without any oversight from courts.) But a system of justice that accords varying levels of due process based on the defendant's likelihood of being convicted isn't a justice system at all. It's a rigged game of show trials.

The former air force lawyer Morris Davis was the chief prosecutor of the Guantánamo military commissions system during the Bush years and resigned in protest in 2008 to become one of the system's leading critics. In the *Wall Street Journal*, he laid bare the corrupt essence of the new approach, noting that "the standard of justice for each detainee will depend in large part upon the government's assessment of how high the prosecution's evidence can jump and which evidentiary bar it can clear."

But the fact that this perverse situation is tolerated should not be surprising. Such fundamental violations of the core precept of the rule of law—whereby the most powerless are subjected to explicitly different rules and degrees of punishment than the elites—are now commonplace in the American justice system; indeed they have become one of its defining features.

America's poor and racial minorities are so marginalized that their vastly different treatment provokes few objections. Those accused of being terrorists, particularly when they are Muslims, are more marginalized still, and therefore their plight triggers even less controversy.

This is how the multitiered justice system preserves itself: by targeting those with the weakest voices, the smallest constituencies, and the least ability to resist. Indeed, those who abuse state power virtually always follow the same playbook. By initially targeting new abuses at groups that are sufficiently demonized, they guarantee that few will object. But abuses of power rarely, if ever, remain confined to these demonized groups. Rather, degraded principles of justice, once embraced in limited circumstances, in time inevitably come to be applied more broadly.

Thus did the pardon of Richard Nixon—justified in 1974 as a onetime exception necessitated by unique circumstances—lay the foundation for elite immunity: a lawbreaking license that spread throughout the political class and then to its partners in the private sector. In the same way, the degradation of basic legal principles that began in the name of "law and order" gave rise to the "war on drugs" and then the "war on terror," with their ever-more-severe erosion of due process and constitutional safeguards.

The result is a "justice system" in name only, one in which outcomes are determined by the status of the parties rather than the merits of their positions. The proclamation of John Adams that we are "a nation of laws, not men," now rings hollow, as does Jefferson's insistence that the essence of America is that "the poorest laborer stands on equal ground with the wealthiest millionaire, and generally on a more favored one whenever their rights seem to jar." And Madison's proud declaration in *Federalist 57* that America's political class, by definition, "can make no law which will not have its full operation on themselves and their friends, as well as the great mass of society," now seems to describe a country entirely other than our own.

EPILOGUE

The founders envisioned the law as the bedrock foundation on which American society would be built, the essential guarantor of fairness and justice. But the multitiered justice system of today's America guarantees nothing of the kind. Indeed, the blatantly unequal legal treatment that we've seen throughout this book accomplishes precisely the opposite: it warps the law into a devastating tool used to entrench privilege, entitlement, and unearned wealth.

When political and financial elites are shielded from any consequences for their actions, they are no longer subject to the law. Instead, they become the law's masters, using the legal system for their own purposes: to safeguard and expand their perquisites; to ensure that their cheating and corruption are not punished but rather rewarded; and to keep any outsiders from challenging their superior status. The law, which was meant to keep the powerful in check, is now used instead to sustain and perpetuate their power.

The degradation of the rule of law as an equalizing force in the United States is both a *cause* and an *effect* of rapidly intensifying inequality in other areas of American life. The greater the disparities in wealth and power become, the more unequal the law becomes—and the more unequal the law is, the more opportunities it creates for the wealthy and powerful to reinforce their advantages. Eventually, favorable treatment in the justice system becomes nothing more than another commodity distributed in accordance with wealth and power. And once the disparities in wealth and power become too great, they overwhelm the law along with everything else. That dynamic—legal inequality and wealth inequality feeding each other in a vicious cycle—is exactly what we see in today's United States.

When a privileged few are able to do whatever they wish while all others are bound by ever-harsher constraints, the former group will naturally win more and more from the latter. It is no surprise, then, that after four decades of growing legal inequality America also finds itself saddled with economic inequality that is reaching crisis proportions. Even mainstream sources are now speaking of the U.S. economy in terms that until recently would have been unthinkable. Nicholas Kristof, the longtime *New York Times* columnist, has argued that when it comes to income distribution, the United States increasingly resembles the world's most corrupt and unbalanced regimes. In a November 2010 column, he described the situation bluntly.

> In my reporting, I regularly travel to banana republics notorious for their inequality. In some of these plutocracies, the richest 1 percent of the population gobbles up 20 percent of the national pie. But guess what? You no longer need to travel to distant and dangerous countries to observe such rapacious inequality. We now have it right here at home.

Kristof reviewed a litany of depressingly familiar statistics to demonstrate how stark this economic inequality has become. The richest 1 percent of Americans now take home almost 24 percent of the nation's income, up from less than 9 percent in 1976. From 1980 to 2005, more than four-fifths of the total increase in American incomes went to that richest one-hundredth of all Americans. Citing Timothy Noah's detailed 2010 *Slate* series on inequality, Kristof noted that "the United States now arguably has a more unequal distribution of wealth than traditional banana republics like Nicaragua, Venezuela and Guyana."

As a chart compiled by the University of Arizona professor Lane Kenworthy demonstrates, income levels for the top 1 percent of America's earners have quadrupled since 1979 while remaining almost completely stagnant for everyone else.

In the face of such massive financial inequality, the notion of equal legal treatment for everyone has crumbled away completely. And this decline of the founding American ideal is not just a matter of isolated incidents and outrageous news headlines; it can be measured in objective numbers, such as those provided by the 2010 "Rule of Law Index" from the World Justice Project. The WJP employs a large team of international experts to gauge the extent to which the rule of law prevails in countries across the globe, and its findings leave no room for doubt: when it comes to fairness and justice, the United States now ranks near the bottom of the Western world.

The fundamental principles promoted by the WJP are uncontroversial. The rule of law prevails, they say, when laws are "clear, publicized, stable, and fair, and protect fundamental rights"; when they are enacted through an "accessible, fair, and efficient" process; when "competent, independent, and ethical adjudicators" are available in sufficient numbers and have adequate

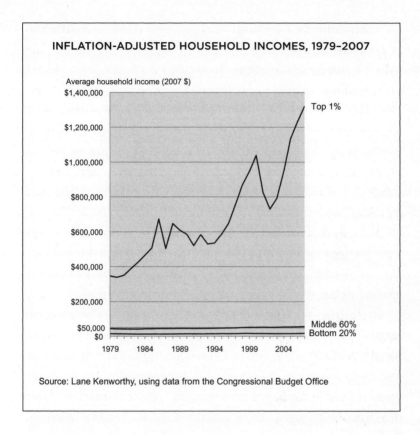

INFLATION-ADJUSTED HOUSEHOLD INCOMES, 1979–2007

Average household income (2007 $)

Source: Lane Kenworthy, using data from the Congressional Budget Office

resources; and when "the government and its officials and agents are accountable under the law." To evaluate adherence to these principles, WJP's 2010 report gathered information from each country in nine overall categories.

- Limited government powers
- Absence of corruption
- Order and security
- Fundamental rights
- Open government

- Regulatory enforcement
- Access to civil justice
- Effective criminal justice
- Informal justice

These broad categories were divided into numerous subcategories, resulting in more than seven hundred variables, and the WJP ran its detailed evaluation in thirty-five representative countries spread out across all continents. To ensure that the comparisons were matching up nations with relatively similar cultural, historical, and legal backgrounds, the report split up the countries into geographic groupings. The United States, Canada, Spain, Sweden, the Netherlands, Austria, and France were all classed under the "Western Europe & North America" heading.

To say that the United States underperformed its peers would be putting it mildly. In four out of the nine overall categories that were studied by the WJP, the United States placed dead last in its group. In two more categories, it only managed a second-to-last finish. Aside from "open government," where the United States was third in its group, there was not a single category where the U.S. ranking was anywhere in the top half of the Western nations.

What's more, the study's methodology might have actually made the United States look far better than it actually is. As the civil liberties writer David Swanson pointed out, the launching of aggressive wars was not counted by the WJP as a "rule of law" violation, even though such wars are clearly illegal under international standards. Similarly, Swanson notes that while the WJP report gave U.S. government officials fairly high marks for not taking bribes, it overlooked the fact that many campaign contributions are little more than bribes in a different guise.

Even with those helpful biases, the WJP report paints a grim picture indeed. And it is telling that one of the categories in which the United States finished last among Western nations was "Limited Government Powers"—which measures, as the report put it, "the extent to which those who govern are subject to law." Included under that rubric were such basic questions as whether "government officials are sanctioned for misconduct" and whether "government powers are effectively limited by the fundamental law, the legislature, and the judiciary." These sorts of restrictions on government authority were at the core of the American founding, yet they are clearly nowhere to be found in our country today.

Of course, high-level politicians have not been the only ones to benefit from this lack of legal checks and balances on their activity. Those at the top of the wealth pyramid have also reaped the rewards. Again, while disparities of wealth have always been tolerated in the United States, and even endorsed by the founders, the crucial difference is that these days financial power has become easily convertible into political power—and political power, in turn, is being exploited to repeatedly rewrite the laws to the advantage of the very rich, making them richer and more powerful still. In other words, the United States has taken on the classic attributes of *oligarchy* (government by a small dominant class) and *plutocracy* (government by the wealthy). Like *banana republic*, such derogatory terms were once reserved for other nations, and it was unthinkable to apply them to the United States; yet now they are being commonly, even casually, used by mainstream sources to describe the facts of life in contemporary America.

Given these developments, the dystopic future toward which the United States is inexorably heading is not difficult to imagine. Even the most slothful and slumbering citizenry, trained to accept political impotence, has its limits. At some point, serious social unrest is the inevitable result when a population is forced to suffer mass joblessness and deprivations of every kind while it sees a tiny sliver of elites enjoying gilded prosperity; when ordinary people are threatened with imprisonment for petty offenses while they see elites illegally spying, invading, torturing, and plundering with nearly total impunity. Such a two-tiered setup is simply unsustainable.

The American elites have, to be sure, gained tremendous short-term benefits from the pervasive corruption that shields the powerful from legal scrutiny. But in the long run, eviscerating the rule of law is likely to prove their undoing. The United States was founded on the notion that the law must apply equally to everyone, and it is now clear that this principle is not just a matter of basic fairness. If a privileged few are exempt from the rule of law, ever-greater inequality will result, and the inevitable discord that such inequality provokes will come to threaten the country itself. Only as a nation of laws, not men, can America hope to endure.

ACKNOWLEDGMENTS

Numerous people played a vital role in shaping this book. One of the most valuable aspects of writing on a daily basis on the Internet is the constant interaction with (and feedback from) readers, commenters, and other writers. So many of the ideas expressed in this book, and the evidence marshaled to support them, come from that interactive process. It is not always possible to trace or acknowledge the genesis of every point but, in general, the role played by my readers is indispensable.

This is the fourth book I've written, and I've learned that few things are more important in determining the quality of the finished product than one's editor. I was genuinely fortunate to have the very wise and experienced hand of Sara Bershtel guiding every part of this process. Sara's unyielding commitment to create the best possible book—no matter the time or work required—and her unique ability to achieve that is the perfect editorial combination for any author. Sara's colleague at Metropolitan Books, Grigory Tovbis, was just as rigorous in finding ways to make the manuscript better, on matters both large and small, and his contributions substantially improved the final outcome.

Two law students provided invaluable research and ideas:

Daniel Novack of NYU and Ariel Schneller of Harvard. Both were able to find needed evidence with astonishing ease. Prior to my submitting the manuscript, Mona Holland wielded a merciless editorial scalpel to make the prose more focused and succinct. My literary agent, Daniel Conaway of Writers House, did his typically superb job of shepherding the book proposal and finding the ideal place to publish it.

And, as always, the anchor for everything I do is my partner for life, David Miranda, whose love, support, and insight make everything possible.

INDEX

Page numbers in *italics* refer to figures and tables.

ABOUT THE AUTHOR

GLENN GREENWALD is the author of the *New York Times* bestsellers *How Would a Patriot Act?* and *A Tragic Legacy*. Proclaimed one of the "25 Most Influential Political Commentators" by *The Atlantic*, Greenwald is a former constitutional law and civil rights attorney and a contributing writer at *Salon*. He lives in Brazil and New York City.